BRITISH STEAM MILITARY CONNECTIONS:

LONDON, MIDLAND AND SCOTTISH RAILWAY STEAM LOCOMOTIVES

ROYAL SCOT in SAN FRANSISCO

In 1933 locomotive 'Royal Scot' class LMS No 6152 THE KINGS DRAGOON GUARDSMAN (built by North British Locomotive Co – July 1927) swapped name and number with the first of the class LMS No 6100 ROYAL SCOT (built at LMS Derby Works – July 1930). Subsequently, LMS No 6152 went to Canada and North America in order to tour, and then attend the Century of Progress Exhibition in Chicago as LMS No 6100 ROYAL SCOT. The 'on tour' mileage completed was 11,194 which included crossing the Rocky Mountains. The two locomotives never reverted back to their original identities. Royal Scot arrived back in UK at Tilbury Docks on 5 December 1933. LMS No 6100 (BR 46100) survives as a preserved working locomotive however, the locomotive numbered BR No 46152 (formerly LMS 6100) was scrapped by British Railways in July 1965.

These two images show the locomotive during the aforementioned tour, and whilst visiting San Francisco, California. The date information relating to the images is recorded as 22 October 1933. *Both images Mike Morant Collection*

BRITISH STEAM MILITARY CONNECTIONS:

LONDON, MIDLAND AND SCOTTISH RAILWAY STEAM LOCOMOTIVES

Keith Langston

PEN & SWORD
TRANSPORT

First published in Great Britain in 2019 by
Pen & Sword Transport
An imprint of
Pen & Sword Books Ltd
47 Church Street
Barnsley
South Yorkshire
S70 2AS

ISBN 978 1 47387 853 2

A CIP catalogue record for this book is
available from the British Library.

Typeset in 11pt Minion by Mac Style Ltd, Bridlington, East Yorkshire
Printed and bound in India by Replika Press Pvt. Ltd.

Pen & Sword Books Limited incorporates the imprints of Atlas,
Archaeology, Aviation, Discovery, Family History, Fiction, History, Maritime, Military,
Military Classics, Politics, Select, Transport, True Crime, Air World, Frontline Publishing,
Leo Cooper, Remember When, Seaforth Publishing, The Praetorian Press, Wharncliffe Local
History, Wharncliffe Transport, Wharncliffe True Crime and White Owl.

For a complete list of Pen & Sword titles please contact
PEN & SWORD BOOKS LIMITED
47 Church Street, Barnsley, South Yorkshire, S70 2AS, England
E-mail: enquiries@pen-and-sword.co.uk
Website: www.pen-and-sword.co.uk

CONTENTS

A selection of QR codes are listed which when scanned with a hand-held device open appropriate film clips.

 The documentary 'Night Mail' (1936).

 Britain's Railways in WW2 Part 2.

 Preserved BR No 46100 ROYAL SCOT in action, 2016.

 THE UNKNOWN WARRIOR 2017 progress film.

 LMS No 6114 COLDSTREAM GUARDSMAN filmed in 1938.

Preserved military named LMS Stanier 'Jubilee' class 4-6-0 BR No 45699 GALATEA is seen slowly but positively climbing past Angrholm towards the summit of Ais Gill on the Settle Carlisle route. This working was the return southbound leg of the service 1Z53, 15:34 Carlisle to Lancaster 'The Fellsman' on Wednesday 2 July 2014. *Gordon Edgar/Rail Photoprints*

Chapter 1

INTRODUCTION

Naming

The naming of steam locomotives in particular, and other railway locomotives and rolling stock in general has been an accepted practice since the very first railway locomotives appeared in 1804.

The practice can fairly be said to be a 'very British tradition'. Numbers were also used to identify individual locomotives, although interestingly the Great Western Railway (GWR) Swindon-built 'Broad Gauge' locomotives at first carried only names.

The relevant locomotive classes concerned are of importance in that they represent the amazing engineering achievements of an industry now long gone, which in its time employed literally thousands of people. Accordingly, the names of aircraft and naval vessels are a tribute to the workers who built them, often in the most testing of circumstances. The chosen locomotive names are a tribute to the military personnel and citizens of our country, commonwealth and allies who lost their lives in conflicts.

Locomotive names have been inspired by a wide variety of topics and those connected with the military have figured prominently. This publication highlights steam locomotives given names with a military connection and originally built/ designed by the London Midland & Scottish Railway (LMSR) or their constituent companies, which then came into British Railways (BR) stock in 1948.

The people who chose and bestowed locomotive names obviously thought it significantly important to do so, and as such those names and their origins are worthy of investigation and explanation. We must take into account that choices made so many years ago, may not have obvious rationale when judged using 21st century ideals. The majority of name choice origins highlighted are obvious in having been conferred to mark significant historic events, military groups, prominent personnel, battles and machines of war etc. However, all are interesting and in their individual ways help to provide snapshots of Britain's military and social history.

After a railway company had decided to allocate names to a class of its locomotives suggestions, often within a predetermined category, were then made by that company's officials and/or other interested parties. Not all of those choices necessarily met with complete approval, and whilst some were rejected others were accepted and indeed occasionally modified after further discussion. Where names were chosen by committees it is good to remember the old maxim 'A camel is a horse, designed by a committee'. However, the choices of military names were less contentious and therefore easier to define.

Constraints did of course apply and those mainly related to the style and size of nameplate and accordingly the amount of space available for the lettering etc. For example, some listings for 'Royal Scot' class LMS No 6145 recorded the name as THE DUKE OF WELLINGTON'S REGIMENT (WEST RIDING) however the locomotive nameplate actually contained an abbreviation of the word regiment i.e. THE DUKE OF WELLINGTON'S REGT. (WEST RIDING). As can be seen this nameplate additionally carried a crest mounted above the name.

LMS locomotive number 6145 (BR 46145) nameplate. *David Anderson Collection.*

Locomotives included are for the main part those which came into British Railways stock in 1948, or others outside that remit but of significant importance. For primary identification BR numbers are used, and in the listings preserved locomotives are identified by the letter **P**.

In some instances, the requested name did not always meet with the approval of railway officials. The following previously unpublished LMS documents serve to illustrate the fact that internal differences of opinion did occur.

A portion of a letter dated 6 October 1936 from The Old Contemptibles' Association concerning their request for a 'Royal Scot' class locomotive to be named in their honour. It was received by G.H. Loftus Allen of the LMS Publicity Department, which after signing he forwarded to the office of W.A. Stanier. The request was made after the LMS agreed to name a locomotive for the British Legion.

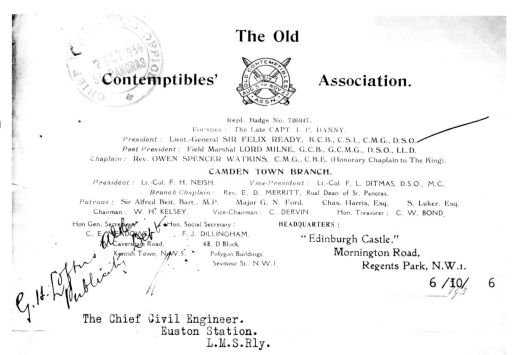

Having received the request Mr Stanier then sent this internal memorandum to the publicity office on 14 November 1936. This copy carries the signature of Mr Riddles. The stamp of W.A. STANIER can be seen at the bottom right of the memo. It can be deduced that Stanier was not in favour of the name!

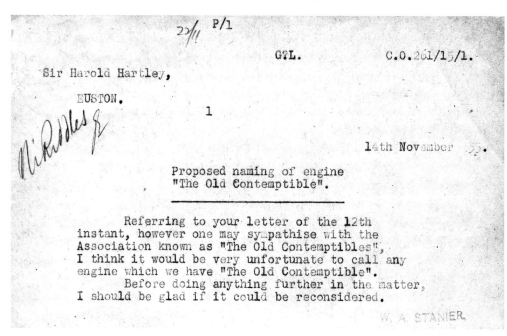

All LMS documents courtesy of John Magnall.
johnmagnall@btinternet.com

A51/SS/X.   C.O.261/15/1.

E.J.H. Lemon, Esq.,
EUSTON.

Copy

1

18th November   35

**Proposed naming of engine
"The Old Contemptible".**

_____

In reply to your letter of the
12th November, I have carefully considered this matter
in conjunction with Mr. Stanier, and we are both
agreed that, however laudable the objective in view,
there would be unfortunate repercussions from
naming any engine "The Old Contemptible".   There
is no doubt that this name would arouse a good deal
of derisive comment on the part of both the
public and the staff.

Perhaps therefore you may care to reconsider
the matter in this light.

(Signed) Loftus Allen

A further memorandum dated 18 November 1935 and copied to E.J.H. Lemon at Euston also highlights objection to the use of the name stating that '*this name would arouse a great deal of derisive comment*'.

LMSR Personnel concerned with this correspondence.

G.H. Loftus Allen *Publicity and Advertising Department. During WWI he was Deputy Assistant Director of Railway Transport, with the rank of major.*

Sir Harold Hartley *Vice-President (Works and Ancillary Undertakings) and Director of Scientific Research. Also known as Brigadier General Sir Harold Brewer Hartley GCVO, CH, CBE, MC, FRS.*

W.A. Stanier (later Sir) *M.I.Mech.E., Chief Mechanical Engineer.*

E.J.H. Lemon O.B.E., *M.I.Mech.E., Vice-President, Railway Traffic, Operating and Commercial Section.*

R.A. Riddles *Stanier's Principal Assistant.*

F.A. Lemon *Works Superintendent (Locomotives), Crewe.*

This copy of an internal LMS memorandum from Sir Harold Hartley, Office of the Vice President was sent to Stanier on 20 November 1935. The Vice President makes it quite clear that objections which amount to a "mere dislike of the title" are of no importance. Hartley then finishes his polite but firm missive saying that he would "be pleased to hear in due course what engine you (Stanier) decide to name".

L.M.S. INTERNAL CORRESPONDENCE.

Our Reference. C.O.261/15/1   Your Reference. G.L.

TO   W. A. Stanier, Esq.,
      EUSTON.

(Centre No.   ).

From OFFICE OF VICE-PRESIDENT,

EUSTON STATION.
(Centre No 1).
E.R.O. 1019
O.P. 4/1

20th November, 1935.

PROPOSED NAMING OF ENGINE
"THE OLD CONTEMPTIBLE".

In reply to yours of the 14th; when this suggestion was originally put forward by one of the local branches of the Old Contemptible Association, it was felt that it should be sympathetically received and Mr. Lemon was of opinion that it would be only in keeping with the spirit in which we have named "British Legion" to adopt it. The Old Contemptibles feel, and probably with justification, that they have a prior claim to consideration in such a connection.

Since I wrote you on the 12th, however, the same suggestion has been put forward, with a strong plea for its adoption, by an influential personal friend of Mr. Lemon, who is quite unconnected with the source from which the original suggestion came, and you may take it that unless there is any difficulty in the way, apart from mere dislike of the title, it is desired that the matter should be pursued.

I shall be pleased to hear in due course what engine you decide to name.

H. H₂₅

Sir Harold Hartley then received this reply from the office of F.A. Lemon at Crewe. After having nameplates fitted No 6127 then went back into traffic. The new nameplates were covered up and thus not intended to be publicly viewed. In the event that nameplate style was not the one which was unveiled almost a year later! See the entry for LMS No 6127.

Sir Harold Hartley,

EUSTON.

1

21st November,   35.

PROPOSED NAMING OF ENGINE "THE OLD CONTEMPTIBLE".

I am in receipt of your letter of the 20th instant, and note what you say. There is no physical difficulty whatever in the naming of an engine "The Old Contemptible".

I have selected engine No. 6127, now named "Novelty", and have given instructions for appropriate nameplates to be prepared and fitted.

Engine No.6127 "The Old Contemptible".

Naming Ceremony at Euston, 28th November, 1936.

P R O G R A M M E

2 p.m.	Members of the Association assemble in Euston Square.
2.10 p.m.	Party move off from Euston Square and proceed via Seymour Street and the entrance near to the Railway Clearing House to No.1 Platform.
2.25 p.m.	General Sir Felix Ready - Mr. E.J.H. Lemon leave Euston Hotel.
2.30 p.m.	General Sir Felix Ready arrives on No.1 Platform. General Salute.
	General Sir Felix Ready and Mr. E.J.H. Lemon mount a special platform.
	Mr. Lemon welcomes General Sir Felix Ready and the members of the Association.
	General Sir Felix Ready replies.
	Mr. Lemon formally invites General Sir Felix Ready to unveil and christen the engine. As he does so the Band play "Tipperary".
	After the Ceremony an opportunity will afford members of the Association to inspect the engine.

The programme for the 1936 naming ceremony at Euston Station on 28 November 1936 is seen in this LMS internal memorandum. Approximately a year had elapsed between the fitting of the original new nameplates at Crewe Works and the naming ceremony.

FOUNDED 1963

Visit http://www.lmssociety.org.uk/

Chapter 2

LONDON MIDLAND & SCOTTISH RAILWAY – BRITISH RAILWAYS

LMS Crest *Keith Langston Collection*

The London Midland & Scottish Railway (LMSR) was formed during the railway period referred to as 'Grouping', as detailed in the Railways Act 1921 and which took effect on 1 January 1923.

Many classes of locomotives included in the original listing subsequently came into British Railways stock in 1948.

Principal members of the 1923 LMSR grouping included the Caledonian Railway (CR), London& North Western Railway (LNWR), Midland Railway (MR) and the Somerset & Dorset Joint Railway (SDJR). Numerically the ex LMS BR locomotives carried numbers in the series 40001 to 58937.

A total of 7,717 steam locomotives surviving from that grouping were listed in the December 1948 BR stock list.

1948

British Railways (BR), which from 1965 traded as British Rail, was the state-owned company that operated most of the rail transport in Great Britain between 1948 and 1997. It was formed from the nationalisation of the so called 'Big Four' British railway companies (LMS, LNER, GWR, SR) and lasted until the gradual privatisation of British Rail, in stages between 1994 and 1997. Originally a trading brand of the Railway Executive of the British Transport Commission, it became an independent statutory corporation in 1962 designated as the British Railways Board.

At the beginning of the BR era locomotives carried the company's name on the tender. As can be seen from this 1950 image taken at Glasgow Corkerhill shed. BR later adopted the use of logos as shown below. *Rail Photoprints Collection*

'Lion on a Bike' (cycling lion) emblem from 1950.

'Ferret & Dartboard' crest used 1956 onwards.

Both images Keith Langston Collection

'The Welsh Mountaineer' was a special train which ran along the Conwy Valley line, Llandudno Junction–Blaenau Ffestiniog–Llandudno Junction, on 2 May 2009. Preserved 'Black Five' class locomotive BR No 45231 carried the name SHERWOOD FORESTER, formerly carried by 'Royal Scot' class BR No 46112, and BR No 45407 carried the name LANCASHIRE FUSILIER, formerly carried by 'Royal Scot' class BR No 46119. The special train is seen approaching Roman Bridge en-route to Blaenau Ffestiniog. *Keith Langston Collection*

Stanier 'Black Five' class

In the history of British steam locomotives, it is possible none were ever as universally popular as the Stanier '5MT' 2-cylinder 4-6-0 engines, which became colloquially known as the 'Black Five' class. They were said to be the most efficient design of mixed traffic locomotives ever seen in Great Britain. There were some 842 locomotives of the class built by the LMS and BR between 1934 and 1951. They were built at Crewe Works (241 engines), Horwich Works (120 engines), Derby Works (54 engines) and by the contractors Armstrong Whitworth (327 engines) and Vulcan Foundry (100 engines).

In traffic they could be seen at work all over the LMS system from Thurso in the north to Bournemouth in the south, and there were several modifications in design. All of the class remained in service until 1961, and many worked until the last days of steam on BR in August 1968. For the majority of their working lives these locomotives were paired with 9 ton/4000 gallon tenders.

Only four 'Black Five' engines were ever named and all of those had names with a direct military link. There have always existed rumours that a fifth member of the class was also allocated a military name, but it is doubtful if that name was ever carried. Fortunately, 18 members of the class survived into preservation, but the militarily named examples are not amongst that number.

For more detailed information relating to this iconic class see *Stanier Black Five Locomotives,* by the same author and published by Pen & Sword Books in their *Locomotive Portfolio* series. https://www.pen-and-sword.co.uk/Locomotive-Portfolios/s/91

William A. Stanier (later Sir)

Stanier was famously 'headhunted' in late 1931 by the London Midland & Scottish Railway (LMS) when that organisation's chairman Sir Josiah Stamp recognised his burgeoning talents. Early promotion chances for Stanier were limited at his then employer the GWR, therefore he was reportedly happy to switch from Swindon to Crewe, doing so in January 1932. Employing the benefit of hindsight, it is easy to see that the GWR's loss was very much the LMS's gain. It is said that Stanier brought with him a chest containing a large number of working drawings, but undoubtedly his greatest asset was 40 years of locomotive design and operational experience. Stanier designed/converted 14 LMS steam locomotive classes (comprising 2431 engines) of which the 'Black Fives' (with a build total of 842 locomotives) were his fifth project.

The original nameplates (2) as carried by 'Black Five' LMS No 5157 (BR 45157). The nameplates on this class of locomotives were mounted on the running plate and located above the leading driving wheel. Three of the four named locomotives had a regimental crest mounted below the name whilst THE GLASGOW HIGHLANDER nameplate (as seen) carried a crest above the name. *David Anderson Collection*

45154 LANARKSHIRE YEOMANRY (LMS 5154) built by Armstrong Whitworth, Lot No 124 – Works No 1195 it entered traffic July 1935. It was withdrawn by BR in November 1966 and cut up at Drapers, Hull during May 1967.

'Black Five' BR No 45154 (LMS 5154) is seen at Wigan North Western station, with the Railway Correspondence and Travel Society (RCTS) 'South Lancashire Rail Tour' reporting number 1T54. The special was hauled throughout by this loco which started at Wigan North Western and terminated at Wigan Wallgate on 24 September 1966. Note that the regimental crest is mounted below the name. *M Whittaker*

The *Lanarkshire Yeomanry* was a regiment of the British Army, first raised in 1819 and disbanded in 1999.

During the First World War the regiment served as a dismounted infantry regiment and in the Second World War provided two field artillery regiments. In 1956 it was amalgamated into The Queen's Own Lowland Yeomanry. When created the Yeomanry was not intended to serve overseas, but due to the string of defeats during the so called 'Black Week' (10-17 December 1899) during the Second Boer War the British government realised they were going to need more troops. A Royal Warrant was required allowing volunteer forces to serve in the aforementioned war. In 1901, the regiment was reorganized as mounted infantry as the Lanarkshire Imperial Yeomanry. In 1908 it was transferred into the Territorial Force, returning to a cavalry role and equipping as lancers, under the new title Lanarkshire Yeomanry.

The Lanarkshire Yeomanry was part of 74th (Yeomanry) Division – First World War.
The Royal Artillery – Second World War.
Royal Armoured Corps – thereafter.
Engagements included
Second Boer War
First World War, Gallipoli 1915, Egypt 1915–17, Palestine 1917-18, France and Flanders 1918
Second World War, Malaya 1941–42, Sicily 1943, Italy 1943–45, North-West Europe 1945.

The regiment transferred into the Royal Artillery in February 1940 as 155th (Lanarkshire Yeomanry) Field Regiment, RA; in April 1940, 156th (Lanarkshire Yeomanry) Field Regiment, RA was formed as a second-line duplicate. Both served as field artillery regiments.

Worthy of note is the fact that then future Prime Minister Alec Douglas-Home (then Lord Dunglass) served in the regiment from commission as a Lieutenant in 1924, he subsequently rose to the rank of Major in 1933. For more information visit www.lanarkshireyeomanry.com

156th field gunners seen in Italy during 1940.

45156 AYRSHIRE YEOMANRY (LMS 5156) built by Armstrong Whitworth it entered traffic July 1935, Lot No 124 – Works No 1197. It was withdrawn by BR in August 1968 and cut up at Wards, Beighton during December of that year.

'Black Five' BR No 45156 (LMS 5156) is seen over the ash pit at Carnforth depot, on 4 August 1968 whilst being serviced. Note that the nameplates had already been removed and that the smokebox number plate has been replaced by a painted version. The occasion was the G.C. Enterprises 'Farewell to Steam' railtour (reporting number 1T80) which ran Stockport-Carnforth and return. *A. W. Nokes/Rail Photoprints*

The style of the original AYRSHIRE YEOMANRY nameplate is seen in this 1950s image. Note the regimental crest below the name and below that the words EARL OF CARRICK'S OWN. The regiment was granted permission to use the title Ayrshire Yeomanry Cavalry (Earl of Carrick's* Own) in honour of the future King Edward VII.

* Earl of Carrick is a subsidiary title of Princes of Wales deriving from the Ayrshire district of Carrick.

Gunners of 'E' Troup 124 Battery, 151st Regiment are seen filling 25-pounder shells with propaganda leaflets. Roermond, Holland during January 1945. *Imperial War Museum Collection*

Ayrshire (Earl of Carrick's Own) Yeomanry cap badge. *Ayrshire Yeomanry Museum* Visit www.armymuseums.org.uk/museum/ayrshire-yeomanry

The **Ayrshire (Earl of Carrick's Own) Yeomanry** was formed as an independent troop of Fencible Cavalry by The Earl of Cassillis in around 1794. Originally raised from amongst the local farmers and townsmen, as a troop of yeomanry known as 'The Earl of Carrick's Own Yeomanry'.

By 1798 it was formally adopted into the Army List as The Ayrshire Regiment of Yeomanry Cavalry making them the senior yeomanry regiment in Scotland, and the seventh yeomanry regiment in Great Britain's Army. The Yeomanry were established at this time to provide Britain with a defence against any possible invasion by Napoleon and French forces.

As with the Lanarkshire Yeomanry this regiment was not intended to serve overseas, but due to several heavy defeats during the so called 'Black Week' (10-17 December 1899) during the Second Boer War the British government realised they were going to need more troops. A Royal Warrant was required allowing volunteer forces to serve overseas. With the Lanarkshire Yeomanry, the regiment co-sponsored the 17th (Ayrshire and Lanarkshire) Company for the 6th (Scottish) Battalion in 1900.

In 1901 the Regiment was given a new title of the Ayrshire (Earl of Carrick's Own) Yeomanry and reorganised as a mounted infantry. In 1908 it returned to its Cavalry role and transferred into the then new Territorial Force.

The Ayrshire was part of the Royal Armoured Corps – First World War.
The Royal Artillery – Second World War.
Royal Armoured Corps – thereafter.
Engagements included
Second Boer War
First World War, Gallipoli 1915, Egypt 1916–17, Palestine 1917–18, France and Flanders 1918.
Second World War, North Africa 1942–43, Italy 1944–45, North-West Europe 1944–45.

After WWII, the regiment reconstituted in the Territorial Army, under its old title of The Ayrshire (Earl of Carrick's Own) Yeomanry, and transferred into the Royal Armoured Corps.

The regiment became part of 30 (Lowland) Independent Armoured Brigade. The Ayrshire Yeomanry continued as an independent Regiment until 1969 when it was reduced to a cadre of just a few men. On 1 April 1971 this cadre gave rise to two new units; B Squadron of the 2nd Armoured Car Regiment, later renamed the Queen's Own Yeomanry and 251 Squadron of 154th (Lowland) Transport Regiment. In 1992, the Squadron was transferred to the newly formed Scottish Yeomanry.

In 1999, following a 'Strategic Defence Review', the Scottish Yeomanry amalgamated with the Queen's Own Yeomanry. Two of the Scottish Yeomanry's four Squadrons – The Ayrshire Yeomanry based in Ayr, and The Fife and Forfar Yeomanry/Scottish Horse based in Cupar, continued to operate under command of The Queen's Own Yeomanry. On 1 July 2014 the Squadron left The Queens Own Yeomanry to form the Scottish and North Irish Yeomanry. Following a later defence review the Squadron was designated as 'light' cavalry.

'Black Five' BR No 45156 (LMS 5156) AYRSHIRE YEOMANRY passes Manchester Victoria with an empty stock working circa 1960. *Alan H. Bryant ARPS/Rail Photoprints*

45157 THE GLASGOW HIGHLANDER (LMS 5157) built by Armstrong Whitworth it entered traffic July 1935, Lot No 124 – Works No 1198. It was withdrawn by BR in December 1962 and cut up at Arnott Young, Troon during July 1963.

Preserved 'Black Five' BR No 45407 is seen with nameplates in the style of BR No 45157 THE GLASGOW HIGHLANDER at the East Lancashire Railway. *Keith Langston Collection*

The **Glasgow Highlanders** was a former infantry regiment of the British Army, part of the Territorial Force (the Territorial Army). Active 1868-1973.

The regiment was originally formed as the 105th Lanarkshire Rifle Volunteers, also known as the Glasgow Highland Regiment, which was formed in 1868 by a group of Highland migrants to Glasgow as part of the civilian Volunteer Force and initially wore the uniform and based its cap badge upon that of the Black Watch (Royal Highland Regiment). It consisted of 12 companies. The various battalions of the Lanarkshire Rifle Volunteers eventually became volunteer battalions of either the Highland Light Infantry or the Cameronians (Scottish Rifles) after the Childers Reforms of 1881, with the 105th becoming part of the former, and renumbered as the '10th Lanarkshire Volunteer Rifles', which was changed to the '5th (Glasgow Highland) Volunteer Battalion' in 1887. The regiment's personnel were distinctive in that they continued to wear their kilts in contrast to the rest of the Highland Light Infantry, who wore trews. Detachments of the regiment were sent to South Africa during the Second Boer War. Visit http://highlandlightinfantry.org.uk/

Part of		
Lanarkshire Rifle Volunteers	*1868–1881*	
Highland Light Infantry	*1881–1959*	
Royal Highland Fusiliers	*1959–1967*	
(Princess Margaret's Own Glasgow & Ayrshire Regiment)		
52nd Lowland Volunteers	*1967–1973*	

Glasgow Highlander Cap Badge

Glasgow Highlanders training in trench warfare Prior to WWI.
The Amalgamated Press Ltd

'Black Five' LMS No 5157 THE GLASGOW HIGHLANDER is seen on shed at Inverness during 1947. *Rail Photoprints Collection*

Preserved 'Black Five' BR No 45407 is seen crossing the River Clwyd near Rhyl, with an up train whilst in the guise of her scrapped sister locomotive BR No 45157 THE GLASGOW HIGHLANDER during August 2000. *Dave Jones*

45158 GLASGOW YEOMANRY (LMS 5158) built Armstrong Whitworth it entered traffic July 1935, Lot No 124 – Works No 1199. It was withdrawn by BR in July 1964, cut up at Arnott Young, Troon during October 1964.

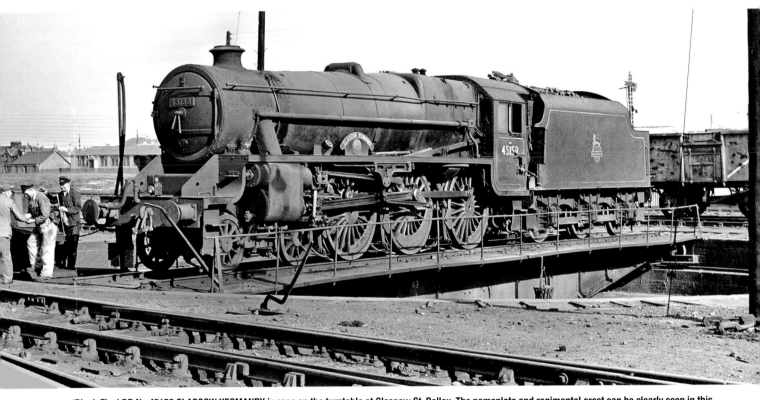

'Black Five' BR No 45158 GLASGOW YEOMANRY is seen on the turntable at Glasgow St. Rollox. The nameplate and regimental crest can be clearly seen in this March 1959 image. *Rail Photoprints*

'Black Five' BR No 45158 GLASGOW YEOMANRY is seen again this time at Callander station whilst heading an Oban-Glasgow service during April 1961. *Sid Rickard-J&J Collection/Rail Photoprints*

Glasgow Yeomanry officer's cap badge.

The Queen's Own Royal **Glasgow Yeomanry** was a yeomanry regiment of the British Army that can trace their formation back to 1796. It saw action in the Second Boer War, the First World War and the Second World War. It amalgamated with the Lanarkshire Yeomanry and the 1st/2nd Lothians and Border Horse to form the Queen's Own Lowland Yeomanry in 1956. Its lineage was revived by B (Lanarkshire and Queen's Own Royal Glasgow Yeomanry) Squadron, the Scottish Yeomanry in 1992 until that unit was disbanded in 1999.

In 1793, the prime minister, William Pitt the Younger, proposed that the English Counties form a force of Volunteer Yeoman Cavalry that could be called on by the king to defend the country against invasion or alternatively could be called upon by the Lord Lieutenant to subdue civil disorders. Whilst north of the border 'The Glasgow Light Horse' was first raised in 1796, it was subsequently disbanded in 1822 but re-raised as 'The Glasgow and Lower Ward of Lanarkshire Yeomanry Cavalry' in 1848. The additional title of 'Queen's Own Royal' was conferred by Queen Victoria the following year.

Roles of the Queens Own Royal Glasgow Yeomanry   – Boer War, *Imperial Yeomanry*
  – World War I, *Yeomanry Infantry*
  – World War II, *Royal Artillery*
  – Post War, *Royal Armoured Corps*
Size, World War I – Three Regiments. World War II   – Two Regiments. Post War – One Squadron

45110 named in preservation RAF BIGGIN HILL (LMS 5110) built by Vulcan Foundry it entered traffic June 1935, Lot No 123 – Works No 4653 and was withdrawn by BR in August 1968. Name not carried during LMS/BR service.

Several of the preserved 'Black Five' class locomotives were given names in preservation. One such is BR No 45110 and it is seen between turns at Bewdley on the Severn Valley Railway, during September 2003. For a period in preservation this locomotive carried the name R.A.F. BIGGIN HILL. In 2018 the locomotive was reportedly stored out of service. *Keith Langston Collection*

The name BIGGIN HILL (famous Battle of Britain airfield) was carried by the Southern Railway (SR) 'Battle of Britain' class Pacific BR No 34057 (SR No 21C157). See *British Steam – Military Connections GWR, SR, BR and WD*, by the same author and published by Pen & Sword Books. https://www.pen-and-sword.co.uk/British-Steam-Military-Connections-Hardback/p/12151

One of the new welcome signs at Biggin Hill unveiled in October 2010. www.bigginhill-history.co.uk

LMS Fowler 4-6-0 'Patriot' class.

A total of 52 Patriot 4-6-0 5XP locomotives designed by Sir Henry Fowler C.B.E. were built by the London Midland & Scottish Railway (LMS) between 1930 and 1934 (reclassified 6P5F in 1951). The complete class of 3-cylinder locomotives were taken into stock by British Railways (BR) in 1948, BR Nos 45500–45551). Of those engines 42 were named. Under BR, 18 of the class were rebuilt with larger boilers, tapered chimneys, new cylinders and later Royal Scot style smoke deflectors (between 1946 and 1949) they were then given a BR power rating of 7P.

The construction of the 52 Patriot locomotives was carried out at Crewe Works (40 locomotives LMS 5502–5519, 5523–5524, 5529-5532 and 5536-5551, and Derby Works (12 locomotives LMS 5500-5501, 5520-5522, 5525-5528 and 5533–5535. In several instances those names were changed/re-allocated during the working lives of the locomotives. A total of 23 Patriots carried names with military connections. The curved nameplates were carried over the leading driving wheel splasher.

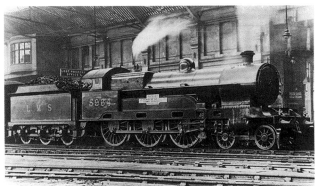

The nameplate from the first of the class LMS No 5500 fitted in 1937, which became BR 45500. Thereafter the 52 engines, became known as the 'Patriot' class. *LMS Patriot Project*

'Claughton' class LMS No 5964 with the original LNWR memorial nameplate. *Crewe Archive*

The original parallel boiler Patriots were given the LMS power rating of 5XP which was changed to 6P5F by British Railways in 1951 and given the BR power rating of 7P. The rebuilt tapered boiler Patriots were considered to be at the least equal in performance to the 'rebuilt Royal Scots' and reportedly were much better riding engines.

The first two locomotives LMS Nos 5500 and 5501 (original numbers 5971 and 5902) were built using component parts from withdrawn LNWR 'Claughton' 4-6-0 class. The driving wheel diameter of the Patriot class was set at 6′ 9″ however, the centre bosses of the ex 'Claughton' engines were noticeably larger. Motive power depots generally reported overall satisfaction with the performance of their Fowler designed Patriot locomotives and right through to the end of the 1950s were rostered for top flight express duties. When first observed in service the Crewe and Derby built 3-cylinder engines quickly earned the name 'Baby Scots' because they were strikingly similar in appearance to the Royal Scot class locomotives introduced by the LMS between 1927 and 1930.

Class leader seen as LMS No. 5971. Pictured un-named at Nottingham Midland, circa 1931. Note the Fowler tender without coal rails. *Steve Armitage Archive/Rail Photoprints*

The 'Baby Scots' did not become officially named as 'Patriots' until 1937 when the first built of the class received the name PATRIOT, and also proudly took on the mantle of LNWR/LMSR national memorial engine. The name was bestowed by the LNWR in memory of the companies' employees who lost their lives during the First World War (1914–1918).

Tender types

Originally paired with a Fowler 3,500-gallon tender (later fitted with double coal rails) carrying 5½ tons of coal. Later in their working lives the engines received other types of tender which included the Stanier 4000-gallon, 9-ton tender and the LMS straight high-sided 3500-gallon, 7-ton tender. Interchanging of tenders took place during the working life of the locomotives. None of the class were preserved however, an enterprise known as The Patriot Project was formally launched in 2008 with the stated purpose of constructing a new-build Patriot class 4-6-0 locomotive.

45500 PATRIOT (LMS 5971 and 5500) built Derby Works entered traffic November 1930 as LMS 5971 CROXTETH, Lot/Works No 074 renamed PATRIOT in 1937. Withdrawn by BR in March 1961 and cut up at Crewe Works in March 1961.

Patriot class BR No 45500 PATRIOT pictured at speed on the West Coast Main Line (WCML) near Symington with a Liverpool/Manchester–Glasgow express on 25 June 1960. Note the driving wheels with large centre bosses, inherited from the LNWR 'Claughton' class engine it replaced. Locomotive No 5500 originally carried the name and number of 'Claughton' No 5971 CROXTETH, when introduced by the London Midland & Scottish Railway (LMS) in November 1930. The locomotive was renumbered and subsequently named PATRIOT in 1937. *David Anderson*

Patriot class BR No 45500 PATRIOT, with a Fowler tender with coal rails is seen prior to departing Manchester London Road station with a service for the capital on 31 March 1954. To the right of the train the footplateman of BR Standard 'Britannia' Pacific No 70033 CHARLES DICKENS looks on admiringly. Manchester London Road so named in 1947, was renovated and renamed Manchester Piccadilly station in 1960. The impressive train shed at Piccadilly has been given 'Grade 2' listed status. *Norman Preedy Collection*

45501 ST. DUNSTANS (LMS 5902 and 5501) built Derby Works, entered traffic November 1930 as LMS 5902 SIR FRANK REE, Lot/Works No 074 renamed ST. DUNSTANS in 1937. Withdrawn by BR in August 1961 and cut up at Crewe Works in September 1961.

Patriot class BR No 45501 ST. DUNSTAN'S is seen passing Bushbury in the West Midlands circa 1960. *Norman Preedy Collection*

The name St. Dunstan's (bestowed in 1937) was carried on a 'badge plate' thus honouring the former War Blinded Association, London. *David Anderson*

St. Dunstan's to this day helps ex-Service men and women who have lost their sight, whatever the circumstances. Some St. Dunstaners lost their sight during active service; others experienced an accident on a training exercise, or suffered vision problems as a result of illness or old age.

Her Majesty the Queen is the Patron of the St. Dunstan's organisation and notable Vice Patrons include General Sir Peter de la Billière, KCB, KBE, DSO, MC, DL, Rear Admiral Sir Donald Gosling, KCVO, Admiral Sir Jonathon Band GCB DL, General Sir Richard Dannatt GCB CBE MC and Air Chief Marshal Sir Joe French KCB CBE FRAeS RAF.

The organisation was founded by Sir Arthur Pearson, Bt, GBE (1866-1921) who was a prominent British newspaper proprietor and publisher, perhaps best remembered for founding the Daily Express. Sir Arthur suffered failing eyesight during the early 1900s and later became totally blind. In 1914 he became president of the National Institute for the Blind and in 1915 he founded St Dunstan's Home for Soldiers, originally in order to help troops blinded by World War 1 gas attacks and the associated traumas.

Saint Dunstan was educated by Irish monks at Glastonbury Abbey. In addition to his ecclesiastical work he was a silversmith and accomplished harpist. He was appointed Abbot of Glastonbury in 944 and Archbishop of Canterbury in 960.

45502 ROYAL NAVAL DIVISION (LMS 5959 and 5502) built Crewe Works, entered traffic unnamed in July 1932. Lot /Works No 087. Named in 1937. Withdrawn by BR in September 1960 and cut up at Crewe Works in October/November 1960.

Patriot class BR No 45502 ROYAL NAVAL DIVISION is seen passing the location of Farrington Junction with a partially fitted express freight train, mainly comprised of vans. *Norman Preedy Collection*

Recruiting poster 1914/15. *Courtesy of John Keegan*

45502 nameplate. *David Anderson*

The name **ROYAL NAVAL DIVISION** was bestowed on the locomotive in June 1937 whilst No 5959, the Claughton locomotive it replaced (withdrawn July 1932) was unnamed. The Royal Naval Division was founded at the beginning of the First World War when it was realised that the Royal Navy had thousands of surplus sailors, even after manning all the vessels of the fleet. The military hierarchy concluded that the war would be mainly fought on land and decided not to expand the navy. Personnel from the Royal Naval Reserve, Royal Fleet Reserve, Royal Naval Volunteer Reserve, a full brigade of Royal Marines and sundry Royal Navy and army personnel were brought together and mustered at Crystal Palace in September 1914 in order to form the Royal Navy Division (RND). The new division was often referred to as 'Winston's Little Army' as it was founded by the great man when he held the position of First Lord of the Admiralty. The RND fought alongside the army, but originally flew the White Ensign and maintained naval traditions, for example being allowed to grow beards and remain seated during a toast to the King's health. When in France during 1916 the RND came under direct army control and from that time onward were known as the 63rd (Royal Naval) Division, 'Winston's Little Army' fought with great distinction. The division was demobilised in April 1919 following an inspection by the Prince of Wales and was disbanded in June of that year.

45503 THE ROYAL LEICESTERSHIRE REGIMENT (LMS 5985 and 5503) built Crewe Works, entered traffic unnamed in July 1932 as LMS 5985. Lot/Works No 087. Named THE LEICESTERSHIRE REGIMENT in 1938 and renamed THE ROYAL LEICESTERSHIRE REGIMENT in 1948. Withdrawn by BR in August 1961 and cut up at Crewe Works in September 1961.

Patriot class BR No 45503 carrying **THE ROYAL LEICESTERSHIRE REGIMENT** nameplate with regimental plaque, is seen over the ashpit at Edinburgh Dalry Road shed on 14 July 1955. This view shows clearly the similarity in appearance between the 'Baby Scots' and the 'Royal Scots'. *Both images David Anderson*

The name **THE LEICESTERSHIRE REGIMENT** was bestowed on the locomotive in 1938 and was changed to THE ROYAL LEICESTERSHIRE REGIMENT in 1948, the name plate incorporated a regimental crest. Locomotive No 5959, the Claughton locomotive it replaced (withdrawn July 1932) was unnamed.

The Leicestershire Regiment was raised in 1688. In 1777 it was awarded the unbroken Laurel Wreath emblem for its bravery at the Battle of Princetown, during the American War of Independence. In 1825 the Regiment was awarded the Honour of wearing the insignia of the Royal Tiger superimposed with the word Hindoostan, in recognition of its exemplary service and conduct during its campaigning and long tour in India from 1804–1823. In the First World War the regiment increased from 5 to 19 battalions. Since that time the Regiment was always proudly called 'The Tigers'. The Regiment became The Royal Leicestershire Regiment in 1946, becoming in 1964 the 4th Leicestershire Battalion the Royal Anglian Regiment and in 1968 the 4th Battalion the Royal Anglian Regiment. The regiment which became known as Tiger Company in 1970. The 'Leicestershire' subtitle was removed on 1 July 1968 and the battalion was subsequently disbanded in 1975.

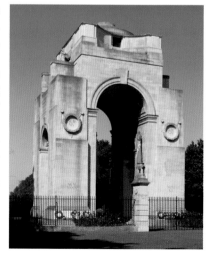

The War Memorial in Victoria Park, Leicester: designed by Edwin Lutyens and erected in 1923. *Len Mills*

45504 ROYAL SIGNALS (LMS 5987 and 5504) built Crewe Works, entered traffic unnamed in July 1932. Lot /Works No 087. Named in 1937. Withdrawn by BR in March 1962 and cut up at Crewe Works in March 1962.

Patriot class BR No 45504 ROYAL SIGNALS is seen departing from Manchester with an express service for London Euston on 15 March 1954. Note the 'as designed' smaller size driving wheel centre bosses. *Norman Preedy Collection*

The **Corps of Signals** was formed in 1920 and its history in the field of British military communications is a long and illustrious one. Swift and accurate passage of information has always been paramount to military success – after all the ancient Greek armies had Torch and Water Telegraph systems whilst the Roman armies communicated with coloured smoke. A Royal Warrant was signed by the Secretary of State for War, the Rt. Hon Winston S Churchill, who gave the Sovereign's approval for the formation of a 'Corps of Signals' on 28th June 1920. Six weeks later, His Majesty the King conferred the title 'Royal Corps of Signals'. During the 1920s and 1930s the strength of the signal 'Corps' steadily increased and during WW11 the Royal Signals had serving totals of approximately 8,518 officers and 142,472 other ranks. The 'Corps' still provide vital communications for the British military and NATO in modern times. It is responsible for installing, maintaining and operating all types of telecommunications equipment and information systems, providing command support to commanders and their headquarters, and conducting electronic warfare against enemy communications. The 'Corps' Motto is 'Certa Cito', which freely translated means 'Swift and Sure'.

The year 2020 is the centenary year of the Royal Signals.

5XP

5504

Official locomotive naming ceremonies would have been quite impressive affairs. The naming of ROYAL SIGNALS took place at Euston station on 10 April 1937. The locomotive was named by Brigadier Clementi-Smith Colonel Commandant of the regiment and the LMS was represented by William Stanier. The pair are seen with the engine crew who are wearing their WW1 medals. It was customary to try and roster enginemen for the occasion who had served in the respective regiments. *John Magnall Collection*

Members of regiment formed a guard of honour and the band played the Royal Signals march.

Brigadier Clementi-Smith Colonel Commandant of the regiment. It seems that prior to the photograph, the ribbon attached to the curtain draw gear had come unattached. Some resourceful individual had tied the ribbon to the handrail! *Both images John Magnall Collection*

45505 THE ROYAL ARMY ORDNANCE CORPS (LMS 5949 and 5505) built Crewe Works, entered traffic unnamed in July 1932. Lot /Works No 087. Named in 1947. Withdrawn by BR in June 1962 and cut up at Crewe Works in August 1962.

Patriot class BR No 45505 THE ROYAL ARMY ORDNANCE CORPS is seen in the stunning WCML setting of Dillicar Troughs on 2 May 1953. The water troughs, which allowed moving locomotives to take on water, were situated on both up and down lines near to Tebay. *Norman Preedy Collection.* Nameplate image *David Anderson.*

The name **Royal Army Ordnance Corps** was bestowed in 1947, and incorporated a regimental crest. This loco was originally allocated the name WEMYSS BAY, which it never carried. Locomotive No 5949 the Claughton locomotive it replaced (withdrawn July 1932) was unnamed.

Coat of Arms of the Royal Army Ordnance Corps (in reign of George VI), as inscribed on the grave of late Warrant Officer I F.H.W. Haynes (died 1943), at Stanley Military Cemetery, Hong Kong. *Nxn 0405 chl*

The Royal Army Ordnance Corps RAOC can trace its ancestry back to the year 1414 when a civilian 'Office of Ordnance' was created and that organisation became a Military Board of Ordnance in 1683. Under that title it supplied weapons and ammunition to the whole British army being also responsible for the Royal Artillery (RA) and the Royal Engineers (RE) in the period up to 1855. The Field Train Department was formed in 1792 and was directly under the Boards' control, numerous other titles were thereafter used and indeed officers and other ranks at that time belonged to different organisations. In order to clarify the situation a change in structure came about in 1896, officers were assigned to the Army Ordnance Department (AOD) whilst warrant officers, NCOs and soldiers were placed in the Army Ordnance Corps. After the end of WW1 in 1918 the two groups were merged to form the Royal Army Ordnance Corps which remained an independent part of the British army until reorganisation in 1993. The Corps motto is *Sua Tela Tonanti* which literally translated means 'His missiles thundering (of Jupiter)' But within the 'Corps' the historical usage was 'Unto the Thunderer his Arms' which was later changed to 'To the Warrior his Arms.'

45506 THE ROYAL PIONEER CORPS (LMS 5974 and 5506) built Crewe Works, entered traffic unnamed in August 1932. Lot /Works No 087. Named in 1948. Withdrawn by BR in March 1962 and cut up at Crewe Works in March/April 1962.

Patriot class BR No 45506 THE ROYAL PIONEER CORPS is seen departing Tebay station on 11 May 1950, Tebay station opened in 1852, and closed on 1 July 1968. The locomotive name plate, which incorporated a military crest, was unveiled by Viscount Montgomery of Alamein in a special ceremony at Euston Station on 15 September 1948. *Norman Preedy Collection*

The British Army raised the Auxiliary Military **Pioneer Corps** as a solo entity on 17 October 1939, for many years prior to that event several British regiments had benefited greatly from the support of their own 'Pioneer' elements. In October 1939 the Auxiliary Military Pioneer Corps (AMPC) came into being. On 22 November 1940 the name was changed from the AMPC to the Pioneer Corps. Pioneers were additionally recruited from throughout Africa, Mauritius and India. They performed a wide variety of tasks in all theatres of war. These tasks range from handling all types of stores, laying prefabricated track on the beaches, airfield building, numerous essential support duties and also stretcher bearing. In 1946, King George VI conferred upon the Pioneers the title 'Royal' for its 'meritorious work during the 1939–1945 war'. On 5 April 1993, the Royal Pioneer Corps united with the Royal Corps of Transport, the Royal Army Ordnance Corps, the Army Catering Corps, and the Postal and Courier Service of the Royal Engineers, to form the Royal Logistics Corps. The regiment's motto is Labor Omnia Vincit (Work Conquers All).

Royal Pioneer Corps Association, representative badge.

45507 ROYAL TANK CORPS (LMS 5936 and 5507) built Crewe Works, entered traffic unnamed in August 1932. Lot /Works No 087. Named in 1937. Withdrawn by BR in October 1962 and cut up at Crewe Works in March 1963.

Patriot class original LMS No 5936 is pictured in 1935 with an up 'milk and parcels' service. This locomotive later became LMS No 5507 and then BR No 45507. It appears that the locomotive fireman has just lifted the scoop after taking water as his engine approaches the end of the 'up' water trough. The location is Hademore Troughs, near to Whittington in the district of Lichfield. There was an LNWR signal box near to the troughs at Hademore Crossing and the original top section of that box has been preserved and reunited with an appropriate brick base at the Chasewater Railway, Staffordshire. The locomotive nameplate ROYAL TANK CORPS was bestowed in 1937, and incorporated a regimental crest. *PS Kendrick/Edward Talbot Collection*

The Royal Tank Regiment was formed almost immediately after the invention of the armoured tank. British tanks were first used in great numbers during the Battle of the Somme in 1916 (WW1). At that time the six tank companies were grouped as the Heavy Branch of the Machine Gun Corps (MGC). In November 1916 eight companies (by then in existence) were each expanded to form battalions lettered A through H; another seven battalions, I through O, were formed by January 1918, when they all were converted to numbered units. On 28 July 1917 the Heavy Branch was by Royal Warrant separated from the

rest of the MGC and given official status as the Tank Corps. More battalions continued to be formed, and by December 1918, 26 had been created. On 18 October 1923, it was officially named Royal (making it the Royal Tank Corps) by Colonel-in-Chief King George V. At that time the famous motto *'Fear Naught'*, the distinctive black beret with unit badge were all adopted. The word Corps was replaced in 1939 with Regiment to give the unit its current name. At the time of writing the Colonel in Chief of the Royal Tank Regiment was HRH Queen Elizabeth II.

45509 THE DERBYSHIRE YEOMANRY (LMS 6005 and 5509) built Crewe Works, entered traffic unnamed in August 1932. Lot /Works No 087. Named in 1951. Withdrawn by BR in August 1961 and cut up at Crewe Works in September 1961.

This fascinating official LMS image was taken in 1939, Patriot class LMS No 5509 (then unnamed) is pictured with a rake of Southern Railway (SR) stock heading a train from the south coast north over Bushey Troughs. This locomotive was originally allocated the name COMMANDO, which it never carried, and was subsequently named THE DERBYSHIRE YEOMANRY in November 1951. *David Anderson Collection*

Troops of 2nd Derbyshire Yeomanry, 51st Highland Division, take cover in a ditch during an attack on St Michielsgestel, 24 October 1944.
Sgt. Carpenter, British Army Photographic Unit

The regiment was first formed as the Derbyshire Corps of Fencible Cavalry in 1794, as a regiment of full-time soldiers intended for home defensive duties. The regiment changed shortly thereafter to the Derbyshire Corps of Yeomanry Cavalry (a part-time yeomanry regiment). In 1834, the various yeomanry troops were regimented as the Derbyshire Yeomanry Cavalry.

The regiment sponsored two companies of the Imperial Yeomanry in 1900, for service in the South African War, and in 1901 was itself reorganized as mounted infantry as the Derbyshire Imperial Yeomanry. In 1908 it was transferred into the Territorial Force, returning to a cavalry role and equipping as dragoons, under the new title of **The Derbyshire Yeomanry**. During the First World War the regiment was based in the Middle East and associated with all major military actions in that region. Returning to that region in the early years of World War 2 the regiment fought during the battle for El Alamien as part of 4th Armoured Brigade within the 7th Armoured Division (The Desert Rats).

45516 THE BEDFORDSHIRE AND HERTFORDSHIRE REGIMENT (LMS 5982 and 5516) built Crewe Works, entered traffic unnamed in October 1932. Named in 1938. Lot /Works No 088. Withdrawn by BR in July 1961 and cut up at Crewe Works in September 1961.

Patriot class BR No 45516 THE BEDFORDSHIRE AND HERTFORDSHIRE REGIMENT stands outside the erecting shop at Crewe Works. This locomotive at that time carried an unusual livery, BR numbers on LMS maroon paint. Note the 5XP power rating under the BR cabside number also a chalk written note on the cab informs interested parties that the 'loco's boiler has been filled with water'. *Edward Talbot Collection*

The locomotive was named THE BEDFORDSHIRE AND HERTFORDSHIRE REGIMENT in 1938 and being comprised of 49 letters was the longest name of any locomotive in the class, a regimental crest was carried above the name plate. The regimental badge/crest incorporates the famous motto *'Honi soit qui mal y pense'*, translated as 'May he be shamed who thinks badly'.

The regiment was known as the **Bedfordshire Regiment** until after World War 1 and was an infantry regiment originally formed in 1881 from other historically significant corps of military. That regiment had a truly illustrious past and served in theatres of war and trouble spots throughout the former British Empire and beyond, including seeing action in the Nine Years War, the War of Spanish Succession and the American War of Independence. On 29 July 1919 the regiment was renamed as the Bedfordshire and Hertfordshire Regiment in recognition of the huge contribution made during the Great War by men recruited from the county of Hertfordshire. The regiment was in 1925 awarded in excess of 70 honours for service in the Great War and in 1957 some 18 Second World War honours were additionally bestowed upon the regiment. Following the later reorganisation of the British Army the Bedfordshire and Hertfordshire Regiment became part of the East Anglian Regiment.

On 17 February 1950 BR No 45516 worked a special troop train from Southampton Docks hauling members of the 1st Battalion of the regiment after which it was named. A group of officers are pictured with the locomotive prior to its departure. *David Anderson Collection*

45524 which as LMS 5907 and 5524 was **SIR FREDERICK HARRISON** from 1933 until 1936, when it was renamed **BLACKPOOL**. The locomotive was built at Crewe Works, and entered traffic March 1933. Lot /Works No 095. Withdrawn by BR in September 1962 and cut up at Crewe Works in October 1962.

Patriot class BR No 45524 then named BLACKPOOL, is seen at Old Milverton on 7 April 1953. *Dick Blenkinsop/Patriot Project*

Lieutenant Colonel Sir Frederick Harrison (1844 – 1914) was railway manager and an officer in the British Army's Engineer and Railway Volunteer Staff Corps. The Engineer and Logistic Staff Corps is a part of the Royal Engineers in the British Army Reserve.

At the age of twenty, Harrison became a clerk on the London and North Western Railway (LNWR) at Shrewsbury. He rose through the ranks, working under George Findlay, the General Goods Manager; a later post was that of Assistant District Superintendent at Liverpool, and in 1874 he moved to the equivalent job at Chester. He remained there for a year before, aged 31, becoming Assistant Superintendent of the Line. Ten years after this he was appointed Chief Goods Manager of the LNWR. In 1893 he became General Manager of the LNWR, a post he held until the end of 1908. In 1909 he joined the Board of the South Eastern Railway, becoming Deputy Chairman, and also being appointed to the South Eastern & Chatham Railway Companies Joint Management Committee; he served these bodies until his death. He was made a knight bachelor in 1902.

45531 which as LMS 6027 and 5531 was named **SIR FREDERICK HARRISON** in 1937. The locomotive was built at Crewe Works, and entered traffic April 1933. Lot /Works No 095. Re-built with a type 2A boiler by BR during 1947. Withdrawn by BR in October 1965 and cut up at Campbells, Airdrie in January 1966.

Re-built Patriot class BR No 45531 SIR FREDERICK HARRISON is seen at Crewe Works, 24 April 1955. *Norman Preedy Collection*

45528 R.E.M.E. (LMS 5996 and 5528) built Crewe Works, entered traffic unnamed in April 1933. Lot /Works No 098. Named in 1960. Rebuilt by BR and re-entered service in August 1947 and named in September 1959. Withdrawn by BR in January 1963 and cut up at Crewe Works in March 1963.

Re-built Patriot class BR No 45528 R.E.M.E. is seen passing Cheadle Hulme on 19 February 1955 with a football special from Manchester (Luton Town v Manchester City). The other Patriots bore names at the time of BR rebuilding however No 45528 did not, it being named some 12 years later. *Norman Preedy Collection*

R.E.M.E. Royal Corps Electrical and Mechanical Engineers was formed during the Second World War. Following the findings of a review into the British army's employment of technical manpower by Sir William Beveridge, the war cabinet decided that a specialist engineering regiment was an essential requisite of modern warfare. R.E.M.E. thus came into being on 1 October 1942. The first of many crucially important actions for the new regiment was to provide engineering support to the troops engaged in the famous Battle of El Alamein. R.E.M.E. has played a vital role in all of the British army's operations, being present in Palestine, Korea, Kenya, Malaya, Suez, Cyprus, Northern Ireland, the Falklands, Afghanistan and both Gulf Wars. It has also been involved in peacekeeping duties all over the globe, from the Balkans to Sierra Leone and including the former republic of Yugoslavia. R.E.M.E. has been a 'Royal' corps since its formation. Interestingly a R.E.M.E. major set up the VW factory in occupied Germany after World War 2, a factory which produced the famous 'Beetle' design. With minor exceptions only, the Corps is now responsible for the examination, modification, repair and recovery of all mechanical, electronic, electrical and optical equipment of the Army, deemed beyond the capacity of unit non-technical personnel. The regiment's motto is *'Art et Marte'* which translates as 'By Skill and by Fighting'.

Helmet of the Band of the Corps of Royal Electrical and Mechanical Engineers. *Rama*

45532 ILLUSTRIOUS (LMS 6011 and 5532) built Crewe Works, entered traffic unnamed in April 1933. Lot /Works No 095. Named in 1933. Rebuilt by BR and re-entered service in July 1948. the Claughton locomotive it replaced (withdrawn February 1933) was also named **ILLUSTRIOUS** (from May 1923). Withdrawn by BR in February 1964 and cut up at Campbells, Airdrie in January 1965.

Re-built Patriot class BR No 45532 ILLUSTRIOUS is seen on Shap with a down London Euston – Glasgow Central express in this 1955 image. *Norman Preedy Collection*

Illustrious is a long-established name associated with Royal Navy warships. A total of five ships have carried the famous name. The first of which was a 74-gun fighting vessel built in 1789 which having been damaged beyond repair during the battles against the French navy in 1793 was set on fire and abandoned. The next HMS *Illustrious* was another 74-gun ship which was launched in 1803 and after a long service career broken up at Portsmouth in 1869. The third ship of the line to carry the name was a 'Majestic class' battleship with 12″ guns, launched in 1896 and scrapped in 1920. The fourth vessel to carry the name was an 'Illustrious class' aircraft carrier commissioned in 1940 and which served the Royal Navy until 1954. An 'Invincible class' aircraft carrier launched in 1981 was the fifth HMS *Illustrious*. A strategic review in 2010 concluded that the vessel should be withdrawn in 2014. The ships motto is '*Vox Non Incerta*' which translates as 'No Uncertain Voice'.

'Majestic class' battleship HMS *Illustrious* is seen at anchor in 1905. *Official image*

45536 PRIVATE W. WOOD V.C. (LMS 6018 and 5536) built Crewe Works, entered traffic unnamed in May 1933. Named in 1936, Loco No 6018 the Claughton locomotive it replaced (withdrawn February 1933) also carried that name, from April 1926. Lot /Works No 095. Rebuilt by BR and re-entered service in November 1948. Withdrawn by BR in December 1962 and cut up at Crewe Works in March 1964.

Re-built Patriot class BR No 45536 PRIVATE W. WOOD, V.C. is seen on shed at Trafford Park, Manchester on 13 June 1958. In the company of LMS Stanier 2-6-2T BR No 40077 and LMS Fowler 4-4-0 BR No 40674. *Anistr.com/Bernard Brown*

Private W. Wood V.C. (1897-1982) was a soldier of the 10th Battalion Northumberland Fusiliers, who was born in Stockport, UK. The Victoria Cross (V.C.) is the highest most prestigious award for gallantry in the face of the enemy which can be awarded to British and Commonwealth forces. At the age of 21 and during the World War I battle for Vittorio Veneto (28 October 1918) in Italy Private Wood carried out the brave and selfless deeds which earned him his V.C. A British advance near to the town of Casa Vana was being held up by hostile enemy machine gun and sniper fire. Private Wood on his own initiative advanced with his Lewis gun and directed his fire towards the flank of an enemy machine gun nest (the military term for such an action being *enfilade)* his action caused 140 men to surrender. Later during the same advance, after a hidden machine gun had opened fire on the Allied troops, Private Wood returned fire at point blank range and advanced singlehandedly towards the enemy position, he continually fired his Lewis gun from the hip as he did so. Having silenced the machine gun Private Wood, without waiting for further orders, took control of an enemy occupied ditch by raining fire upon it. This action subsequently caused a further 160 men and 3 officers to surrender. Wilfred Wood worked as a locomotive driver and the name plate from the withdrawn loco (No 45536) was placed on display inside Norbury Primary School, Hazel Grove until being transferred to the Northumberland Fusiliers regimental museum. Wilfred Wood joined the LNWR at Stockport in 1915 transferring to Newton Heath; after war service he became a passed fireman in 1919 and a driver in June 1936.

THE FIFTH REGIMENT of FOOT, THE ROYAL NORTHUMBERLAND FUSILIERS.

1918

Pte.. WILFRED WOOD (10th Service Battalion)

V.C. picture card kindly loaned for publication by *David Anderson*

45537 PRIVATE E. SYKES, V.C. (LMS 6015 and 5537) built Crewe Works, entered traffic in July 1933. Loco No 6015 the Claughton locomotive it replaced (withdrawn February 1933) also carried that name, from April 1926. Lot /Works No 095. Withdrawn by BR in June 1962 and cut up at Crewe Works in September 1962.

Patriot class BR No 45537 PRIVATE E. SYKES, V.C. is seen near Diggle on the trans Pennine route with a Manchester – Leeds service circa 1954, note the rake of mixed ex LNER and BR coaching stock. *Norman Preedy Collection*

Private E. Sykes V.C. (1885-1945) was a soldier of the 27th Battalion Northumberland Fusiliers, who was born in Mossley, Lancashire, UK. The Victoria Cross (V.C.) is the highest most prestigious award for gallantry in the face of the enemy which can be awarded to British and Commonwealth forces. At the age of 32, and during the World War I battle for the control of Arras in France Private Sykes carried out the brave and selfless deeds which earned him his V.C. During that battle on the 19 April 1917 the battalion was pinned down by heavy enemy fire from the front and flank, the Northumberland Fusiliers were taking casualties at an alarming rate. Despite the heavy fire Private Sykes went forward and brought back four wounded colleagues. He then made a fifth foray into that extremely dangerous territory and remained there, in life threatening conditions whilst bandaging all those who were too severely wounded to be moved. During the Second World War Private Sykes, (a London & North Western Railway company employee) returned to serve with the 25th Battalion West Riding Home Guard. His V.C. is displayed at the Northumberland Fusiliers regimental museum in Alnwick, as is the locomotive's nameplate. Following war service Ernest Sykes returned to the railways and served the LNWR and LMS for a period as a train guard. Sykes is honoured by a Tameside Metropolitan Borough Council blue plaque erected in 1996 at the George Lawton Hall in his home town of Mossley, Greater Manchester. A second plaque was erected in 2004 at his workplace of Mossley railway station.

The Northumberland Fusiliers motto, '*Quo Fata Vocant*' is translated as 'Whither the Fates Call'.

THE FIFTH REGIMENT of FOOT, THE ROYAL NORTHUMBERLAND FUSILIERS.

1917

PTE. ERNEST SYKES
(27th Service Battalion (Tyneside Irish))

V.C. picture card kindly loaned for publication by *David Anderson*

Patriot class BR No 45539 E.C. TRENCH is seen as LMS No 5539 and is pictured on shed at Aston, in this 1934 image. *Edward Talbot Collection*

Ernest Frederic Crosbie Trench CBE, TD (1869–1960) was a British civil engineer who had a close association with railways. He was born to a noble family with his mother (Frances Charlotte Talbot Crosbie) being particularly well connected to British aristocracy. Trench studied at Trinity College Dublin for a Master of Arts degree. Thereafter he chose to pursue a career in engineering in general, and railway engineering in particular. He became an active associate member of the Institute of Civil Engineers in 1897, attaining full membership status in 1904. He was elected to the organisation's ruling council in 1915 and served on it for the next 17 years, being elected vice president in 1924 and then serving as president between 1927/28. Trench was created a Commander of the British Empire (C.B.E.) for wartime services and further honoured with the Territorial Decoration (T.D.) after serving as a volunteer Colonel in the Engineer and Railway Staff Corps. In 1923 he was appointed to the post of Chief Engineer at the London, Midland and Scottish Railway, he retired from that post in April 1930.

Engineer and Railway Staff Corps was founded by William McMurdo in 1865 to ensure 'the combined action among all the railways when the country is in danger' and tasked particularly with 'the preparation, during peace, of schemes for drawing troops from given distant parts and for concentrating them within given areas in the shortest possible time'.

BR No 45539 is seen in familiar territory, descending Beattock Bank on the WCML, at speed with a Glasgow-Carlisle stopping train on 9 July 1960. *David Anderson*

45540 SIR ROBERT TURNBULL (LMS 5901 and 5540) built Crewe Works, entered traffic in August 1933. Lot / Works No 095. Rebuilt by BR and re-entered service in November 1947. Withdrawn by BR in April 1963 and cut up at Crewe Works in July 1963.

Rebuilt Patriot class BR No 45540 SIR ROBERT TURNBULL is seen at Cheadle Hulme in charge of 'The Comet' which was a titled express service. The train ran between London Euston and Manchester London Road (Piccadilly from 12 September 1960). The first titled run took place on 12 September 1932, with a break between September 1939 and September 1949. The last titled run of this train took place on 7 September 1962. *Norman Preedy Collection*

Sir Robert Turnbull MVO (21 February 1852 – 22 February 1925) was a British railway manager. He was made a member of the Royal Victorian Order in the 1911 New Year Honours and knighted in 1913. He served as a Lieutenant Colonel in the Engineer and Railway Staff Corps.

He was a major player during the growth of Britain's railway industry in general, and in particular during the development of the London & North Western Railway (LNWR).

Robert Turnbull was educated at Whitchurch Grammar School in Shropshire. He joined the London and North Western Railway (L&NWR/LNWR) in 1868 and some seven years later became assistant district superintendent at Liverpool, moving to London to take up the post of Superintendent Southern Division in 1885. Two years later he became assistant superintendent of the line and then superintendent in 1895. He was promoted to the post of General Manager in 1914 but left that post in 1915 and joined the LNWR board of directors. He was also a director of the London, Brighton & South Coast Railway (LBSCR). In 1917 Turnbull returned to the LNWR so that his brother in law, Sir Guy Calthrop could be released from the company for war service as controller of mines (coal).

The offices of L&NWR company on the quay at Waterford, Ireland circa 1910. *National Library of Ireland*

45543 HOME GUARD (LMS 5543) built Crewe Works, entered traffic unnamed in March 1934. Lot /Works No 095. The locomotive was named in 1940. Withdrawn by BR in November 1962 and cut up at Crewe Works in September 1963.

Patriot class BR No 45543 HOME GUARD is seen at Brock troughs near Bamber Bridge, Garstang on 19 September 1955. These particular water troughs were approximately 560 yards in length. *Norman Preedy Collection*

The Home Guard (initially 'Local Defence Volunteers' (LDV) or in a popular slang term of the period, 'Look Duck Vanish', (hence the name change) was a defence organisation of the British Army during the Second World War. Operational from 1940 until 1944, the Home Guard, comprising approximately 1.5 million local volunteers (otherwise ineligible for military service) usually owing to age, hence the well-known nickname 'Dad's Army', acted as a secondary defence force, in case of invasion by the forces of Nazi Germany and their allies. The force guarded the coastal areas of Britain and other important places such as airfields, factories, explosives stores and critical areas of the civilian infrastructure.

Patriot class BR No 45543 HOME GUARD is seen in glorious sunshine at Carnforth depot in 1962. *LMS Patriot Project*

WW2 Home Guard Serviceman's lapel badge.

Other Patriot locomotives

BR Number/Name	Loco Period in Service	HMS – Date Launched
45515 CAERNARVON	09/1932–06/1962	1 ship 1905
45520 LLANDUDNO	02/1933–05/1962	1 ship 1941
45521 RHYL	03/1933–09/1963	2 ships 1940, 1959
45522 PRESTATYN	03/1933–09/1964	1 ship 1918
45523 BANGOR	03/1933–01/1964	1 ship 1940
45546 FLEETWOOD	03/1934–06/1962	2 ships 1655, 1959

The 'Patriot class' listings have included names which are commonly accepted to have been selected by the LMS naming committee because of their obvious military connection. However, other locomotives of the class have names which could be linked to the military for a secondary reason. For example, names having associations with British/Allied naval vessels. See table above.

Locomotive LMS No 5509 (BR 45509) was allocated the name COMMANDO but never carried that name and became THE DERBYSHIRE YEOMANRY in 1951. Locomotive LMS No 5549 (BR 45549) was allocated the name R.A.M.C. (Royal Army Medical Corps) but never carried that name and remained unnamed.

Rebuilt Patriot class BR No 45522 PRESTATYN is seen between turns at Buxton depot during the summer of 1963. *Keith Langston Collection*

Patriot class BR No 45546 FLEETWOOD is pictured at speed on the WCML near Symington with a Liverpool/Manchester–Glasgow Central express on 14 June 1958. *David Anderson*

The Patriot Project – No 45551 THE UNKNOWN WARRIOR

The scrapping of the last of the original Patriot class engines was a cause of great sadness for all admirers of this unique design. Preserving large locomotives hadn't got off the ground at the time of the withdrawal of the final engine of the class in December 1962.

By this time withdrawal and scrapping of certain classes often had nothing to do with their condition, but was more to do with the directives of British Railways accountants.

This fiscal driven approach led to the withdrawal of all 34 of original Patriots in a little less than two years, an act often described with hindsight as 'indecent haste'. In fact, one Patriot (BR No 45547 an unnamed engine) had only just been given a full works overhaul before being put into store and subsequently scrapped.

Following the successful launch of a number of new build projects during the late nineteen eighties and nineties it became clear that almost anything was possible provided the money could be raised. Fast forward to 2007 and a chance conversation between the then editor of 'Steam Railway' magazine and David Bradshaw (founder of the County of Glamorgan new build project) which led to the launch of the LMS Patriot Project.

The stated intention of the project group was identified as 'recreating a fully functioning example of the iconic Patriot 4-6-0 design', but built to modern standards. A public appeal was launched. The results were immediate, generous and gratifying. As the project reached the mid-point of 2018 approximately £2.5 million had been raised. The group decided to reuse the running number of the last member of the class, BR No 45551(an unnamed engine withdrawn in 1962). Following a ballot of 'Steam Railway' readers, the name THE UNKNOWN WARRIOR was chosen. The new build engine was subsequently recognised as the National Memorial engine.

THE UNKNOWN WARRIOR, a work in progress. A front-end mock up seen at the Llangollen Railway in July 2013. *Keith Langston Collection*

The original BR No 45551 seen at speed on the WCML during the summer of 1960. *David Anderson*

The crest adorning the original locomotive nameplate, had to be redesigned following a change of heart by the Royal British Legion (RBL). The nameplate with a new crest was unveiled during a ceremony at the Heritage Centre, Crewe. During November 2018 the firebox and boiler were trial fitted into the locomotive frames. *LMS Patriot Project*

Wheels on the move. *LMS-Patriot Project*

The frames were ordered from Corus Steel, Cradley Heath and were Plasma cut to shape in March 2009, after which they were delivered to the works of Boro' Foundry in Lyle, Worcestershire so that they could be drilled (300 holes on each plate), in order to facilitate construction (as a pair). Progress on building what is only the second full size steam locomotive in the UK since 1960 has been fairly rapid. However, the unfortunate need to find an alternative contractor in order to complete the boiler (following the decision by the original builder to discontinue contract work) added between six and nine months to the overall completion date; at the time of writing that was expected to be September 2019.

Towards the end of 2010 the 6 driving wheels were cast by Boro' Foundry. After casting, the wheels were delivered to South Devon Engineering. Thereafter, the finished wheels and axles were transported to

The new nameplate was unveiled by Falkland's veteran Simon Weston CBE, during a ceremony held on 10 November 2018. Pictured at the ceremony, which also included a dedication are L to R, Ian Dudson HM Lord Lieutenant for Staffordshire, Simon Weston CBE, Reverend Mike Roberts Chaplain Rail Industry and BT Police Manchester Area, and David Bradshaw Chairman LMS-Patriot Project. *Bob Sweet/LMS Patriot Project*

the Llangollen Railway works. In the meantime, the rolling chassis was described as an advanced 'work in progress' at contractors Llangollen Railway Works, during early 2018.

The intention is to run the locomotive on the mainline and once commissioning and running-in are completed, work will start on fitting the electronic equipment necessary to allow the engine to run on the national network and hopefully haul the 'Cavell Van', used originally to bring the body of the Unknown Warrior from Dover to London Victoria station in a re-enactment of this historical event, scheduled to take place on 11 November 2020.

Monetary support is crucial and will be needed for some time to come. Membership and Regular Donation forms can be downloaded from www.lms-patriot.org.uk and can also be requested in writing, or by telephoning 01785 244156. Card donations can be made at www.lms-patriot.org.uk.

The Ribblehead Viaduct carries the Settle–Carlisle Railway across Batty Moss in the valley of the River Ribble at Ribblehead, in North Yorkshire, England. The viaduct, built by the Midland Railway opened 3 August 1875. Preserved 'Jubilee' class BR No 45699 GALATEA in silhouette against the darkening sky. The locomotive is seen on Ribblehead Viaduct (Settle & Carlisle route) in this stunning image of the 'Cumbrian Mountain Express' charter taken on 17 February 2018. *Dave Hewitt*

Stanier 4-6-0 'Jubilee' class

The LMS order for the last five 'Patriot' class engines (5552–5557) was instead built by Stanier with taper boilers and top feeds, thus becoming the first of the 4-6-0 5XP (reclassified 6P5F in 1951) 3-cylinder 'Jubilee' class. In total 191 'Jubilee' class engines were built, 141 at Crewe Works (LMS Nos 5552–5556 and 5607-5742) and 50 locomotives, by the contractor North British Locomotive Co in Glasgow (LMS Nos 5557–5606). The building programme commenced in 1934 and continued until the last locomotive LMS No 5742 entered service in December 1936.

The engines came into service concurrently with the 'Black Five' class. They were intended for all ordinary main line work with the exception of the heaviest 'top link' jobs which were at that time carried out by the '8P' class engines. In service the 'Jubilee' class worked extremely successfully, with notable performances achieved on principal express trains over the former Midland Railway (MR) route. Basically, the locomotives were coupled to Stanier 9 ton 4000-gallon and 3500-gallon tenders, and alternatively to smaller Fowler 9 ton 3500-gallon and high sided tenders, the inter changing of which did take place. Locomotive LMS No 5552 was named SILVER JUBILEE to celebrate the Silver Jubilee of King George V, giving the class its name.

The locomotives carried names associated with the then British Empire, some being named specifically after admirals and warships whilst other carried names of engines from an earlier age. There were several modifications during service including the addition of double chimneys and larger boilers. Under British Railways the class was numbered in the series 45552–45742. The curved nameplates were carried over the leading driving wheel splasher.

The nameplates of preserved 'Jubilee' LMS No 5690 (BR No 45690) as seen on 30 September 2017. On the left (driver's side) the fitted nameplate had a 'Red' background. On the right hand (fireman's side), the fitted nameplate had a 'Black' background. The locomotive at that time was finished in British Railways (BR) lined black livery. *David Moyle*

The LMS selected the class to celebrate the Silver Jubilee of King George V and Queen Mary. All 191 of the class came into British Railways stock in 1948 and, three years later, their power classification was revised to 6P. Apart from locomotive BR No 45637, which was damaged beyond repair in the 1952 Harrow disaster, the class survived intact until 1960, when scrapping proper began. The final three of the class were retired in 1967. They were the last working Stanier designed express passenger locomotives, four of which have been privately preserved.

Tender Types

No less than four tender types were attached to the Jubilee engines as built, although the tenders were not always new and often had been originally attached to other LMS locomotives e.g. 'Royal Scot' class.

In the London Midland & Scottish Railway nomenclature of the time the types were:

(a)   Old standard straight sides, 3,500 gallons, 5½ tons of coal. (Fowler type low sides with double coal rails often referred to as 'greedy bars'). Wheelbase 13ft 0in, width 7ft 1in (overall length of engine and tender 62ft 8¾in).

(b)   Modified old standard with higher straight sides, 3,500 gallons, 7 tons of coal. (Fowler type without coal rails but with higher sides). Only ten of this type were constructed. Wheelbase 13ft 0in, width 7ft 1in (overall length of engine and tender 62ft 8¾ in).

(c)   New type higher sides with inward curving top edge, 3,500 gallons and 7 tons of coal. (a mixture of Fowler and Stanier styles). Wheelbase 13ft 0in, width 7ft 1in (overall length of engine and tender 62ft 8¾in,).

(d)   Stanier type curved top sides, 4,000 gallons and 9 tons of coal. When first built, and initially fitted to LMS locomotives 5682–5690 they were almost certainly the first railway-built all-welded tenders (as opposed to rivetted/part welded rivetted construction). Wheelbase 15ft 0in (overall length of engine and tender 64ft 8¾ in, width 8ft 6in).

The Fowler and Stanier types each had three axles with 51in diameter 12 spoke wheels.

This 1957 image of 'Jubilee' class BR No 45710 IRRESISTIBLE leaving Manchester Victoria station, as the 'train engine' of a double header shows clearly the narrower 7ft 1in width of the Fowler style 3,500 gallon/7ton tender, in comparison to the locomotive footplate width of 8ft 6in. Note that the coal has been stacked high by utilising the 'greedy bars'. *Keith Langston Collection*

'Jubilee' class BR No 45731 PERSEVERANCE with a Stanier type curved top sides, 4,000 gallons/9 tons tender is seen on shed at Carlisle Kingmoor in the spring of 1962. *Mike Stokes Archive*

'Jubilee' class BR No 45717 DAUNTLESS with a Stanier type curved top sides, 4,000 gallons/9 tons tender is seen at Elvanfoot whilst climbing Beattock Bank on 18 April 1959, with a Liverpool/Manchester – Glasgow express. Beattock Summit is a high point of the West Coast Main Line (WCML) railway and of the A74(M) motorway as they cross between Dumfries and Galloway and South Lanarkshire in south west Scotland. The height of the summit is 1,033 feet (315 m) above sea level. However, the trackside signboard records the railway elevation as being 1,016 feet. *David Anderson*

'Jubilee' class BR No 45696 ARETHUSA with a Fowler type 3,500 gallons/7 ton tender with coal rails, is also seen on Beattock Bank with a down express on 22 August 1955. Note that the driver seems keen to be in the photograph. *David Anderson*

45616 MALTA (LMS 5616) built Crewe Works entered traffic August 1936, Lot No 112 – Works No 177, the locomotive was renamed MALTA G.C. on 23 October 1943. Withdrawn by BR in January 1961 and cut up at Crewe Works in February 1961.

'Jubilee' class BR No 45616 MALTA G.C. is seen at Crewe in the summer of 1948. Note that the locomotive has at that time been renumbered, and is in British Railways livery whilst the Fowler style tender (complete with coal / 'greedy rails') still carries LMS markings.

'Jubilee' class BR No 45616 MALTA G.C. is seen passing Trent Station on 19 May 1951, note Trent Station North Junction signal box and the impressive array of signals. *Both images Norman Preedy Collection*

Trent railway station was situated near Long Eaton in Derbyshire at the junction of the Midland Railway line from London to Derby and Nottingham. The station which opened in May 1862 was closed 1 January 1968. It was unusual in that it did not serve any community, simply having been built to serve as an interchange. It was particularly remarkable in that, although there was an up and a down platform, trains for a given destination might face in either direction.

Malta – The George Cross Island

The George Cross medal was famously awarded directly to the Mediterranean island of Malta by the British Monarch King George VI. A letter from Buckingham Palace signed by the King and addressed to Lieutenant-General Sir William Dobbie, the island's then Governor stated that the reason for the award was to 'bear witness to the heroism and devotion of its people' during the great siege they underwent in the early part of World War II. This award was made by King George VI by a letter in his own hand. The naval and air forces of Italy and Germany besieged the then British colony from 1940 to 1942. The George Cross was incorporated into the Flag of Malta beginning in 1943 and remains on the current design of the flag.

RN Maltese ratings seen mounting guard over the displayed George Cross in 1943.

The George Cross was instituted by King George VI, on 24 September 1940, replacing the Empire Gallantry Medal. It is the civilian equivalent to the Victoria Cross. While intended mainly for civilians, it is awarded also to certain fighting services, confined however to actions for which purely military honours are not normally given. This medal is awarded only for acts of the greatest heroism or the most conspicuous courage in circumstances of extreme danger.

George Cross.

During the siege heavy bombardment by Italian and German bombers wreaked havoc upon the Maltese islands, creating huge shortages of supplies. However, an invasion threat in July 1941 ended in failure when stoic coastal defenders spotted approaching torpedo boats, of the Italian Decima MAS special forces. With the people suffering hunger, a final assault to neutralise the island was ordered by the German Field Marshal Albert Kesselring. History showed that the people's heroism withstood every attack.

At the time of the George Cross award, military resources and food rations in Malta were practically finished. Fuel was restricted to military action and heavily rationed, the population was on the brink of starvation, and even ammunition was running out, so much that Anti-Aircraft (AA) guns could only fire a few rounds per day.

Italian battleships outgunned the Royal Navy, but they were far from outclassed. The German air force attacked with superior aircraft against the RAF's ageing Gloster Gladiator biplane fighter aircraft but towards the end of the siege Supermarine Spitfires were finally sent to help defend the Maltese islands. German and Italian strategists were reportedly planning 'Operation Herkules', a sea and air invasion of the islands, often postponed and eventually abandoned because the Maltese Islands finally received supplies of food, fuel and munitions.

On 15 August 1942 (feast of Santa Maria) a convoy of Royal and Merchant Navy ships reached the Grand Harbour, Valletta, after completing what historians described as one of the most heroic maritime episodes in recent history. A public award ceremony in Valletta was held on 13 September 1942, after the arrival of the 'Santa Maria Convoy'. That event is still commemorated annually in St. Georges Square.

George V1's letter to the people of the island is seen displayed on the wall of the 'Grandmaster's Palace' Valleta, Malta.

45639 RALEIGH (LMS 5639) built Crewe Works entered traffic December 1934, Lot No 112 – Works No 200. It was withdrawn by BR in October 1963, cut up at Crewe Works during January 1964.

'Jubilee' class BR No 45639 RALEIGH, is noted by a stylishly dressed train-spotter at Leeds Holbeck depot circa 1958. Railway Images (sales@railwayimages.com)

Walter Raleigh

He was born in East Budleigh, Devon (c.1554 – 29 October 1618). He was an English gentleman, writer, poet, soldier, politician, courtier, spy, and explorer cousin to Sir Richard Grenville and younger half-brother of Sir Humphrey Gilbert. He is perhaps mainly remembered for popularizing tobacco in England. He rose rapidly to favour with Queen Elizabeth I who bestowed a knighthood on him in 1585. In what could be rightly described as an eventful life Raleigh was twice imprisoned in the Tower of London, firstly for marrying, without permission, one of the Queen's ladies in waiting and secondly for his part in a plot against King James I (1603). After his release, he led an expedition in search of the so called *El Dorado* during which he took part in an unsuccessful military action against a Spanish outpost in South America. On his return to England, and despite his previous good deeds on behalf of the nation, he was arrested and executed apparently in order to appease the Spanish rulers of the time.

He was beheaded at the Palace of Westminster in the Old Palace Yard on 29 October 1618; having asked to see and been shown the axe he reportedly remarked that it was 'sharp medicine, but a physician for all diseases and miseries'. His headless body was laid to rest at St. Margaret's, Westminster but gruesomely Raleigh's head was embalmed and presented to his wife, which she kept. After her death 29 years later, his head was returned to his tomb.

Six ships and one shore establishment of the Royal Navy have borne the name HMS *Raleigh*. The first a 32-gun vessel captured in 1778 and the last a 'Hawkins-class' heavy cruiser launched in 1919. The vessel ran aground off Labrador in April 1922 and was eventually declared a total loss and blown up by the Royal Navy in September 1926.

Shore-based HMS *Raleigh* is the largest Royal Navy training establishment in the South West of England. The centre also trains members of the Royal Marines, Royal Fleet Auxiliary and the Royal Navy Reserve.

The name SIR WALTER RALEIGH was also carried by the Southern Railway (SR) 'Lord Nelson' class locomotive BR No 30852 (SR No 852). See *British Steam-Military Connections GWR, SR, BR and WD*, by the same author and published by Pen & Sword Books.

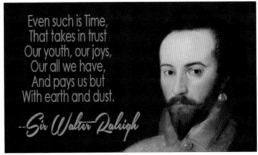

Even such is Time,
That takes in trust
Our youth, our joys,
Our all we have,
And pays us but
With earth and dust.

Sir Walter Raleigh

Many quotations attributed to Raleigh have been recorded, this being one such.

45640 FROBISHER (LMS 5640) built Crewe Works entered traffic December 1934, Lot No 112 – Works No 201. It was withdrawn by BR in March 1964, cut up at Campbells Airdrie during January 1965.

'Jubilee' BR No 45640 FROBISHER is seen hard at work passing Harthope on Beattock Bank with a Euston-Perth express during August 1955. *David Anderson*

Sir Martin Frobisher

He was an eminent mariner during the reign of Queen Elizabeth I (1558-1603).

Martin Frobisher was born circa 1539. From his educational background Frobisher developed an interest in the mysteries that lay overseas. In his early life he crewed a number of voyages to the African coast (1550s) and fought for the Protestants during the 'Revolt of the Spanish Netherlands'.

As a 'privateer' Frobisher embarked on trading voyages which included his three journeys to find the North West Passage resulting in the infamous 'Fools Gold' voyage in 1576 when he returned home with tons of black rocks, wrongly thinking that they contained gold. His searches for the North West Passage resulted in the naming of the Frobisher Strait. He also visited Greenland and returned with some iron nails, which perchance indicated that other European sailors had got there before the English.

He returned to military service between 1579-1580. Then promoted to Vice Admiral he fought victoriously with Sir Francis Drake against the Spanish Armada and was knighted for his part in the action.

He was given the command of *Primrose* during Drake's attacks on the West Indies between September 1585 and July 1586. He served as a Vice-Admiral. In the period 1589-1592 he made three expeditions to the Azores and when doing so captured a number of Spanish ships. During 1594 he commanded a force sent to Brest in order to aid the Huguenots and he was wounded during an attack at Croon. Frobisher died on 15 November 1594 and was subsequently buried in Plymouth, Devon.

Also, HMS *Frobisher* a 'Hawkins Class' heavy cruiser, pennant number D81 (namesake Sir Martin Frobisher) which was launched 20 March 1920 and sold for scrap after WWII in March 1949.

The name SIR MARTIN FROBISHER was also carried by the Southern Railway (SR) 'Lord Nelson' class locomotive BR No 30864 (SR No 864).

Plaque in St. Giles-without-Cripplegate, London. *Edward Hands*

54

45641 SANDWICH (LMS 5641) built Crewe Works entered traffic December 1934, Lot No 112 – Works No 202. It was withdrawn by BR in September 1964, cut up by Cashmores, Great Bridge during January 1965.

1928 built *HMS Sandwich* (Bridgewater-class sloop) is seen on WWII convoy escort duty. *Imperial War Museum*

Six ships of the Royal Navy have borne the name **HMS** *Sandwich*, either after the Kentish seaside town of Sandwich, or one of the holders of the title Earl of Sandwich, particularly Vice-Admiral Edward Montagu, 1st Earl of Sandwich, or First Lord of the Admiralty John Montagu, 4th Earl of Sandwich. A seventh ship was planned, but apparently never completed:

HMS *Sandwich* was a 90-gun second rate launched in 1679. She was rebuilt in 1712 and hulked in 1752. She was broken up in 1770.

HMS *Sandwich* was a 98-gun second rate launched in 1759. She was converted to a floating battery in 1780 and used for harbour service from 1790. She was broken up in 1810.

HMS *Sandwich* was a 24-gun armed ship, formerly the civilian *Marjory*. The Royal Navy purchased her in 1780 but on 24 August 1781 she had the misfortune to encounter the French fleet under Admiral de Grasse off the coast of the Carolinas. The French 74-gun *Souverain* captured her. The French sold her in North America in December.

HMS *Sandwich* was a 12-gun hired armed cutter that the Royal Navy hired in 1798, the French captured in 1799, and the Royal Navy recaptured in 1803, purchased in 1804, commissioned in 1805, and sold in 1805.

HMS *Sandwich* was a 12-gun schooner purchased in 1805 as HMS *Pitt*. She was renamed HMS *Sandwich* in 1807 and was broken up in 1809.

HMS *Sandwich* was to have been a 74-gun third rate. She was laid down in 1809 but was reportedly cancelled in 1811.

HMS *Sandwich* was a 'Bridgewater-class sloop' launched in 1928 and sold for breaking up in 1946.

45642 BOSCAWEN (LMS 5642) built Crewe Works entered traffic May 1934, Lot No 112 – Works No 203. It was withdrawn by BR in January 1965, cut up at Wards, Killamarsh during April 1965.

'Jubilee' BR No 45642 BOSCAWEN is seen heading a train northbound in the Lune Gorge circa 1949. *Rail Photoprints Collection*

Edward Boscawen

He was an Admiral, Privy Councillor and also a Member of Parliament for the borough of Truro, Cornwall. He was born in Tregothnan, Cornwall, on 19 August 1711, the third son of Hugh Boscawen, 1st Viscount Falmouth.

The young Edward joined the navy when 12 years old and first served aboard HMS *Superb*. That vessel was sent to the West Indies with Admiral Francis Hosier. Boscawen stayed with the ship for three years during the Anglo-Spanish War. He is known principally for his various naval commands during the 18th century and the engagements that he won, including the Siege of Louisburg in 1758 and Battle of Lagos in 1759. He is also remembered as the officer who signed the warrant authorising the execution of Admiral John Byng in 1757, for failing to engage the enemy at the Battle of Minorca (1756). On 12 March 1736 Boscawen was promoted by Admiral Sir John Norris to the temporary command of the 50-gun HMS *Leopard*.

He was also given the Freedom of the City of Edinburgh. Admiral Boscawen returned to sea for the final time and took his station off the west coast of France around Quiberon Bay. After a violent attack of typhoid fever, the Admiral came ashore where, on 10 January 1761, he died at his home in Hatchlands Park in Surrey. His body was taken to St. Michael's Church, St Michael Penkevil, Cornwall, where he was buried.

In his political role, he served as a Member of Parliament for Truro from 1742 until his death, although due to almost constant naval employment he seems not to have been particularly active. He also served as one of the Lords Commissioners of the Admiralty on the Board of Admiralty from 1751 and as a member of the Privy Council from 1758 until his death. Two Royal Navy vessels (1763 and 1844) and a shore establishment carried the name HMS *Boscawen*.

45643 RODNEY (LMS 5643) built Crewe Works entered traffic December 1934, Lot No 112 – Works No 204. It was withdrawn by BR in January 1966, cut up by Cashmores, Great Bridge during May 1966.

'Jubilee' BR No 45643 RODNEY waits to leave Lichfield Trent Valley station (WCML) with a down express, circa 1960. *Rail Photoprints Collection*

George Brydges Rodney

1st Baron Rodney, KB (baptised 13 February 1718–24 May 1792) was a Royal Navy officer.

Rodney came from a distinguished but poor background and went to sea at the age of fourteen. His first major action was the Second Battle of Cape Finisterre in 1747. During the Seven Years' War, Rodney was involved in a number of amphibious operations such as the raids on Rochefort and Le Havre and the Siege of Louisbourg. He became well known for his role in the capture of Martinique in 1762. He made a large amount of prize money during the 1740s, allowing him to purchase a large country estate and a seat in the House of Commons. Following the Treaty of Paris (1763) Rodney's financial situation stagnated. He spent large sums of money pursuing his political ambitions. By 1774 he had run up large debts and was forced to flee Britain to avoid his creditors, being incarcerated in a French jail when war was declared in 1778 (Anglo-French war). Rodney however secured his release and returned to Britain where he was appointed to a new command. He is perhaps best known for his commands in the American War of Independence. It is often claimed that he was the commander to have pioneered the naval battle tactic of 'breaking the line'. Rodney's victory at the Battle of the Saintes in April 1782, ended the French threat to Jamaica, and on returning to Britain he was made a peer.

Rodney died in 1792 and was buried in the church of St. Mary the Virgin, Old Alresford, Hampshire which adjoined his family seat.

Six ships of the Royal Navy have been named HMS *Rodney* the first being a 4-gun cutter launched in 1759.

Monument of George Brydges Rodney, in Memorial Spanish Town, Jamaica. *Anatoly Terentiev*

The last being a 'Nelson-class' battleship launched in 1925 (Pennant No 29). The vessel played a major role in the sinking of the *Bismarck* in May 1941 and was scrapped in 1948.

The name LORD RODNEY was also carried by the Southern Railway (SR) 'Lord Nelson' class locomotive BR No 30863 (SR No 863).

'Jubilee' BR No 45643 RODNEY is seen preparing to depart from Edinburgh Princes Street station with a service for Glasgow during February 1955. *David Anderson*

45644 HOWE (LMS 5644) built Crewe Works entered traffic December 1934 Lot No 112 – Works No 205. It was withdrawn by BR in November 1963, cut up at Crewe Works during January 1964.

'Jubilee' class LMS No 5644 HOWE is seen at Aberdeen station with a Glasgow express during 1947. *Rail Photoprints Collection*

Richard Howe

1st Earl Howe, KG (8 March 1726 – 5 August 1799) Admiral of the Fleet.

He was born in Albemarle Street, London, the second son of Emanuel Howe, 2nd Viscount Howe, who died as governor of Barbados in March 1735, and of Charlotte, a daughter of Baroness von Kielmansegg, afterwards Countess of Darlington, the half-sister of King George I. Howe was educated at Eton College and entered the navy by joining the crew of HMS *Pearl* in July 1739. He was notable for his service during the American War of Independence and French revolutionary wars. Howe served throughout the war of the Austrian Succession having joined the navy at the age of thirteen. During the 'Seven Years War' he gained a reputation for his role in amphibious operations against the French coast. He took part in the decisive British naval victory at the Battle of Quiberon Bay in 1759. He is perhaps best known for his service during the American War of Independence, when he acted as a naval commander and a peace commissioner with the American rebels. He served as First Lord of the Admiralty for two periods, firstly January 1783 to April 1983 when he resigned but was then re-appointed by Prime Minister William Pitt the Younger in December 1783. He resigned from that position in 1788 and was awarded an Earldom in that year.

He also commanded the British fleet during the mid-Atlantic battle and blockade against the French in 1794, referred to as the 'Glorious First of June; remarkably Howe was then 68 years of age.

Howe died at his Grafton Street London home on 5 August 1799 and was buried in the family vault at St. Andrew's Church, Langar, Nottinghamshire.

Several ships of the Royal Navy have been named HMS *Howe* the first in 1805, the last being a 'King George V-class' battleship launched in 1940 (Pennant No 32) which served throughout WWII and was decommissioned in 1950 and scrapped in 1958.

The name LORD HOWE was also carried by the Southern Railway (SR) 'Lord Nelson' class locomotive BR No 30857 (SR No 857).

'HMS *Howe*' seen in this wartime official image circa 1943.

HMS *Howe*, a ships bell seen in St. Giles Cathedral Edinburgh. The bell was presented to the cathedral in 1957. Interestingly when a baby of an RN crew member was christened at St. Giles it was the custom to up-end the bell, use it as a font and scratch the child's name inside on the lip of the bell. *Ronnie Leask*

45645 COLLINGWOOD (LMS 5645) built Crewe Works entered traffic December 1934 Lot No 112 – Works No 206. It was withdrawn by BR in November 1963, cut up at Crewe Works during that month.

'Jubilee' class BR No 45645 COLLINGWOOD leaves Llandudno Junction with a westbound service, during the summer of 1962. *Jim Carter/Rail Photoprints*

Cuthbert Collingwood

1st Baron Collingwood was born in Newcastle Upon Tyne on 26 September 1748. He was a notable partner with Lord Nelson during several of the British victories of the Napoleonic wars, and frequently as Nelson's successor in various commands. His early education was at Royal Grammar School, Newcastle upon Tyne. He first went to sea as a volunteer onboard the frigate HMS *Shannon* under the command of his cousin Capt. Richard Brathwaite (Braithwaite) who took charge of the young Collingwood's nautical education.

In 1777 Collingwood first met Horatio Nelson when they both served on the frigate HMS *Lowestoffe*. During the Battle of Trafalgar, he commanded HMS *Royal Sovereign*. On 9 November 1805 Collingwood was promoted 'Vice Admiral of the Red' and raised to the peerage as Baron Collingwood of Caldburne and Hethpool in Northumberland.

When not at sea he resided at Collingwood House in the town of Morpeth, which lies some 15 miles north of Newcastle upon Tyne and also at Chirton Hall in Chirton, North Shields. The Maritime Warfare School of the Royal Navy is commissioned as HMS *Collingwood*, it is home to training for warfare, weapon engineering and communications disciplines. In addition, three RN vessels were also named for him. Collingwood died during a voyage home onboard the HMS *Ville de Paris* on 7 March 1810 and he is laid to rest beside Nelson in the crypt of St. Pauls Cathedral. Three Royal Navy ships and one shore establishment were named HMS *Collingwood*. The first being an 80-gun vessel launched in 1841. The third vessel being a 'St. Vincent' class dreadnought battleship launched in 1908 which fought at the Battle of Jutland in 1916 and was scrapped in 1922.

The name LORD COLLINGWOOD was also carried by the Southern Railway (SR) 'Lord Nelson' class locomotive BR No 30862 (SR No 862).

A statue erected in his honour overlooks the River Tyne in the town of Tynemouth. *Len Mills*

45646 NAPIER (LMS 5646) built Crewe Works entered traffic December 1934, Lot No 112 – Works No 207. It was withdrawn by BR in December 1963, cut up at Darlington Works March 1964.

'Jubilee' class LMS No 5646 NAPIER with a rivetted construction Stanier style tender and in LMS red livery with sans lettering, is seen when still unnamed at Carlisle Kingmoor depot, on 10 June 1936, the locomotive was named in the September of that year. The 12A shed plate refers to the LMS shed identification number. *Rail Photoprints Collection*

45647 STURDEE (LMS 5647) built Crewe Works entered traffic January 1935, Lot No 112 – Works No 208. It was withdrawn by BR in April 1967, cut up at Cashmores, Great Bridge in September of that year.

'Jubilee' class LMS No 5647 STURDEE in LMS wartime black livery with unshaded lettering but in this case with maroon lining along the running plate and on cab and tender, is seen at Liverpool Edge Hill depot circa 1939. Note the power classification 5XP below the cabside number. *Rail Photoprints Collection*

Sir Charles John Napier KCB GOTE RN

Napier was born at Merchiston Hall near Falkirk, Scotland on 6 March 1786 and was educated at The Royal High School in Edinburgh. In addition to his naval career (1799-1853) he was active in politics as a Liberal Member of Parliament (elected 1855). In 1799 he became a midshipman aboard the 16-Gun sloop HMS *Martin* but left her in May 1800 before she was lost with all hands. Thereafter he played a prominent part in the capture of the Caribbean island of Martinique and the capture of the French flagship *Hautpoult* which resulted in a promotion to acting post captain, and then in 1811 to captain of the frigate HMS *Thames*. Serving both the British and Portuguese navies Napier, who had a reputation for humane reform within the service and a deep interest in the development of iron ships, was awarded the rank of Admiral.

An Edwin T. Dolby sketch of the quarter deck of *HMS Bulldog* in Bomarsund, 1854. Napier is the figure in the slouch hat carrying a telescope.

His gravestone incorporates a cross made with timbers from Nelson's *HMS Victory*. Len Mills

He was active in several prominent battles during the campaigns: *Napoleonic Wars, War of 1812 (United States), Liberal Wars (Portugal), Egyptian – Ottoman War/ Syrian War, Crimean War (Russian Empire).*

Napier was made a Knight Commander of the Order of the Bath in 1840. He continued to campaign vigorously for the improvement of the way common seamen were treated during and after service, and maintained his parliamentary seat, even though he was in poor health, until his death on 6 November 1860. His tomb is in the churchyard of All Saints, Catherington in Hampshire.

Historians have commented that Napier was, although a man of great energy and courage, ofttimes vain and certainly eccentric. He is also said to have been abrupt and perchance even rude in his dealings with fellow officers and indeed the Admiralty.

Three ships of the British Royal Navy have been named HMS *Napier*, an iron gunboat launched in 1844, an Admiralty 'M-class' destroyer launched in 1916 and an 'N-class' destroyer (Pennant No G97) launched in 1940 and served the Royal Australian Navy (RAN) throughout WWII and was broken up in 1956.

Sturdee on board *HMS Hercules*, circa 1916/17.

Sir Frederick Charles Doveton Sturdee, GCB, KCMG, CVO

1st Baronet Sturdee was born Charlton, London on 9 June 1859 and educated at the Royal Naval School at New Cross. He joined the Royal Navy as a cadet in the training ship HMS *Britannia* in July 1871. When promoted to midshipman in 1873 he joined the crew of the frigate HMS *Undaunted* which became flagship of the China Station in 1876. Specialising in torpedoes he joined HMS *Bellerophon* in 1886. In 1889 he served as a torpedo instructor on HMS *Vernon* later transferring to the Admiralty as a torpedo specialist in the Directorate of Naval Ordnance. He was promoted to full Admiral in 1917 and to Admiral of the Fleet on his retirement in July 1921.

Commands held, Nore Command, 4th Battle Squadron, 2nd and 3rd Cruiser Squadrons, 1st Battle Squadron, HMS *New Zealand*, HMS *King Edward VII*, HMS *Bulwark*, HMS *Bedford* and HMS *Porpoise*. He served in the Anglo-Egyptian War and the First World War. Awards, Knight Grand Cross of the Order of the Bath, Knight Commander of the Order of St. Michael and St. George and Commander of the Royal Victorian Order.

He died in Camberley, Surrey on 7 May 1925 and was buried at St. Peter's churchyard in Frimley.

Rosslyn Erskine Wemyss, GCB, CMG

1st Baron Wester Wemyss was a Royal Navy officer. Wemyss was born in London on 12 April 1864 and joined the Royal Navy as a cadet in the training ship HMS *Britannia* in 1877. After promotion to midshipman in 1879 he joined the crew of corvette HMS *Bacchant* and transferred to the battleship HMS *Northumberland* in 1883.

During the First World War he served as commander of the 12th Cruiser Squadron and then as Governor of Moudros, Greece before leading the British landings at Cape Helles and at Suvla Bay during the Gallipoli Campaign. He went on to be commander of the East Indies and Egyptian Squadron in January 1916 and then First Sea Lord in December 1917, in which role he encouraged Admiral Roger Keyes, commander of the Dover Patrol, to undertake more vigorous operations in the Channel, ultimately leading to the launch of the Zeebrugge Raid in April 1918.

Wemyss was the senior British representative at the signing of the armistice that ended active hostilities in the 1st World War. He is seen seated third from right. The signing took place aboard a railway carriage in the Forest of Compiègne, France. The same railway carriage was also used when France surrendered to the Germans in 1940 (2nd World War). Unfortunately, the historic vehicle was destroyed in 1945. The coloured picture is from a postcard.

Commands held: First Sea Lord, East Indies and Egyptian Squadron, 12th Cruiser Squadron, 2nd Battle Squadron, HMS *Implacable* and HMS *Suffolk*. Served throughout Second Boer War and First World War.

Awards: Knight Grand Cross of the Order of the Bath, Companion of the Order of St. Michael and St. George, Member of the Royal Victorian Order, Grand Cross of the Legion of Honour and Croix de Guerre (France), Grand Cross of the Order of the Crown (Romania) and the Navy Distinguished Service Medal. On his retirement in 1919 he was promoted to Admiral of the Fleet and raised to the peerage as Baron Wester Wemyss of Wemyss (Fife). He died in Cannes on 24 May 1933 and was buried at Wemyss Castle.

Admiral Sir John Hawkins (also spelled as Hawkyns)

He was born in 1532 in Plymouth, Devon and he first went to sea in 1562 as a trader. He is variously described as English slave trader, naval commander and administrator, merchant, navigator, ship builder and privateer. As treasurer and comptroller of the Royal Navy Hawkins rebuilt older ships in addition to helping with the design of faster ships the like of which withstood the Spanish Armada in 1588. He died on 12 November 1595 and was buried at sea, off Puerto Rico.

One Royal Navy vessel was named for Sir John Hawkins, launched in 1917 (Pennant No D86) it was a 'Hawkins class' heavy crusier which was retired in 1947.

Admiral Sir John Hawkins

Admiral Sir Richard Hawkins

Admiral Sir Richard Hawkins (also spelled as Hawkyns)

He was born in 1562 and was the son of Admiral Sir John Hawkins. Richard Hawkins was a 17th century English seaman, explorer and pirate. In 1585 during Drake's expedition to the Spanish main he captained a galliot, he also commanded a Queen's ship against the Armada in 1588. In 1593 he purchased the discovery ship *Dainty* and it seemed clear that he would utilize that vessel to prey on the overseas possessions of the Spanish crown. In 1594 the *Dainty* was successfully attacked by two Spanish ships and Hawkins, after a promise of safe conduct, surrendered. However, the promise was not kept and he was imprisoned in Spain in 1597. After being released he returned to England, being knighted in 1603, and also in that year being elected Mayor of Plymouth. In 1604 he became Vice Admiral of Devon and Member of Parliament for Plymouth.

He died in London on 17 April 1622.

The name SIR JOHN HAWKINS was also carried by the Southern Railway (SR) 'Lord Nelson' class locomotive BR No 30865 (SR No 865).

45648 WEMYSS (LMS 5648) built Crewe Works entered traffic January 1935, Lot No 112 – Works No 209. It was withdrawn by BR in February 1963, cut up at Crewe Works in the same month.

'Jubilee' class BR No 45648 WEMYSS is seen undergoing servicing at Dalry Road, Edinburgh after arriving with the Birmingham – Edinburgh service, on 12 July 1954. *David Anderson*

45649 HAWKINS (LMS 5649) built Crewe Works entered traffic January 1935, Lot No 112 – Works No 210. It was withdrawn by BR in September 1963, cut up at Crewe Works in October 1963.

'Jubilee' class BR No 45649 HAWKINS is seen between turns at Annesley Depot in 1962. *Mike Stokes Archive*

45650 BLAKE (LMS 5650) built Crewe Works entered traffic January 1935, Lot No 112 – Works No 211. It was withdrawn by BR in January 1963, cut up at Crewe Works in June of that year.

'Jubilee' class BR No 45650 BLAKE is seen with 'The Waverley' at Leeds City on 2 August 1958. 'The Waverley' St. Pancras-Edinburgh (Waverley). First titled run 17 June 1957 and the last titled run 28 September 1968. *Keith Langston Collection*

45651 SHOVELL (LMS 5651) built Crewe Works entered traffic January 1935, Lot No 212 – Works No 212. It was withdrawn by BR in November 1962, cut up at Crewe Works in December of that year.

'Jubilee' class BR No 45651 SHOVELL is seen passing London Road signal box as it leaves Derby for the south west during 1959. Note the DMUs to the left of the image. *Rail Photoprints Collection*

Admiral Robert Blake

He was born on 27 September 1598 in Bridgwater, Somerset, the son of a merchant and one of thirteen siblings. He was educated at Bridgwater Grammar School for Boys and thereafter attended Wadham College, Oxford. Before he went to sea Blake followed a career in politics after being elected as the Member of Parliament for Bridgwater in 1640. At the onset of the English Civil War and after failing to be re-elected Blake began a military career on the side of the Parliamentarians despite having no previous experience of military matters. Having distinguished himself during the Siege of Bristol he was given the rank of Lieutenant Colonel (1643). He was appointed 'General at Sea' in 1649 as the parliamentarian navy did not use the rank of admiral, his actual role being a combination of an admiral and commissioner of the Navy.

Blake has often been referred to as 'Father of the Royal Navy' as he was largely responsible for building the largest navy the country had at that time ever known. He was the first commander to keep a fleet at sea during the winter and additionally produced the navy's first set of rules and regulations which were called 'The Laws of War and Ordinances of the Sea'. Holding the rank of General at Sea and also Colonel he took part in the English Civil War, First Anglo-Dutch War, Barbary pirate Campaign and the Anglo-Spanish War.

Statue of Robert Blake in his home town of Bridgwater Somerset. *Len Mills*

He died at sea off Plymouth on 7 August 1657 and after lying in state at Greenwich he was given a full state funeral and was initially buried in Westminster Abbey. However, in 1661 King Charles II ordered his body to be exhumed and 'dumped in a common grave' in St. Margaret's churchyard.

Four ships of the Royal Navy have carried the name HMS *Blake*

The first in 1808 and the fourth a 'Tiger-class' guided missile cruiser, completed in 1961 and scrapped in 1982.

The name ROBERT BLAKE was also carried by the Southern Railway (SR) 'Lord Nelson' class locomotive BR No 30855 (SR No 855).

Sir Cloudesley Shovell

He was born November 1650 in Cockthorpe, Norfolk the son of a Norfolk gentleman. He first went to sea as a cabin boy in 1663. Promoted to midshipman in January 1672 he joined the crew of HMS *Royal Prince*, the flagship of the Duke of York. His first command as captain was HMS *Sapphire*, which he joined in September 1677. He was promoted to Vice Admiral in 1694 and to the rank of full Admiral in 1702.

Commands held were HMS *Sapphire*, HMS *Phoenix*, HMS *Nonsuch*, HMS *James Galley*, HMS *Anne*, HMS *Dover*, HMS *Edgar* and HMS *Monck*. He took part in the Third Anglo-Dutch War (battles of Sole Bay and Texel), Nine Years War (battles of Bantry Bay and Barfleur), War of the Spanish Succession (capture of Gibraltar, Siege of Barcelona and Battle of Toulon). He also served two terms as Member of Parliament for Rochester, Kent 1695-1701 and 1705-1707.

18th century engraving of the 'Scilly Naval Disaster' October 1707. *HMS Association* is seen in the centre of the image.

He died off the coast of Scilly during the Naval Disaster of 22 and 23 October 1707 when in the region of 2000 sailors lost their lives. Shovel's flagship HMS *Association* with three other vessels, HMS *Eagle*, HMS *Romney*, and HMS *Firebrand* all sank. The fleet was returning from the Battle of Toulon on what was described as 'a difficult voyage'. Reportedly Shovell mistakenly thought that he was off the coast of Brittany but he was actually approaching the Isles of Scilly. Shovell's body was washed up at Porthellick Cove St Marys, Isle of Scilly. He was temporarily buried on the beach but later interred at Westminster Abbey on 22 December 1707, having been carried in state to London by the order of Queen Anne.

Edward Hawke, KB, PC, Admiral of the Fleet

1st Baron Hawke was born the only son of a barrister on 21 February 1705 at Lincolns Inn, London. He joined the navy as a volunteer in February 1720 and joined the crew of HMS *Seahorse* and in 1725 after being promoted to lieutenant he transferred to HMS *Kingsale*. On 13 April 1733 Hawke was promoted to commander of the sloop HMS *Wolf* and was promoted to captain of that vessel on 20 March 1734.

Hawke portrait by Francis Cotes.

As captain of *HMS Berwick* he took part in the Battle of Toulon in February 1744 during the War of the Austrian Succession. He also captured six ships of a French squadron in the Bay of Biscay in the Second Battle of Cape Finisterre in October 1747. Hawke went on to achieve his most famous victory over a French fleet at the Battle of Quiberon Bay in November 1759 during the Seven Years' War, thereby preventing a French invasion of Britain. He developed the concept of a Western Squadron, keeping an almost continuous blockade of the French coast throughout the war.

Commands held were HMS *Wolf,* HMS *Flamborough,* HMS *Portland,* HMS *Berwick,* HMS *Neptune,* Western Squadron and Commander in Chief Portsmouth. He took part in the War of the Austrian Succession and the Seven Years War. Hawke also sat in the House of Commons from 1747 to 1776 and served as First Lord of the Admiralty for five years between 1766 and 1771. In this post, he was successful in bringing the navy's spending under control, and also oversaw the mobilisation of the navy during the 1770 Falklands Crisis. He died at home in Sunbury-on-Thames on 17 October 1781 and was buried at St. Nicolas' Church, North Stoneham.

Seven ships of the Royal Navy carried the name HMS *Hawke* after an old English spelling of the bird's name, but two vessels were actually named after Edward Hawke. They were a 74-gun ship of the line in 1820 and an 'Edgar-class' cruiser launched in 1891, which was sunk by a U Boat in 1914 (WWI) with a loss of 524 crew members, including the captain.

The name LORD HAWKE was also carried by the Southern Railway (SR) 'Lord Nelson' class locomotive BR No 30860 (SR No 860).

Charles Middleton, PC

1st Baron Barham, Admiral, was born 14 October 1726 in Leith, Midlothian to Robert Middleton a customs collector of Bo'ness, Linlithgowshire. He joined the Royal Navy in 1741 as a captain's servant assigned in turn to the vessels HMS *Sandwich* and HMS *Duke*. He later served as a midshipman and masters mate aboard HMS *Flamborough* and became a lieutenant in 1745 whilst serving aboard HMS *Chesterfield*. In January 1757 during a dispute over rum rations and whilst in a fit of temper he physically attacked a sailor which resulted in the sailor being court martialled and Middleton being promoted to command of the sloop HMS *Speaker*.

In 1775 he was given a guardship at the Nore and subsequently appointed comptroller of the navy in 1778, a position he held for 12 years. He was created a baronet in 1781. On 1 February 1793 he was promoted to Vice Admiral and in May 1794 he was appointed to the Board of Admiralty becoming 1st Naval Lord in March 1795 and full admiral on 1 June of that year. Commands held were

Launched in 1914 the 'Queen Elizabeth' class battleship HMS *Barham* was reconstructed (refitted) in the period 1931 to 1934. This image was taken during the mid-1930s. The vessel was damaged by German aircraft during the evacuation of Crete before being sunk by the German Submarine 'U-331'.

HMS *Arundel,* HMS *Emerald* and HMS *Adventure*. He took part in the Seven Years War, American War of Independence, French Revolutionary Wars and the Napoleonic Wars. He died 17 June 1813 at Barham Court, Teston, Kent.

Three warships of the Royal Navy have been given the name HMS *Barham*, the first in 1811 and the most recent of which being a 'Queen Elizabeth-class' battleship launched in 1914 (Pennant No 04) which was sunk by a 'U-Boat' off the Egyptian coast on 25th November 1941 with a loss of 862 lives, approximately two thirds of her crew.

45652 HAWKE (LMS 5652) built Crewe Works entered traffic January 1935, Lot No 112 – Works No 213. It was withdrawn by BR in January 1965, cut up at Maden & McKee, Liverpool in June of that year.

'Jubilee' class BR No 45652 HAWKE, is seen arriving at Carstairs station with a local service during 1961. Carstairs No 3-signal box can be seen on the end of the platform. *Keith Langston Collection*

45653 BARHAM (LMS 5653) built Crewe Works entered traffic January 1935, Lot No 112 – Works No 214. It was withdrawn by BR in April 1965, cut up at Drapers, Hull in August of that year.

'Jubilee' class BR No 45653 BARHAM is seen heading north through Warrington with what appears to be a rake of Lancaster-Morecambe stock together with a guard's van, in September 1963. *Colin Whitfield/Rail Photoprints*

45654 HOOD (LMS 5654) built Crewe Works entered traffic February 1935, Lot No 112 – Works No 215. It was withdrawn by BR in June 1966, cut up at Wards, Beighton in October of that year.

'Jubilee' class BR No 45654 HOOD is seen at Manchester Exchange station with the RCTS's Jubilee Commemorative Tour to York on 4 December 1965. A 4-coach train portion ran from Liverpool Lime Street behind BR No 45654 and an 8-coach train hauled by 'Jubilee' No 45596 BAHAMAS left from Crewe, the 2 portions were combined at Manchester Victoria with the locos then double-heading the special to York. *Mike Morant Collection*

For Rail Tour information visit www.sixbellsjunction.co.uk

Samuel Hood

1st Viscount Hood, Admiral. He was born in Butleigh Somerset on 12 December 1724, the son of the Reverend Samuel Hood. He joined the Royal Navy in 1741 and subsequently served part of his early period as a midshipman attached to the crew of HMS *Ludlow* and then became a lieutenant in 1746.

His first command was HMS *Jamaica* which he joined in July 1754. While serving in the Caribbean he became acquainted with Horatio Nelson, then a young frigate commander, to whom he became a mentor.

Commands held, HMS *Jamaica*, HMS *Lively*, HMS *Grafton*, HMS *Antelope*, HMS *Bideford*, HMS *Bestal* and Greenwich Hospital. He took part in the Seven Years War (Raid on Le Havre), American Revolutionary War (Battles of Chesapeake, Saintes and Mona Passage), French Revolutionary Wars (Siege of Toulon and British Occupation of Corsica).

He was made an Irish peer as Baron Hood of Catherington in September 1782 and entered the British Parliament as Member for Westminster in 1784 where he was a supporter of the government of William Pitt the Younger. He was appointed to the Board of Admiralty in July 1788 and became First Naval Lord in August 1789

Portrait of Admiral Hood by *James Northcote*

and Commander in Chief Portsmouth in June 1792. He was created Viscount Hood of Whitley, Warwickshire in 1796. On his retirement (1794) he was granted a lifetime pension of £2000 a year which in 2017 was equivalent to approximately £220,000 p.a. Hood died in Greenwich, London on 27 January 1816 and is buried in Greenwich Hospital Cemetery.

The name LORD HOOD was also carried by the Southern Railway (SR) 'Lord Nelson' class locomotive BR No 30859 (SR 859)

HMS *Hood* – *Bismarck*

Three Royal Navy ships have been named HMS *Hood* after several members of the Hood family who were notable naval officers. The first which was launched in 1859 being a 91-gun ship of the line.

However, the most well-known being a 'Admiral-class' battlecruiser launched in 1918 and built by John Brown & Company on Clydeside (Pennant No 51). That ship of some 46,680 tons was overhauled in the mid-1930s and at that time had a complement of 1,418 men.

During World War Two, on 24 May 1941 two mighty ships engaged in a deadly battle – the respective pride of the German and British navies, the *Bismarck* and HMS *Hood*. Regarding *Bismarck*, German propagandists claimed that 'there had never been a warship like her'. She was named after the 19th century German chancellor, Otto von Bismarck and launched in February 1939 by his great granddaughter. The ship was an impressive sight being one sixth of a mile long, 120 feet wide and with a weight of 50,300 tons.

The German warship left the Polish port of Gdynia on 18 May 1941 on her first mission. The *Bismarck* was accompanied by the heavy cruiser *Prinz Eugen* and their mission was to head for the Atlantic and cause as much damage to British/Allied convoys as possible.

After leaving Poland, the two German ships passed Norway where their presence was picked up by the allies. British aircraft and ships then monitored their progress as the German ships passed north of Iceland and then turned south towards the Denmark Straits, between Iceland and Greenland. It was in the Denmark Straits that the British fleet, led by HMS *Hood* and HMS *Prince of Wales*, was ordered to intercept. The *Hood* had between the wars been described as 'the embodiment of British sea-power'. However, the mighty vessel was built to First World War requirements where shells were likely to come in low and strike the sides of a ship below the waterline. The decks of the Hood had never been reinforced and therein lay a weakness, she had been built for a different war.

In the early hours of 24 May, the opposing fleets with their imposing ships engaged. Thirteen miles apart the ships fired one-ton shells that, travelling at 1,600 miles per hour, took almost a minute to reach their intended target. The noise, which could be heard in Iceland, was described as being horrendous. The battle lasted only twenty minutes with both of the British ships taking several direct hits. But it was the fate of HMS *Hood* which stunned the world.

The battle cruiser took a hit from the *Bismarck* on her vulnerable upper deck which tore through the ship and penetrated its ammunition room. The resultant huge explosion sliced the once great ship in two and rocketed a fireball into the sky with the molten metal fragments forming what one German sailor later described as 'a display of white stars'.

Within five minutes, the HMS *Hood*, former pride of the Royal Navy, had sunk. It was no more! Of its crew of 1,421 souls only three men survived. Although badly damaged HMS *Prince of Wales* lived to fight another day. The *Bismarck* was damaged, leaking fuel and listing badly it aborted the Atlantic mission and tried to limp into port in France for repair. The morale of the British nation was badly shaken and Winston Churchill issued the cry 'Sink the Bismarck'. The Royal Navy located the stricken German vessel off Brest, and three days after the battle aircraft from the carrier HMS *Ark Royal* torpedoed and further damaged the vessel by destroying her steering gear (rudder etc) thus preventing her from continuing to a port of safety. Thereafter action from a British battle fleet comprising, 2 battleships, 3 cruisers and 6 destroyers resulted in the sinking of the *Bismarck* on 27 May 1941 with a loss of approximately 2,220 souls, a further 110 crew members were taken prisoner.

HMS *Hood* is seen in Australia during a world tour on 17 March 1924. *Allan C. Green as restored by Adam Cuerden*

45655 KEITH (LMS 5655) built Derby Works entered traffic December 1934, Lot No 113 and was withdrawn by BR in April 1965, cut up at R.S. Hayes/Birds, Bridgend in June 1966.

'Jubilee' class LMS No 5655 KEITH is seen between turns at Bedford on 2 August 1937. This Derby built engine is sporting an LMS (later BR) 16A Nottingham shedplate. *Rail Photoprints Collection*

45656 COCHRANE (LMS 5656) built Derby Works entered traffic December 1934, Lot No 113 and was withdrawn by BR in December 1962, cut up at Crewe Works in March 1963.

'Jubilee' class BR No 45656 COCHRANE is seen at an unknown Midland Route location during 1957. *Rail Photoprints Collection*

George Keith Elphinstone, GCB

1st Viscount Keith, Admiral, was born in Stirling, Scotland on 7 January 1746 and he was the fifth son of the 10th Lord Elphinstone. Two of his siblings went to sea in 1761; he followed them when he joined HMS *Royal Sovereign* later transferring to HMS *Gosport*. In 1767 he voyaged to the East Indies in the service of the British East India Company and with £2000 borrowed from an uncle he started the process of amassing a handsome fortune in private trading ventures. He became a lieutenant in 1770 and thereafter a commander in 1772 and post captain in 1775. During the

HMS Keith seen in 1937. *Royal Navy Photographer*

American Revolution he was employed against the privateers together with a naval brigade during the occupation of Charleston, South Carolina. As commander of HMS *Warwick* he captured a Dutch 50-gun ship in 1781 which had beaten off a British vessel of equal strength a few days before. Amongst other actions Keith was the leader of a squadron that captured a French 38-gun ship *Aigle*. After peace was signed he remained on shore for ten years, serving in Parliament as member first for Dunbartonshire, and then for Stirlingshire. He was elected a fellow of the Royal Society in 1790. Commands held, Cape of Good Hope Station, Mediterranean Fleet and Nore Command. He died on 10 March 1823 at Tulliallan Castle, near Kincardine-on-Forth, Fife and was buried in the parish church.

One Royal Navy ship a B-class destroyer was named HMS *Keith* which was built by Vickers-Armstrong at Barrow (Pennant No D06) and launched 10 July 1930. The vessel was sunk by German aircraft on 1 June 1940. At the time of the German bombing HMS *Keith* was the flagship of Rear-Admiral Frederic Wake-Walker, commander of the Dunkirk evacuation. The ship was attacked by aircraft which at first damaged her steering gear and, in a later attack, a bomb went down the aft funnel and exploded in the No. 2 boiler room. With no power available, she anchored and 'abandon ship' was ordered. HMS *Keith* sank from her damage at 0945. The lives of 36 souls were lost, but 131 crew members were saved.

Thomas Cochrane GCB ODM

10th Earl of Dundonald, Marquess of Maranhao, Admiral, was born at Annsfield, near Hamilton Scotland on 14 December 1775. He was the son of the 9th Earl of Dundonald and one of seven male siblings. He joined the navy 23 July 1793 as a midshipman, joining the crew of HMS *Hind*. He was appointed acting lieutenant in 1795 and commissioned lieutenant in the following year. He was dismissed from the Royal Navy in 1814 after a conviction for fraud involving Stock Exchange dealings, the 'Great Stock Exchange Fraud of 1814'. However, he was pardoned by the Crown in 1832 and reinstated in the Royal Navy with the rank of Admiral of the Blue.

During his military career he also served in the navies of Republic of Chile, Empire of Brazil and the Kingdom of Greece. Command held, North America and West Indies Station. He took part in Napoleonic Wars, Chilean War of Independence, Peruvian War of

Admiral Cochrane bust, Culross, Fife. *Kim Traynor*

Independence, Brazilian War of Independence and Greek War of Independence. In addition to British decorations he was awarded Order of the Merit of Chile and Order of the Southern Cross. He rejoiced in the nick name 'Le Loup des Mers' roughly translated as 'Old Sea Dog'.

At his second attempt of running for parliament he successfully won the seat of Honiton, Devon in 1806 and served in parliament until taking the title of 10th Earl of Dundonald on the death of his father in 1831. In 1818 Cochrane patented the tunnelling shield, together with engineer Marc Isambard Brunel and he was also a great supporter of the early development of steam ships. He also held patents in his own right covering some development aspects of naval steam power. He died at Kensington, London on 31 October 1860 and his remains were interred in Westminster Abbey.

Two Royal Naval vessels and a shore establishment carried the name HMS *Cochrane*.

Sir Reginald Yorke Tyrwhitt GCB DSO

1st Baronet, Admiral of the Fleet was born in Oxford on 10 May 1870 the son of Reverend Richard St. John Tyrwhitt. His naval career began at the training ship HMS *Britannia* as a cadet which he joined on 15 July 1883. Assigned to the battleship HMS *Alexandra* as a midshipman during December 1885 he was appointed to the Training Squadron cruiser HMS *Calypso* in November 1888. He rose to the rank of Commanding Officer HMS *Hart* in January 1896.

During World War One he led a supporting naval force of 31 destroyers and two cruisers at the Battle of Heligoland Bight, during which three German cruisers and one destroyer were sunk, August 1914. In a further notable action Tyrwhitt led the forces assigned to the Cuxhaven Raid when British seaplanes successfully destroyed German Zeppelin airships and associated shore installations, December 1914. He also served as commander of the support force to Admiral Beatty's battlecruiser squadron during the Battle of Dogger Bank, January 1915.

An artist impression of the Cuxhaven Raid, from a French post card.

Commands held, HMS *Hart,* HMS *Waveney,* HMS *Attentive,* HMS *Skirmisher,* 4th Destroyer Flotilla, HMS *Bacchante,* HMS *Good Hope,* 2nd Destroyer Flotilla, Destroyer Flotilla of the First Fleet, Harwich Force, Senior Naval Officer, Gibraltar, 3rd Light Cruiser Squadron, Coast of Scotland, China Station and Nore Command. He hauled down his flag for the last time in May 1933 and was promoted to Admiral of the Fleet in 1934. He did not see active service during the Second World War but for a short period served in the Home Guard. He died on 30 May 1951 at Sandhurst in Kent.

HMS *Arethusa*, Tyrwhitt's flagship during the Battle of Heligoland Bight, 1914. *Royal Navy Photographer*

Roger John Brownlow Keyes GCB, KCVO, CMG, DSO

Ist Baron Keyes, Admiral of the Fleet was born in Punjab, British India on 4 October 1872 as the second son of General Sir Charles Patton Keyes of the Indian Army. He attended a preparatory school in Margate, Kent and from there he joined the Royal Navy as a cadet at HMS *Britannia* on 15 July 1885. As a junior officer he served in a corvette operating from Zanzibar on slavery suppression missions. During the Boxer Rebellion, Keyes led a mission to capture a flotilla of four Chinese destroyers on the Peiho River. He was one of the first men to climb over the Peking walls, in order to free the besieged diplomatic legations.

During the First World War Keyes was heavily involved in the organisation of the Dardanelles Campaign. Keyes took charge in an operation when six trawlers and a cruiser attempted to clear the Kephez minefield. He became Director of Plans at the Admiralty and subsequently took command of the Dover Patrol. Working to a new plan he devised, the patrol sank five U-Boats in the first month after implementation, compared with just two in the previous two years. Keyes also planned and led the famous raids on the German submarine pens in the Belgian ports of Zeebrugge and Ostend.

Between the wars Keyes commanded the Battlecruiser Squadron, the Atlantic Fleet and then the Mediterranean Fleet before becoming Commander-in-Chief, Portsmouth. During the Second World War he initially became liaison officer to Leopold III, King of the Belgians. He went on to be the first Director of Combined Operations. Commands held HMS *Opossum,* HMS *Hart,* HMS *Fame,* HMS *Bat,* HMS *Falcon,* HMS *Sprightly,* HMS *Venus,* Commodore-in-Charge Submarine Service, HMS *Centurion,* Dover Patrol, Battlecruiser Squadron Atlantic Fleet, Commander-in-Chief Mediterranean Fleet, Commander-in Chief Portsmouth and Director of Combined Operations. He took part in the Boxer Rising, First and Second World Wars.

Keyes was elected Member of Parliament for Portsmouth North in January 1934 and served that constituency until January 1943. He was opposed to the Munich Agreement that Neville Chamberlain had reached with Adolf Hitler in 1938 and, along with Winston Churchill was one of the few who withheld support from the Government on this issue. He died in Tingewick, Buckinghamshire 26 December 1945 and was interred at St. James's cemetery in Dover.

The ships crest of Keyes's ninth command HMS *Centurion* as displayed at Shugborough Hall, Staffordshire. *Martin Evans*

45657 TWRWHITT (LMS 5657) built Derby Works entered traffic December 1934, Lot No 113 and was withdrawn by BR in September 1964, cut up at Central Wagon Company, Ince in May 1965.

'Jubilee' class BR No 45657 TYRWHITT is seen on Beattock Bank with a Creative Tourist Agents Conference (CTAC) 'Scottish Tours Express' on 5 July 1958. The Creative Tourist Agent's Conference was a consortium of nine UK travel agents and firms which chartered special trains in the periods 1933–1939 and 1945–1968. *David Anderson*

45658 KEYES (LMS 5658) built Derby Works entered traffic December 1934, Lot No 113 and was withdrawn by BR in October 1965, cut up at Drapers, Hull in December 1965.

'Jubilee' class BR No 45658 KEYES with a Stanier tender, is seen on the West Coast Main Line (WCML) at Elvanfoot on 15 August 1955. *David Anderson*

45659 DRAKE (LMS 5659) built Derby Works entered traffic December 1934, Lot No 113 and was withdrawn by BR in June 1963, cut up at Crewe Works in the same month.

'Jubilee' class BR No 45659 is seen in the Guiseley, Yorkshire area.
Mark A. Hoofe

Sir Francis Drake

Vice Admiral Drake was born in Tavistock, Devon circa 1540 to Edmund Drake a farmer and he was the eldest of 12 sons. He was an Elizabethan sea captain, privateer, navigator, slaver, and politician. He first went to sea in 1563 on one of a fleet of ships owned by his relatives, the Hawkins family of Plymouth. Drake famously carried out the second circumnavigation of the world in a single expedition, from 1577 to 1580 and the vessel concerned was the *Pelican* (later renamed *Golden Hind*).

For his achievements Queen Elizabeth awarded Drake a knighthood in 1581. He was second in command of the English fleet that famously did battle with the Spanish Armada in 1588.

He was a great hero to the English, however King Philip II of Spain considered him to be a pirate (and accordingly nicknamed him *El Draque – The Dragon*); the Spanish ruler reportedly offered a reward of 20,000 ducats (about £4 million by modern standards) for Drake's life. A popular cocktail of the era named *El Draque* (modern times Mojito) is attributed to Drake. His commands were *Golden Hind* (previously known as *Pelican), Bonaventure* and *Revenge* and he took part in the Anglo-Spanish War and Battle of Gravelines.

Drake was politically astute, and although known for his private and military endeavours, he was an influential figure in politics during the time he spent in Britain. Often abroad, there is little evidence to suggest he was active in Westminster, despite being a member of parliament on three occasions.

During a voyage to Panama, Drake contracted dysentery and died. He was buried at sea in a sealed lead lined coffin and dressed in full armour, near Portobelo, Colon, Panama on 28 January 1596. In total nineteen ships and a shore establishment were named HMS *Drake* after Sir Francis Drake, or the drake. The first being a 16-gun vessel launched in 1653 and HMS *Drake* is the name now given to Her Majesty's Naval Base Devonport, Plymouth (HMNB *Devonport*)

The name SIR FRANCIS DRAKE was also carried by the Southern Railway (SR) 'Lord Nelson' class locomotive BR No 30851 (SR No 851).

45660 ROOKE (LMS 5660) built Derby Works entered traffic December 1934, Lot No 113 and was withdrawn by BR in June 1966, cut up at Drapers, Hull in October 1966.

'Jubilee' class BR No 45660 ROOKE is seen climbing the famous Lickey incline (1 in 37.7 gradient) near Vigo, with the 10.30 Bristol–Newcastle service on 7 June 1960. Note the exhaust from the banking engine. *Ian Turnbull/ Rail Photoprints*

Sir George Rooke

Admiral of the Fleet, was born in 1650 at St. Lawrence, Canterbury, Kent and was the son of Colonel Sir William Rooke. He joined the Royal Navy as a volunteer in 1672 and was also promoted to lieutenant in that year upon joining the crew of HMS *London*. As a junior officer Rooke saw action at the battles of Solebay and Schooneveld. He took part in the Battle of Bantry during the Williamite War in Ireland and as a captain he commanded the ship which conveyed William of Orange to England.

When promoted to the position of Flag Officer Rooke commanded a division of the Royal Navy during their defeat at the battle of Beachy Head. He later distinguished himself at the Battle of La Hogue after having successfully commanded a division at the Battle of Barfleur. Rooke commanded the unsuccessful allied expedition against Cádiz (1702) but on the passage home he destroyed the Spanish treasure fleet at the Battle of Vigo Bay in the opening stages of the War of the Spanish Succession. He also commanded the allied naval forces at the capture of Gibraltar (1704) and attacked the French fleet at the Battle of Málaga.

Commands held were, HMS *Holmes,* HMS *Nonsuch,* HMS *Hampshire,* HMS *St. David* and HMS *Deptford.* He took part in the Third Anglo-Dutch War, Nine Years War, Great Northern War and War of the Spanish Succession. Rooke joined the Board of Admiralty in May 1694 and became Commander in Chief of the Mediterranean Fleet in August 1695. He was later promoted to Admiral of the Fleet and given command of the Channel Fleet. In 1698 he was elected member of Parliament for Portsmouth and there played an active part as spokesman for the Admiralty. He became Senior Naval Lord (Admiralty Board) in May 1699. He gave up his seat in Parliament in 1708 and died at Lawrence House Canterbury on 24 January 1709. He was buried at St. Paul's Church, Canterbury. One Royal Navy ship and two shore establishments were named after him (HMS *Rooke*).

Statue of Rooke erected in 2004 to celebrate the capture of Gibraltar and 300 years of British rule. *Terry Bate*

45661 VERNON (LMS 5661) built Derby Works entered traffic December 1934, Lot No 113 and was withdrawn by BR in May 1965, cut up at Drapers Hull, in August 1965.

'Jubilee' class BR No 45661 VERNON is seen heading away from Elvanfoot with an afternoon all stations passenger working from Carlisle to Glasgow Central on 11 April 1960. *David Anderson*

45662 KEMPENFELT (LMS 5662) built Derby Works entered traffic December 1934, Lot No 113 and was withdrawn by BR in November 1962, cut up at Crewe Works, in January 1963.

'Jubilee' class BR No 45662 KEMPENFELT is seen approaching Kilnhurst in this 1961 image. *Mike Stokes Archive*

Edward Vernon

Admiral was born on 12 November 1684 in Westminster London and he was the second son of James Vernon Secretary of State to King William III. He attended Westminster School and thereafter joined the Royal Navy as a volunteer joining the crew of HMS *Shrewsbury* on 10 May 1700. He was appointed to the rank of Captain in 1706 and his first command was HMS *Rye* which was a part of the fleet of Admiral Shovell.

The origin of the navy word 'grog', a term used for rum diluted with water, is attributed to Vernon. He was known for wearing coats made of grogram cloth, earning him the nickname of Old Grog, which in turn came to mean diluted rum. Some historians claim that Vernon instigated the addition of citrus juice in grog which reportedly prevented scurvy. Mount Vernon, the home of the first American president George Washington, was named after Vernon. Washington's elder brother Lawrence served under Edward Vernon.

On 21 November 1739 Vernon captured the then Spanish colonial possession of Porto Bello using just six ships (against the 90-man Spanish garrison). Vernon was subsequently granted the Freedom of the City of London and commemorative medals were produced. The Portobello areas in London, Dublin and Edinburgh are named after this victory. Interestingly the patriotic song 'Rule, Britannia!' was composed by Thomas Arne during the 1740 celebrations of the victory. Commands held, HMS *Rye,* HMS *Dolphin,* HMS *Association,* HMS *Jersey,* HMS *Assistance,* HMS *Mary,* HMS *Grafton,* Commander in Chief

Edward Vernon by Thomas Gainsborough, circa 1753.

Jamaica Station and Commander in Chief North Sea. He took part in War of the Spanish Succession (Capture of Gibraltar, Battle of Velez-Malaga and Siege of Barcelona), War of Jenkins' Ear (Battles of Porto Bello and Cartagena de Indias and Invasion of Cuba).

Vernon was also Member of Parliament for both Penryn and Ipswich on separate occasions. A tower commemorating his victory was erected by members of the Vernon family at Hilton Hall outside Wolverhampton. He died 30 October 1757 at Nacton, Suffolk.

Two Royal Navy ships and a training establishment carried the name HMS *Vernon.*

Richard Kempenfelt

Rear Admiral was born in 1718 at Westminster in London to a Swedish father. Kempenfelt joined the Royal Navy, and he was commissioned a lieutenant in January 1741. He saw service in the West Indies and took part in the capture of Portobello during the War of Jenkins' Ear. In 1746 he returned to Britain, and from that time until 1780 he saw active service in the East Indies and in various quarters of the world with Sir George Pocock, after having been made rear-admiral. In 1779, he was made Chief of Staff (or Captain of the Fleet) under Admiral Sir Charles Hardy on HMS *Victory* which was to lead a hastily assembled fleet to oppose an invasion of England by the combined French and Spanish Armada of 1779. In 1781 he won the Battle of Ushant, with a vastly inferior force, defeating the French fleet and in doing so capturing 20 ships.

Four ships of the Royal Navy were named HMS *Kempenfelt*, this is the second of them a destroyer launched in 1931 and pictured in 1933 which was later transferred to the Royal Canadian Navy and renamed HMCS *Assiniboine. Royal Navy Photographer*

In 1782 Kempenfelt hoisted his flag on HMS *Royal George* and prior to a voyage to Gibraltar the vessel was ordered to Portsmouth for repairs. In order to heel the ship over, the larboard guns had been run out and the starboard guns moved into the centre of the deck. That action being in order to tilt the vessel sufficiently so that the deck wash pump (located three feet below the water level) could be repaired. During that repair the supply vessel *Lark* came alongside in order to transfer a cargo of rum. During that transfer the guns on the centre of the deck apparently broke through rotten timbers an action which fatally accentuated the list, causing water to wash onboard through the gunports and enter the ship's hold.

A sudden breeze against the raised side of the ship forced her further over thus speeding up the ingress of sea water. Despite desperate attempts to lift the cannon the ship rolled on her side and sunk within two minutes. It has been estimated that approximately 900 souls lost their lives and that total included many non-naval personnel, joiners etc and crew family members. Admiral Kempenfelt who was in his cabin at the time, became trapped and also perished, on 29 August 1782.

John Jervis GCB PC

1st Earl of St. Vincent, Admiral of the Fleet was born 9 January 1735 at Meaford Hall, Staffordshire. His father Swynfen Jervis was a barrister who served as a counsellor to the Admiralty Board and in addition was an auditor of Greenwich Hospital. He was initially educated at Burton upon Trent Grammar School and thereafter at Reverend Swinden's Academy in Greenwich. At the tender age of 13 he ran away from school and joined the Royal Navy at Woolwich eventually joining the navy proper as part of the crew of 50-gun HMS *Gloucester* as an able seaman and in January 1749 he voyaged to Jamaica. Jervis served throughout the latter half of the 18th century and into the 19th and was a prominent commander during several notable naval campaigns. He was made lieutenant on 2 January 1755 and given his first command.

Commands held, HMS *Porcupine*, HMS *Scorpion*, HMS *Albany*, HMS *Gosport*, HMS *Alarm*, HMS *Kent*, HMS *Foudroyant*, Leeward Islands Station, Mediterranean and Channel Fleet, First Lord of the Admiralty.

He took part in Seven Years' War (Battle of Quebec), American War of Independence (Battles of Ushant and Cape Spartel), French Revolutionary Wars (Invasion of Guadeloupe and Battle of Cape St. Vincent) and the Napoleonic Wars. He is best known for his victory at the 1797 Battle of Cape Saint Vincent.

He became Member of Parliament for Launceston in 1783 and in the following year he was returned as one of two Members of Parliament for Great Yarmouth. He stood down from that seat in 1790 standing instead for Chipping Wycombe and resigned that seat in 1794. He was created Baron Jervis of Meaford and Earl of St Vincent in 1801 and upon his retirement from the navy took up his seat in the House of Lords.

Memorial to John, Earl of St. Vincent in the crypt of St. Pauls Cathedral. *Len Mills*

He died in March 1823 at Rochetts, Essex and was buried in the family mausoleum at Stone, Staffordshire.

A Royal Navy 'J class' Destroyer launched 9 September 1938 (Pennant No F00-1937-1940, G00 1940-1946) was named HMS *Jervis*. The vessel survived WWII and was sold for scrap 1954. The ship earned the epithet 'Lucky Jervis' as after five and a half years of war and thirteen major actions, no crew member was lost to enemy action.

The name LORD ST. VINCENT was also carried by the Southern Railway (SR) 'Lord Nelson' class locomotive BR No 30856 (SR No 856).

Horatio Nelson KB

1st Viscount Nelson, Vice Admiral, was born Burnham Thorpe, Norfolk on 29 September 1758. He was the 6th of 11 children of the Reverend Edmund Nelson. He attended Paston Grammar School, North Walsham and King Edward VI's Grammar School, Norwich. His naval career began on 1 January 1771 when he joined the crew of HMS *Raisonnable* as an ordinary seaman and coxswain. Nelson was greatly revered for his inspirational leadership and superb grasp of naval strategy. He was wounded several times in combat, losing one arm in the unsuccessful attempt to conquer Santa Cruz de Tenerife and the sight of one eye during action off Corsica. Nelson was shot and killed during his fleet's final victory at the Battle of Trafalgar in 1805, whilst aboard his flag ship HMS *Victory*. The battle was the most decisive naval victory of the war in which 27 British ships of the line defeated 33 French and Spanish ships of the line, commanded by French Admiral Pierre-Charles Villeneuve. The battle took place in the Atlantic off the southwest coast of Spain, west of Cape Trafalgar. The Franco-Spanish fleet lost twenty-two ships, but not a single British vessel was lost. Admiral Lord Nelson's body was brought back to England where he was accorded a state funeral. His most famous, and frequently quoted signal was 'England expects that every man will do his duty'. Commands held, Mediterranean Fleet. He took part in American War of Independence (Battles of Fort San Juan and Grand Turk) War of the First Coalition (Siege of Calvi, Battles of Genoa, Hyeres Islands, Cape St. Vincent, Santa Cruz de Tenerife and Nile, Attack on Cadiz). War of the Second Coalition (Siege of Malta, Battle of Copenhagen and Raid on Boulogne). War of the Third Coalition (Battle of Trafalgar).

Nelsons Column, Trafalgar Square. *Keith Langston*

HMS *Victory* can be visited at the Historic Dockyard, Portsmouth. Visit http://www.hms-victory.com/

Three Royal Navy ships and a shore base were named HMS *Nelson* and two ships named HMS *Lord Nelson*.

The name LORD NELSON was also carried by the Southern Railway (SR) 'Lord Nelson' class locomotive BR No 30850 (SR No 850).

45663 JERVIS (LMS 5663) built Derby Works entered traffic January 1935, Lot No 113 and was withdrawn by BR in October 1964, cut up at Wards Beighton, in April 1965.

'Jubilee' class BR No 45663 JERVIS is seen restarting a southbound service away from Sheffield Midland, circa 1956. *Rail Photoprints Collection*

45664 NELSON (LMS 5664) built Derby Works entered traffic January 1935, Lot No 113 and was withdrawn by BR in May 1965 cut up at Drapers Hull, in July 1965.

'Jubilee' class LMS No 5664 NELSON is seen arriving at Glasgow St. Enoch station during 1936. The enginemen look keen to be in the photograph. *Peter Pescod/Transport Treasury*

45666 CORNWALLIS (LMS 5666) built Crewe Works entered traffic November 1935, Lot No 121 – Works No 264 and was withdrawn by BR in April 1965 cut up at Hayes, Bridgend in August 1965.

'Jubilee' class BR No 45666 CORNWALLIS is seen heading north near Broughton (Preston) with a mixed freight, 21 September 1963. *Paul Claxton – Steve Armitage Collection/Rail Photoprints*

45667 JELLICOE (LMS 5667) built Crewe Works entered traffic November 1935, Lot No 121 – Works No 265 and was withdrawn by BR in January 1965 cut up at Maden & McKee, Liverpool in May 1965.

'Jubilee' class BR No 45667 JELLICOE is seen in BR Green lined livery after being serviced at Newton Heath depot, Manchester in January 1965. *The Railway Correspondence & Travel Society Club archive (RCTS www.rcts.org.uk/)*

Sir William Cornwallis GCB

Admiral was born 10 February 1744 and his father was Charles the fifth baron and first earl Cornwallis.

William Cornwallis entered the Royal Navy in 1755 when he joined the crew of the 80-gun HMS *Newark* which was bound for America in the fleet of Admiral Edward Boscawen. His first command was HMS *Wasp* an 8-gun sloop of war in July 1762. He saw action in several prominent battles but is perhaps best known as a friend of Admiral Lord Nelson.

Commands held, HMS *Wasp*, HMS *Swift*, HMS *Prince Edward*, HMS *Guadeloupe*, HMS *Lion*, HMS *Canada*, HMS *Ganges*, HM *Yacht Charlotte*, HMS *Robust*, HMS *Crown*, Commander in Chief East Indies and Commander in Chief Channel Fleet.

He took part in Seven Years War (Siege of Louisbourg, Battle of Quiberon Bay) American War of Independence (Battles of Grenada, St Kitts and Saintes). Third Anglo-Mysore War (Reduction of

HMS *Cornwallis* and the British Squadron under the walls of Nanking, saluting the peace treaty,1840s. By Rundle Burges Watson

Pondicherry) French Revolutionary Wars (First Battle of Groix) and Napoleonic Wars. In 1796 Cornwallis was promoted Rear Admiral of Great Britain and then in 1814 Vice Admiral of the United Kingdom.

He served as a Member of Parliament for Eye, Suffolk in the periods 1768-1774, 1782–1784, 1790-1800. 1801–1807 and also served as a Member of Parliament for Portsmouth 1782–1790. Cornwallis died 5 July 1819.

Five or six ships of the Royal Navy have been named HMS *Cornwallis* the first in 1777 and the last in 1901.

John Rushworth Jellicoe, GCB, OM, GCVO, SGM, DL

Admiral of the Fleet, 1st Earl Jellicoe was born 5 December 1859 in Southampton, Hampshire, his father was John Henry Jellicoe a captain in the Royal Mail Steam Packet Company and he was educated at Field House School, in Rottingdean. He joined the Royal Navy in 1872 in the training ship HMS *Britannia*. In 1874 he joined the steam frigate HMS *Newcastle* as a midshipman and transferred to the Ironclad HMS *Agincourt* in July 1877. He was promoted to commander in June 1891 and joined the battleship HMS *Sans Pareil* and later was serving on HMS *Victoria* when it collided with HMS *Camperdown* and was wrecked off Tripoli in June 1893. He was then appointed to HMS *Ramillies* in October 1893.

Jellicoe became Director of Naval Ordnance in 1905 and he was made an Aide-de-Camp to King Edward VII on 8 March 1906. He was promoted to rear admiral on 8 February 1907, he was appointed second-in-command of the Atlantic Fleet in August 1907, hoisting his flag in the battleship HMS *Albemarle*. He went on to be Third Sea Lord and Controller of the Navy in October 1908 and he became Commander-in-Chief, Atlantic Fleet in December 1910, hoisting his flag in the battleship HMS *Prince of Wales*. Jellicoe was given the rank of vice admiral on 18 September 1911. He went on to be Second-in-Command of the Home Fleet, hoisting his flag in the battleship HMS *Hercules*, in December 1911, being appointed commander of the 2nd Battle Squadron in May 1912, became Second Sea Lord in December 1912.

JELLICOE
1859-1935

Jellicoe was promoted to full Admiral and assigned command of the Grand Fleet in August 1914 and famously he commanded the fleet at the Battle of Jutland (May 1916). He was appointed First Sea Lord in November 1916 and created Viscount Jellicoe of Scapa Flow in March 1918. Commands held, First Sea Lord, Grand Fleet, Atlantic Fleet, HMS *Drake*, and HMS *Centurion*. He took part in Anglo Egyptian War, Boxer Rebellion and First World War (Battle of Jutland).

He became Admiral of the Fleet in April 1919 and was appointed second Governor General of New Zealand in September 1920 a post he held until December 1924. On his return to Britain he was created Earl Jellicoe and Viscount Brocas of Southampton in July 1925. He died 20 November 1935 in Kensington, London and was buried in St. Pauls' Cathedral and there is a statue (bust) of Jellicoe in Trafalgar Square.

Sir Charles Edward Madden, GCB, OM, GCVO, KCMG

1st Baronet, Admiral of the Fleet was born 5 September 1862 at Gillingham, Kent and he was the second son of Captain John William Madden of the 4th (King's Own) Regiment. He joined the Royal Navy in 1875 on the training ship HMS *Britannia*. In 1877 he was promoted to midshipman and posted to HMS *Alexandra* on which he served until joining HMS *Ruby* in 1880. He was promoted to lieutenant in July 1884 and transferred first to HMS *Assistance* and later attended the Torpedo School at HMS *Vernon*. Promoted to captain in June 1901 and a year later joined HMS *Renown* as an additional officer for duty with torpedo boat destroyers. He became a Rear Admiral in April 1911 and full Admiral in February 1919. He was created a Baronet in 1919.

During World War One he served as Chief of the Staff to Sir John Jellicoe in the Grand Fleet from 1914 to 1916 and was Second in Command of the Fleet under Sir David Beatty from 1916 to 1919. In that year Madden was appointed to the command of the newly constituted Atlantic Fleet with his flag in the battleship HMS *Queen Elizabeth*. Commands held, First Sea Lord, Atlantic Fleet, First Battle Squadron, 2nd and 3rd Cruiser Squadrons, First Division Home Fleet, HMS *Dreadnought* and HMS *Good Hope*. He took part in Anglo-Egyptian War and First World War. Madden was appointed First and Principal

Naval Aide-de-Camp to King George V on 15 August 1922 and was promoted to Admiral of the Fleet in July 1924. He served as chairman of the committee on the functions and training of Royal Marines in 1924. He was appointed First Sea Lord in July 1927. He retired in July 1930 and died at 29 Wimpole Street in London on 5 June 1935.

The Battleship HMS *Queen Elizabeth* seen in the Dardanelles during 1915.

John Arbuthnot Fisher, GCB, OM, GCVO

1st Baron Fisher Admiral of the Fleet, was born on 25 January 1841 in Ramdoda, Ceylon and he was the eldest of 11 children born to Captain William Fisher a British Army officer (78th Highlanders). Fisher formally entered the Royal Navy on 13 July 1854 and served on Nelson's former flagship HMS *Victory*.

He was known for his efforts at naval reform and he hugely influenced the shaping of the Royal Navy in a career spanning more than 60 years, starting in a navy of wooden sailing ships armed with muzzle-loading cannon and ending in one of steel-hulled battlecruisers, submarines and the first aircraft carriers. The argumentative, energetic, reform-minded Fisher is often considered the second most important figure in British naval history, after Lord Nelson.

When appointed First Sea Lord in 1904, he removed 150 ships then on active service which were no longer useful and set about constructing modern replacements, creating a modern fleet and preparing it for war (1914–18). Fisher saw the need to improve the performance of naval guns and was also an early advocate of the use of torpedoes. As Controller, he introduced torpedo boat destroyers. As First Sea Lord, he was responsible for the construction of HMS *Dreadnought*, the first all-big-gun battleship, but he also believed that submarines would become increasingly important and urged their development. He was involved with the introduction of turbine engines to replace reciprocating engines, and the introduction of oil fueling to replace coal. Importantly he introduced daily baked bread on board ships.

Commands held, First Sea Lord, Commander in Chief Portsmouth, Second Naval Lord, Mediterranean Fleet, North America and West Indies Station, Third Naval Lord and Controller, Admiral Superintendent Portsmouth and Director of Naval Ordinance. He took part in Crimean War, Second Opium War, Anglo-Egyptian War and First World War. File Infl

He first officially retired from the Admiralty in 1911 on his 70th birthday but became First Sea Lord again in November 1914. He resigned seven months later in frustration over Churchill's Gallipoli campaign, and then served as chairman of the Government's Board of Invention and Research until the end of the war. He died 10 July 1920 at St. James Square, London and after a funeral service at Westminster Abbey his body was cremated at Golder's Green Crematorium.

Battleship HMS *Inflexible*, on which Fisher served circa 1882, is seen before the full sailing masts were removed (1885).

45668 MADDEN (LMS 5668) built Crewe Works entered traffic December 1935, Lot No 121 – Works No 266 and was withdrawn by BR in December 1963 cut up at Crewe Works in January 1964.

'Jubilee' class BR No 45668 Madden is seen at Manchester Exchange station in the summer of 1949, note that LMS is still shown on the tender. *Rail Photoprints Collection*

45669 FISHER (LMS 5669) built Crewe Works entered traffic December 1935, Lot No 121 – Works No 267 and was withdrawn by BR in May 1963 cut up at Crewe Works in July 1963.

'Jubilee' class BR No 45669 FISHER is seen on the through road at Stafford station with a down express, Diesel BR No 10202 waits in the southbound platform, circa 1962. *Rail Photoprints Collection*

45670 HOWARD OF EFFINGHAM (LMS 5670) built Crewe Works entered traffic December 1935, Lot No 121 – Works No 268 and was withdrawn by BR in October 1964 cut up at Wards, Killamarsh in February 1965.

'Jubilee' class BR No 45670 HOWARD OF EFFINGHAM is seen at Willesden, during 1951. *D.Cobbe collection – C.R.L Coles/Rail Photoprints*

45671 PRINCE RUPERT (LMS 5671) built Crewe Works entered traffic November 1935, Lot No 121 – Works No 269 and was withdrawn by BR in November 1963 cut up at Crewe Works in January 1964.

'Jubilee' class LMS No 5671 PRINCE RUPERT is seen at Crewe in 1946 in LMS lined black livery. Note the 5XP power rating on the cab side and also the connection of test equipment located on the top of the smokebox. *Rail Photoprints Collection*

William Howard (c.1510–1573), 1st Baron Howard of Howard of Effingham.

William Howard 1st Baron Howard of Effingham was born circa 1510 and he served four monarchs. He served in various official capacities, including Lord Admiral and Lord Chamberlain of the Household. In 1541, Lord Howard was charged with concealing the sexual indiscretions of his young niece, Katherine Howard, Henry VIII's fifth Queen, and ordered to stand trial. On 22 December 1541 Lord Howard, his wife, and a number of servants who had been alleged witnesses to the Queen's misconduct were convicted and sentenced to life imprisonment and loss of goods. However, Howard and most of the others were pardoned after Queen Katherine's execution (13 February 1542). William Howard 1st Baron Howard of Effingham died at Hampton Court Palace on 12 January 1573, and was buried at Reigate.

Charles Howard

Admiral Charles Howard 1st Earl of Nottingham and 2nd Baron Howard of Effingham (created 1573 following his father's death) was the eldest son of William Howard, born 1536. He was Lord High Admiral (1585) under Queen Elizabeth I and King James I and was the commander of English forces during the battles against the Spanish Armada. It is said that after Sir Francis Drake he was chiefly responsible for the victory that saved England from invasion by the Spanish Empire. Additionally, Admiral Howard was a patron of the theatre, in 1576 a company of actors originally known as Lord Howard's Men was formed (later referred to as The Admiral's Men) and they are allegedly linked to the first performances of Shakespeare's 'Richard III'. Charles Howard Lord High Admiral 2nd Baron Howard of Effingham died 14 December 1624. A 'Hawkins class' heavy cruiser launched June 1921 was named HMS *Effingham* (Pennant No D98).

The name HOWARD OF EFFINGHAM was also carried by the Southern Railway (SR) 'Lord Nelson' class locomotive BR No 30854 (SR No 854).

Coat of Arms, Sir Charles Howard, 1st Earl of Nottingham.

Coat of arms of Rupert Count Palatine of the Rhine.

Prince Rupert of the Rhine KG PC FRS

He was born on 17 December 1619 in Prague and was a son of the German prince Frederik V and Elizabeth eldest daughter of James 1st, thus he was the nephew of King Charles I. He was a noted German soldier, admiral, scientist, sportsman, colonial governor and amateur artist during the 17th century. He first came to prominence as a Cavalier cavalry commander during the English Civil War.

He fought against Spain in the Netherlands during the Eighty Years War (1568–1648), and against the Holy Roman Emperor in Germany during the Thirty Years War (1618–1648). At the age of 23, he was appointed commander of the Royalist cavalry during the English Civil War, and ultimately became the senior Royalist general. He surrendered after the fall of Bristol and was banished from England.

He served under Louis XIV of France against Spain, and then as a Royalist privateer in the Caribbean. Following the Restoration, Rupert returned to England, becoming a senior English naval commander during the Second and Third Anglo-Dutch wars, also engaging in scientific invention, art, and serving as the first governor of the Hudson's Bay Company. He was also a founding member of the Royal Society. As the head of the Royal Navy in his later years, he is said to have shown great maturity and made impressive and long-lasting contributions to the Royal Navy's doctrine and development. Prince Rupert died at Westminster, London in 1682, and he was buried in the crypt of Westminster Abbey, following a state funeral.

Several ships of the Royal Navy have been named HMS *Rupert* (or derivatives of the name). The first being in 1666 and the last a 'Captain class' frigate, originally launched as United States Navy 'Buckley class' destroyer 31 October 1943 and renamed HMS *Rupert* (Pennant No K561) and subsequently returned to the USA in March 1946.

George Anson, PC, FRS, RN

1st Baron Anson, Admiral of the fleet was born in Staffordshire on 23 April 1697. Anson hailed from a wealthy Staffordshire family of that name, the son of William Anson of Shugborough. He joined the Royal Navy at the age of 15 serving as a volunteer aboard HMS *Ruby*. In 1716 he was promoted to the rank of lieutenant and assigned to HMS *Hampshire*. He is perhaps best remembered for his circumnavigation of the globe and his role overseeing the Royal Navy during the Seven Years War. During his time in office Anson instituted a series of reforms to the Royal Navy. In 1744 he joined the Admiralty Board and from June 1751 until November 1756 and also from 1757 until his death he was First Lord of the Admiralty. Among his reforms were the transfer of the Marines from Army to Navy authority, uniforms for commissioned officers, devising a way to effectively get superannuated Captains and Admirals to retire on half pay and submitting a revision of the Articles of War to Parliament, which reportedly tightened discipline throughout the navy.

Commands held, HMS *Weazel*, HMS *Scarborough*, HMS *Garland*, HMS *Diamond*, HMS *Squirrel* and HMS *Centurion*. He took part in The War of the Spanish Succession, War of the Quadruple Alliance, War of Jenkins' Ear, War of the Austrian Succession and Seven Years War.

Anson was also elected as Member of Parliament for Hedon, Yorkshire in 1744.

Admiral of the Fleet, 1st Baron Anson died at Moor Park, Hertfordshire on 6 June 1762 and was buried at St. Michael and All Angels church, Colwich, Staffordshire.

Eight warships of the Royal Navy were named HMS *Anson*, the first in 1747, and the penultimate being a 'King George V class' battleship (Pennant No 79) launched in 1940 which served throughout World War Two and was decommissioned in November 1951. Currently the eighth, an 'Astute class' nuclear powered submarine, was in 2018 under construction and due into service circa 2020 (Pennant No S123).

The name LORD ANSON was also carried by the Southern Railway (SR) 'Lord Nelson' class locomotive BR No 30861 (SR No 861).

HMS *Anson* firing her gun circa 1942. *Royal Navy photographer*

Augustus Keppel PC

Admiral, First Viscount Keppel was born 25 April 1725 of Willem van Keppel 2nd Earl of Albemarle and he was educated at Westminster School. He went to sea at the tender age of 10 years in 1735 and in 1740 voyaged with Lord Anson round the world trip aboard HMS *Centurion*. He saw action in command of various ships, including the fourth-rate *Maidstone*, during the War of the Austrian Succession. He went on to serve as Commodore on the North American Station and then Commander-in-Chief, Jamaica Station during the Seven Years War, having been promoted to Rear Admiral. After that he served as Senior Naval Lord and then Commander-in-Chief of the Channel Fleet.

During the American Revolutionary War Keppel came into a notorious dispute with

The third and last HMS *Keppel* is seen at sea during February 1972. *Royal Navy Photographer*

Sir Hugh Palliser over Palliser's conduct as his second-in-command at the inconclusive Battle of Ushant in July 1778; The dispute led to Keppel being court-martialled, although he was subsequently acquitted. During the final years of the American Revolutionary War Keppel served as First Lord of the Admiralty.

In 1782 he became First Lord of the Admiralty, was raised to the peerage as Viscount Keppel of Elveden in the County of Suffolk, and sworn of the Privy Council. His career in office was not distinguished, and he broke with his old political associates by resigning as a protest against the Peace of Paris. He finally discredited himself by joining the Coalition ministry formed by North and Fox, and with its fall disappeared from public life in December 1783. Keppel died unmarried on 2 October 1786 and the peerage died with him.

Three Royal Navy warships were named HMS *Keppel*, the first was a 14-gun brig in 1778 and the last a 'Blackwood class' frigate launched in August 1954 (Pennant No F85) and decommissioned circa 1979.

45672 ANSON (LMS 5672) built Crewe Works entered traffic December 1935, Lot No 121 – Works No 270 and was withdrawn by BR in November 1964 cut up at Wards, Beighton in April 1965.

'Jubilee' class BR No 45672 ANSON is seen approaching Winwick Junction (WCML) with a down passenger service, on 29 August 1964. Note that the backing plate remains over the leading wheel splasher but the nameplate has been removed. *Hugh Ballantyne/Rail Photoprints*

45673 KEPPEL (LMS 5673) built Crewe Works entered traffic December 1935, Lot No 121 – Works No 271 and was withdrawn by BR in December 1962 cut up at Campbells, Shieldhall in December 1963.

A great Stanier line up! 'Jubilee' class BR No 45673 is seen with 'Black Five' locomotives BR No 45472 and BR No 44798 on shed at Perth, 9 July 1957. *David Anderson*

45674 DUNCAN (LMS 5674) built Crewe Works entered traffic December 1935, Lot No 121 – Works No 272 and was withdrawn by BR in October 1964 cut up at Drapers, Hull in March 1965.

'Jubilee' class BR No 45674 DUNCAN is seen approaching Sheffield with a train from Manchester during 1963. *Mike Stokes Archive*

45675 HARDY (LMS 5675) built Crewe Works entered traffic December 1935, Lot No 121 – Works No 273 and was withdrawn by BR in June 1967 cut up at Cashmores, Great Bridge in November 1967.

'Jubilee' class BR No 45675 HARDY in poor exterior condition, is seen arriving at Leeds City station with a parcels train during April 1966. Note that although the backing plate remains in place the nameplate has already been removed. *Mike Stokes Archive*

Adam Duncan

Admiral, 1st Viscount Duncan was born 1July 1931 in Dundee, Angus and he was the second son of Alexander Duncan, Baron of Lundy, Provost of Dundee. He was educated in Dundee and joined the Royal Navy in 1746 as part of the crew of HMS *Trial*. In 1755 he attained the rank of lieutenant when serving off the coast of North America aboard HMS *Norwich*. In 1778 he was briefly appointed to HMS *Suffolk* but in only a short time he moved again joining HMS *Monarch* which was part of Admiral Hardy's fleet. He sailed with that vessel to take part in the relief of Gibraltar (December 1779) and in January 1780 he had a prominent part in the action off St. Vincent (this action was also referred to as The Moonlight Battle).

'Type 45' destroyer HMS Duncan is pictured inbound to Portsmouth in June 2016. *Brian Burnell*

He then attained flag rank thus becoming Vice Admiral in February 1793 and was in February 1795 appointed Commander in Chief North Sea. He hoisted his flag on board HMS *Venerable* and was subsequently promoted to Admiral in June 1795. His victory against the Dutch Fleet (Battle of Camperdown) in 1797 was considered one of the most significant actions in naval history. After news of the victory reached England Duncan was at once raised to the peerage as Viscount Duncan of Camperdown (21 October 1797). Duncan was awarded the Large Naval Gold Medal and an annual pension of £3,000, to himself and the next two heirs to his title, this was the biggest pension ever awarded by the British government. Additionally, he was given the freedom of several cities, including Dundee and London.

He died quite suddenly on 4 August 1804 at the inn at Cornhill, a village on the Scottish border, where he had stopped for the night during a journey to Edinburgh. He was buried in Lundie west of Dundee Angus, Scotland. There is a statue of Duncan in the crypt of St. Paul's Cathedral.

In total seven Royal Navy vessels have been named HMS *Duncan* the first in 1804 and the last a 'Type 45' destroyer launched in 2010 (Pennant No D37).

The name LORD DUNCAN was also carried by the Southern Railway (SR) 'Lord Nelson' class locomotive BR No 30858 (SR No 858).

Sir Thomas Masterman Hardy, GCB

Vice Admiral, 1st Baronet was born in Kingston Russell, Dorset on 5 April 1769 the second son of Joseph Hardy. He joined the Royal Navy as a midshipman aboard HMS *Hebe* in February 1790. He served as flag captain to Admiral Lord Nelson, and commanded HMS *Victory* at the Battle of Trafalgar in October 1805 during the Napoleonic Wars. Nelson was shot as he paced the decks with Hardy, and as he lay dying, Nelson's famous remark of 'Kiss me, Hardy' was directed at him. Hardy went on to become First Naval Lord in November 1830 and in that capacity, he refused to become a Member of Parliament. He is remembered for encouraging the introduction of steam warships. He was promoted to Vice Admiral on 10 January 1837.

Hardy's Monument (1842) is located on Blackdown Hill, Dorset. *Sarah Smith*

Commands held, HMS *Mutine*, HMS *Vanguard*, HMS *Foudroyant*, HMS *Princess Charlotte*, HMS *San Josef*, HMS *St. George*, HMS *Isis*, HMS *Amphion*, HMS *Victory*, HMS *Triumph*, HMS *Barfleur*, HMS *Ramillies*, HMS *Princess Augusta*, South America Station and Greenwich Hospital.

He took part in French Revolutionary Wars (Action of 19 December 1796), Battles of Cape St. Vincent-The Nile and Copenhagen). Napoleonic Wars (Battle of Trafalgar), War of 1812. He died 20 September 1839 at Greenwich and he is buried in the officers' vault at Greenwich Hospital Cemetery.

In total there were ten Royal Navy vessels named HMS *Hardy* with most of the later ones being named for Admiral Sir Thomas Masterman Hardy, however the first in 1797 was simply named after the common adjective. The last being a 'Blackwood class' ASW Frigate launched in 1953 (Pennant No F54) and was sunk as a target vessel on 3 July 1984.

Sir Edward Codrington, GCB, FRS

Admiral. He was born in Dodington, Gloucestershire on 27 April 1770. He was educated privately by an uncle and thereafter attended Harrow School for a short time, Codrington entered the Royal Navy in July 1783. He was promoted to lieutenant on 28 May 1793, when Lord Howe selected him to be signal lieutenant on the flagship of the Channel fleet at the beginning of the French Revolutionary Wars. In that capacity he served on the 100-gun HMS *Queen Charlotte*. On 7 October 1794 he was promoted to commander, and on 6 April 1795 attained the rank of post-captain. He became Rear Admiral during June 1814, Vice Admiral in July 1821 and full Admiral in January 1837. Commands held, Portsmouth Command, Mediterranean Fleet, HMS *Orion,* HMS *Druid* and HMS *Babet.* He took part in French Revolutionary Wars (Glorious First of June) Napoleonic Wars (Battle of Trafalgar, Walcheren Campaign) War of 1812 and Greek War of Independence (Battle of Navarino).

HM King George VI visited the British Expeditionary Forces (BEF) in December 1939 and he is seen (7th from the right) on board HMS *Codrington* at Boulogne. *G Keating (Lt) War Office official photographer*

He was elected Member of Parliament for Devonport in 1832 and sat for that constituency until taking the Chiltern Hundreds in 1839. From November 1839 until December 1842 he was Commander in Chief Portsmouth. He died on 28 April 1851 in London and was buried at St. Peters Church, Eaton Square. His three sons all had military connections, Edward Codrington a midshipman aboard HMS *Cambrian* (died circa 1821) Sir William Codrington a commandeer in the Crimean War (died 1884) and Sir Henry Codrington Admiral of the Fleet (died 1877).

An 'A class' destroyer launched 8 August 1929 (Pennant No D65) was named HMS *Codrington* and took part in Operation Dynamo (Dunkirk Evacuation). That vessel was sunk by enemy bombing 27 July 1940 whilst in dock at Dover, fortunately without loss of life, although three crew members were wounded.

David Richard Beatty, GCB, OM, GCVO, DSO, PC

Admiral of the Fleet 1st Earl Beatty was born in Stapeley, Nantwich Cheshire on 17 January 1871. He was Anglo-Irish and the second son of five children born to army Captain David Longfield Beatty. He was educated at Kilkenny College and thereafter at the Burney's Naval Academy, Gosport (1882). Beatty joined the Royal Navy in 1884 as a cadet on the training ship HMS *Britannia*. He was promoted to lieutenant during August 1892, and then to captain in 1900. In 1910 Alfred Winsloe, Fourth Sea Lord requested that Beatty be promoted to Rear Admiral even though he had not completed the requisite time as a captain. In 1912 he was appointed Naval Secretary by the then First Lord of the Admiralty Winston Churchill.

Beatty became Rear Admiral in March 1913, Vice Admiral in February 1915, full Admiral in January 1919 and to Admiral of the Fleet in May 1919. Beatty was created 1st Earl Beatty, Viscount Borodale and Baron Beatty of the North Sea and Brooksby in October 1919.

Commands held, First Sea Lord (a position that Beatty held longer (7 years 9 months) than any other First Sea Lord in history) Grand Fleet, Battle Cruiser Fleet, 1st Battle Cruiser Squadron, HMS *Queen,* HMS *Suffolk,* HMS *Arrogant* and HMS *Juno.* He took part in Mahdist War (Battles of Dongola and Omdurman) Boxer Rebellion, First World War (Battles of Heligoland Bight, Dogger Bank and Jutland).

A bust of Admiral of the Fleet 1st Earl Beatty stands in Trafalgar Square. *Len Mills*

Beatty died on 12 March 1936 in London. His coffin was draped in the Union Flag flown by his flagship HMS *Queen Elizabeth* in 1919. Beatty had requested in his will that he would like to be buried at Dingley Church, Northamptonshire however, he was actually buried at St Paul's Cathedral.

45676 CODRINGTON (LMS 5676) built Crewe Works entered traffic December 1935, Lot No 121 – Works No 274 and was withdrawn by BR in September 1964 cut up at Cashmores, Great Bridge in January 1965.

'Jubilee' class BR No 45676 CODRINGTON is seen between turns at Bristol Barrow Road depot on 10 July 1963. *Rail Photoprints Collection*

45677 BEATTY (LMS 5677) built Crewe Works entered traffic December 1935, Lot No 121 – Works No 275 and was withdrawn by BR in December 1962 cut up at Campbells, Shieldhall in December 1963.

'Jubilee' class BR No 45677 BEATTY is seen nearing Beattock Summit with a Manchester/Liverpool – Glasgow Central service, and without the help of a banking engine during August 1954. *David Anderson*

45678 DE ROBECK (LMS 5678) built Crewe Works entered traffic December 1935, Lot No 121 – Works No 276 and was withdrawn by BR in December 1962 cut up at Taylor Brothers, Trafford Park in January 1964.

'Jubilee' class BR No 45678 DE ROBECK is seen being serviced at Edinburgh Dalry Road depot on 23 July 1953. *David Anderson*

45679 ARMADA (LMS 5679) built Crewe Works entered traffic December 1935, Lot No 121 – Works No 277 and was withdrawn by BR in December 1962 cut up at Darlington Works in November 1963.

'Jubilee' class BR No 45679 Armada with is seen at Stockport during June 1960. *Mike Stokes Archive*

Sir John Michael de Robeck, GCB, GCMG, GCVO

Admiral of the Fleet,1st Baronet was born in Naas, Co Kildare, Republic of Ireland on 10 June 1862. He was the son of John Henry Edward Fock, 4th Baron De Robeck. He joined the Royal Navy in 1875 as a cadet aboard the training ship HMS *Britannia,* he joined HMS *Shannon* as a midshipman in July 1878 and was promoted to lieutenant in September 1885 transferring to the battleship HMS *Audacious.*

De Robeck became gunnery officer in the corvette HMS *Cordelia* on first, the North America, and then the West Indies Station in November 1895. He then gained promotion to commander on 22 June 1897 and was subsequently promoted to captain in January 1902. He gained the rank of Rear Admiral in December 1911 and became Admiral of Patrols, commanding four flotillas of destroyers in April 1912.

De Robeck commanded the allied naval force in the Dardanelles during the First World War.

His campaign to force the straits, launched on 18 March 1915, was not entirely successful, as the Turkish land-based artillery almost ran out of ammunition. However, mines laid in the straits led to the loss of three allied battleships. The subsequent ground campaign was ultimately a failure and the troops had to be taken off the Gallipoli peninsula by de Robeck on 8 January 1916. He was made Vice Admiral in May 1917, created a Baronet in December 1919, full Admiral in March 1920 and Admiral of the Fleet in 1925.

Admiral of the Fleet, Sir John Michael de Robeck, 1st Baronet GCB, GCMG, GCVO, a 1923 image. *NPG*

Commands held, Atlantic Fleet, Commander in Chief Mediterranean Fleet 2nd and 3rd Battle Squadrons. Eastern Mediterranean Squadron 9th Cruiser Squadron. HMS *Dominion,* HMS *Carnarvon,* HMS *Mermaid,* HMS *Angler* and HMS *Desperate.*

In his retirement De Robeck became President of the Marylebone Cricket Club (MCC). He died at his London home on 20 January 1928 and was interred at Bembridge Church, Isle of Wight.

Armada

The name in British history commonly referred to the Spanish Fleet of 130 ships which sailed with a purpose of invading England in the early summer of 1588.

This image depicts the launch of fireships against the Armada on 7 August 1588.

One Royal Navy warship was named HMS *Armada* in honour of the English victory. HMS *Armada* was built by Hawthorn Leslie and Company on the Tyne. She was launched on 9 December 1943, commissioned on 2 July 1945, and decommissioned in 1960.

Battle of Camperdown

The Battle of Camperdown was a major naval action fought on 11 October 1797, between the British North Sea Fleet under Admiral Adam Duncan and a Batavian* Navy fleet under Vice-Admiral Jan de Winter. The battle was the most significant action between British and Dutch forces during the French Revolutionary Wars and resulted in a complete victory for the British, who captured eleven Dutch ships without losing any of their own.

HMS *Camperdown*

Four ships of the Royal Navy were named HMS *Camperdown*, they were a 74-gun ship of the line launched in 1797, 106-gun vessel launched as HMS *Trafalgar* in 1820 and renamed in 1825, an 'Admiral-class' battleship launched in 1885 and 'Battle-class' destroyer launched in 1944 (Pennant No D32) it was placed on the disposal list in 1962 and scrapped in 1970.

HMS *Camperdown* was also a Royal Naval Reserve training centre in Dundee, Scotland between October 1970 and May 1994.

Battle of Aboukir Bay

The Battle of Aboukir Bay (also known as The Battle of the Nile) was a famous and decisive British victory fought between the British Royal Navy and the Navy of the French Republic between 1–3 August 1798. The British Fleet was led by Rear Admiral Sir Horatio Nelson and the French Fleet by Vice Admiral Francois-Paul Brueys d' Aigalliers.

Battle of Aboukir

The Battle of Aboukir (or Aboukir or Abu Qir) was a battle in which Napoleon Bonaparte defeated Seid Mustafa Pasha's Ottoman army on 25 July 1799, during the French campaign in Egypt. It was fought during the French Revolutionary War.

HMS *Aboukir*

Four ships of the Royal Navy were named HMS *Aboukir*. The first a 74-gun ship of the line which was formerly the French ship *Aquilon*, captured at the Battle of the Nile in 1798. The fourth a 'Cressy-class' cruiser launched in May 1900 which was sunk by submarine U-9 on 22 September 1914 with a loss of 527 souls.

'Cressey-class' cruiser HMS *Aboukir* is seen passing Fort St. Angelo, Malta prior to WWI.

Admiral Duncan receiving the surrender of Jan de Winter after the Battle of Camperdown. *Artist Daniel Orme and on display at the National Maritime Museum*

* The Batavian Republic was the successor of the Republic of the Seven United Netherlands. It was proclaimed on 19 January 1795 and ended on 5 June 1806.

45680 CAMPERDOWN (LMS 5680) built Crewe Works entered traffic December 1935, Lot No 121-Works No 278 and was withdrawn by BR in January 1963, cut up at Crewe Works in June 1963.

'Jubilee' class BR No 45680 CAMPERDOWN is seen as it awaits departure from Sefton Arms with a Grand National race special on 31 March 1962. That year the race was won by the 28-1 shot Kilmore. *Paul Claxton/Rail Photoprints Collection*

45681 ABOUKIR (LMS 5681) built Crewe Works entered traffic December 1935, Lot No 121-Works No 279 and was withdrawn by BR in September 1964, cut up at Central Wagon Company, Wigan in January 1965.

'Jubilee' class BR No 45681 ABOUKIR is seen with '4F' 0-6-0 BR No 44548 and 'Black Five' 4-6-0 BR No 45078, stabled inside the shed at Blackpool Central depot on 20 July 1964. *Paul Claxton/Rail Photoprints Collection*

45682 TRAFALGAR (LMS 5682) built Crewe Works entered traffic January 1936, Lot No 121-Works No 280 and was withdrawn by BR in June 1964, cut up at Birds, Morriston in August 1964.

'Jubilee' class BR No 45682 TRAFALGAR is seen approaching Bath Green Park with an Easter Monday Weston-super-Mare–Bournemouth West excursion, in April 1962. *Hugh Ballantyne/Rail Photoprints*

45683 HOGUE (LMS 5683) built Crewe Works entered traffic January 1936, Lot No 121-Works No 281 and was withdrawn by BR in December 1962, cut up at Crewe Works in March 1964.

'Jubilee' class BR No 45683 HOGUE is seen at Chinley station, June 1961. *Rail Photoprints Collection*

45684 JUTLAND (LMS 5684) built Crewe Works entered traffic February 1936, Lot No 121-Works No 282 and was withdrawn by BR in December 1965, cut up at Cashmores, Great Bridge in March 1966.

'Jubilee' class BR No 45684 JUTLAND is seen at Dalry Road, Edinburgh on 31 July 1953. *David Anderson*

Battle of Trafalgar

The Battle of Trafalgar was a naval engagement fought by the Royal Navy against the combined fleets of the French and Spanish Navies, during the War of the Third Coalition of the Napoleonic Wars.

A fleet of twenty-seven British ships of the line, led by Admiral Lord Nelson aboard HMS *Victory* defeated thirty-three French and Spanish ships of the line under the French Admiral Villeneuve. It took place on 21 October 1805 off Cape Trafalgar, Spain (Atlantic Ocean) and it was a decisive British victory.

HMS *Trafalgar*

Five Royal Navy warships have been named in honour of Nelson's famous battle the first being a 106-gun vessel launched in 1820. The fourth vessel was a 'Battle-class' destroyer which served during the later part of the Second World War which was decommissioned in 1963 and scrapped in 1971. The last was a 'Trafalgar-class' submarine launched in 1981 and decommissioned in 2009.

Battle of La Hogue

The Action at La Hogue occurred during the pursuit by the English of the French fleet after the Battle of Barfleur during May 1692 (Nine Years' War). The pursuing English fleet, under the command of Admiral of the Fleet Edward Russell, 1st Earl of Orford, destroyed a number of French ships that had been beached near the port of Saint-Vaast-la-Hougue, Normandy, France.

HMS *Hogue*

HMS *Hogue* was a 'Cressy-class' armoured cruiser built for the Royal Navy around 1900. Upon completion she was assigned to the Channel Fleet and the China Station. In 1906 she became a training ship for the North America and West Indies Station before being placed in reserve in 1908. Recommissioned at the start of World War I, she played a minor role in the Battle of Heligoland Bight a few weeks after the beginning of the war. Hogue was sunk by the German submarine 'U-9' on 22 September 1914, with a loss of 48 crew members.

Battle of Jutland

The Battle of Jutland was a naval battle fought by the Royal Navy's Grand Fleet under Admiral Sir John Jellicoe, against the Imperial German Navy's High Seas Fleet under Vice-Admiral Reinhard Scheer during the First World War, from 31 May to 1 June 1916, off the North Sea coast of Denmark's Jutland Peninsula. It was the largest naval battle and the only full-scale clash of battleships in that war, importantly it was the last major battle in world history fought primarily by battleships.

HMS *Jutland*

Two Royal Navy ships were to have been named for the aforementioned battle however the first launched in November 1945 was never completed and after trial use was broken up in 1957. The second however was a 'Battle-class' destroyer launched in 1946 and broken up in 1965.

Visit www.titanicbelfast.com/

The name JUTLAND was also carried by LNER 'D11' class locomotive BR No 62668 (LNER 2668).

Rear Admiral Sir Horatio Nelson in 1799. *National Maritime Museum*

The launch of *HMS Hogue* in 1900. *Municipal Archives of Trondheim*

HMS *Caroline* is the only surviving warship (still afloat) from the Battle of Jutland. The light cruiser was built at Cammell Laird, Birkenhead and launched on 29 September 1914 and was originally decommissioned in February 1922. The vessel is now designated a Museum Ship and located at Alexandra Dock Belfast, Northern Ireland.

Battle of Barfleur

The action at Barfleur, 29 May – 4 June 1692 was part of the battle of Barfleur-La Hougue during the War of the Grand Alliance. A French fleet under Anne Hilarion de Tourville was seeking to cover an invasion of England by a French army to restore James II to the throne but was intercepted by an Anglo-Dutch fleet under the Admiralship of Edward Russell, 1st Earl of Orford. The battle was a decisive Anglo-Dutch victory and the invasion of Britain was foiled.

HMS *Barfleur*

Five Royal Navy ships were named HMS *Barfleur,* the first being a 90-gun ship of the line launched in 1697. The fifth was a 'Battle-class' destroyer launched in 1943 (Pennant No D80) which was the only ship of the class to see action during the Second World War. The vessel was put into Reserve in 1958 and broken up in 1966.

Battle of Cape St. Vincent

The Battle of Cape St Vincent (14 February 1797) was one of the opening battles of the Anglo-Spanish War (1796–1808), as part of the French Revolutionary Wars, where a British fleet under Admiral Sir John Jervis defeated a larger Spanish fleet under Admiral Don José de Córdoba y Ramos near Cape St. Vincent, Portugal.

HMS *Vincent*

The name was given to four Royal Navy ships and three shore establishments. The first ship being an 8-gun fire ship captured from the French in 1692. The last vessel was a 'St. Vincent-class' dreadnought battleship launched in 1908 and was a participant in the WW1 Battle of Jutland. The vessel survived the war and was decommissioned in March 1921.

Shore Establishments
HMS *St Vincent* (Gosport shore establishment) was a boy/junior training establishment in Gosport from 1927 to 1969.
HMS *St. Vincent* was the home of the Royal Navy section of the Royal Naval Reserve's London centre, HMS *President* between 1983 and 1992.
HMS *St Vincent* (Whitehall shore establishment) was the Navy's communication centre in Whitehall from 1992 to 1998. It then became known as 'MARCOMM COMCEN (St Vincent)'.

Neptune

Roman God of the Ocean.

HMS *Neptune*

Nine Royal Navy ships and one shore establishment were named for the Roman God. The first being a 90-gun ship launched in 1683. The ninth warship was a 'Leander-class' light cruiser launched in 1933 (Pennant No 20) and sunk in a minefield off Tripoli on 19 December 1941 with a loss of 736 souls, of which 150 were New Zealand sailors. The one survivor was Norman Walton, who in 1991 travelled to New Zealand to unveil a memorial to HMS *Neptune* and a memorial service is held each year in the town of Nelson NZ.

Admiral Edward Russell, 1st Earl of Orford. circa 1715, painted by Thomas Gibson. *Royal Museums Greenwich. www. rmg.co.uk*

Crest from the Arms of Admiral Sir John Jervis. *RNA. www.royal-naval-association.co.uk/*

Statue of Neptune in the Louvre Museum, Paris.

45685 BARFLEUR (LMS 5685) built Crewe Works entered traffic February 1936, Lot No 121-Works No 283 and was withdrawn by BR in April 1964, cut up at Birds, Risca in January 1965.

'Jubilee' class BR No 45685 gets under way from Sheffield with a northbound train, in December 1963. Nice smile from the driver! *Rail Photoprints Collection*

45686 ST. VINCENT (LMS 5686) built Crewe Works entered traffic February 1936, Lot No 121-Works No 284 and was withdrawn by BR in November 1962, cut up at Crewe Works in August 1963.

'Jubilee' class early BR No M5686 ST. VINCENT (later 45686) is seen at Crewe circa 1948. The locomotive has been newly painted in lined 'BR Black' livery, the power rating 5XP is on the cabside in addition to the letter M. The token equipment fixing bracket obscures the figure 8. *Rail Photoprints Collection*

45687 NEPTUNE (LMS 5687) built Crewe Works entered traffic February 1936, Lot No 121-Works No 285 and was withdrawn by BR in December 1962, cut up at Campbells, Aidrie in December 1963.

'Jubilee' class BR No 45687 NEPTUNE is seen on 22 May 1961 at Ardrossan depot. *RCTS Archive*

45688 POLYPHEMUS (LMS 5688) built Crewe Works entered traffic February 1936, Lot No 121-Works No 286 and was withdrawn by BR in December 1962, cut up at Crewe Works in June 1963.

45689 AJAX (LMS 5689) built Crewe Works entered traffic February 1936, Lot No 121-Works No 287 and was withdrawn by BR in December 1964, cut up at Wards, Beighton in May 1965.

'Jubilee' class BR No 45689 AJAX is seen heading along the picturesque Welsh coast, whilst approaching Colwyn Bay with a holiday special on 18 July 1959. *Steve Armitage Archive/Rail Photoprints*

45690 LEANDER (LMS 5690) built Crewe Works entered traffic March 1936, Lot No 121-Works No 288 and was withdrawn by BR in March 1964 and saved for preservation.

Preserved 'Jubilee' class BR No 45690 LEANDER in 'BR Lined Black' livery, is seen passing Wem en-route for Shrewsbury on 28 March 2015 with a 'Salopian Express' working. *Keith Langston Collection*

The locomotive was sold for scrap to Woodham Brothers, Barry but rescued from there in 1972. After an initial restoration to working order LEANDER returned to mainline duty in 2008, having first been seen in action on preserved railway metals. In October 2012 the engine was withdrawn and re-restored to working order, this time at the Carnforth works of the West Coast Railway Company. At the time of writing BR No 45690 is in private ownership, operational and mainline certified.

Polyphemus

Polyphemus is the giant son of Poseidon and Thoosa in Greek mythology, one of the Cyclopes (mythical giant with a single eye in the centre of his forehead) as described in Homer's Odyssey.

HMS *Polyphemus*

Three ships of the Royal Navy have been named HMS *Polyphemus* the first a 64-gun vessel launched in 1782. The last a Torpedo Ram launched in 1881 (scrapped 1903) which was a shallow-draft, fast, low-profile vessel, designed to penetrate enemy harbours at speed and sink anchored ships.

AJAX

Ajax is a mythological Greek hero the son of King Telamon and Periboea, often referred to as Ajax the Great.

HMS *Ajax*

Eight ships of the Royal Navy have been named HMS *Ajax* the first being a 74-gun vessel launched in 1677. Included in the list is a 'Leander-class' light cruiser launched in March 1934 (Pennant No 22) which famously took part in The Battle of the River Plate (December 1939) amongst other engagements. In that battle the German warship *Admiral Graf Spee* was cornered, severely damaged and as a result was subsequently scuttled by her own crew. HMS *Exeter* and HMS *Achilles* also took part in the famed sea action which took part off Montevideo, Uruguay.

Commemorative shield made to commemorate the 50th anniversary of the Battle of the River Plate.

This picture by the artist Jan van den Hoecke depicts the sorrowful Hero lamenting the death of Leander.

Leander

Hero and Leander are two characters in the Greek myth relating the story of Hero, a priestess of Aphrodite who dwelt in a tower in Sestos on the European side of the Hellespont, and Leander, a young man from Abydos on the opposite side of the strait.

HMS *Leander*

Six ships of the Royal Navy have been named HMS *Leander* the first a 52-gun vessel launched in 1780. The sixth a 'Leander class' frigate launched in 1961 and expended as a target in 1989.

The fifth HMS *Leander* (Pennant No 75) was launched at Devonport on 24 September 1931. She was commissioned into the Royal Navy on 24 March 1933. From April 1937 she was loaned to the New Zealand Navy (RN New Zealand division). In 1941 the New Zealand Division became the Royal New Zealand Navy (RNZN) and she was commissioned as HMNZS *Leander* in September 1941. She returned to the Royal Navy in August 1945 and was decommissioned in February 1948.

Seen at sea, HMS *Leander* returned to the Royal Navy in 1945. *Royal Navy Photographer*

Preserved 'Jubilee' class BR No 45690 LEANDER is seen in 'LMS Maroon' livery as No 5690 approaching Penmaenmawr with a Vintage Trains 'The Irish Mail' charter on 3 September 2005. 'The Irish Mail' London Euston-Holyhead, was officially introduced on 26 September 1927 with the title being withdrawn during WWII and reintroduced on 31 May 1948, last BR titled run 12 May 1985 (Diesel hauled). *Brian Jones*

The Great Gathering was held on the site of Crewe Works over the weekend of 10-11 September 2005 and preserved 'Jubilee' class LMS No 5690 LEANDER is seen in the company of LMS Stanier 2-6-0 BR No 42968. The GG 'Festival of Rail' being the last time that the works site was used for a public display of locomotives. The event was staged by the Webb Crewe Works Charity Fund, for the benefit of local organisations. *Keith Langston Collection*

Preserved 'Jubilee' class LMS No 5690 LEANDER is seen near Pontypool Road with a southbound Welsh Marches Express on 18 February 1984. *John Chalcraft*

Preserved 'Jubilee' class BR No 45690 LEANDER is seen in LMS livery as No 5690 whilst approaching Llanfairfechan with a Vintage Trains 'The Irish Mail' charter on 3 September 2005. Note the backdrop of the delightful West Shore and Great Orme, Llandudno. *David Jones*

Orion

Orion is a prominent constellation located on the celestial equator and visible throughout the world. It is one of the most conspicuous and recognizable constellations in the night sky and was named after Orion, a hunter in Greek mythology.

HMS *Orion*

Six ships of the Royal Navy were named HMS *Orion* the first being a 74-gun vessel launched in 1787. The fourth vessel, was the first of the so-called 'super dreadnoughts' and a member of the 'Orion-class' which operated during the First World War period including taking part in the Battle of Jutland. The fifth vessel was a 'Leander-class' light cruiser (Pennant No 85) launched in 1932 which served throughout the second world war and received no less than thirteen battle honours. The six and last was interestingly a French submarine seized in 1940.

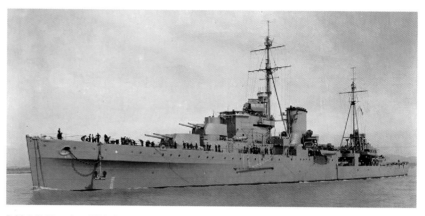

British light cruiser HMS *Orion* underway after completion of a refit at Mare Island Naval Shipyard, California, USA, February 1942. *British Navy Photographer*

Cyclops

A cyclops, in Greek mythology and later Roman mythology, is a member of a primordial race of giants, each with a single eye in the centre of his forehead. The name literally means 'round-eyed' or 'circle-eyed'.

HMS *Cyclops*

Four ships of the Royal Navy were named HMS *Cyclops*, the first a 28-gun vessel launched in 1779 and the last a repair-ship which was formerly the merchant ship *Indrabarah*, built by Sir James Laing & Son, Sunderland, launched in 1905 and commissioned in 1907. The lightly armoured vessel saw service during both world wars and was scrapped in 1947.

Agamemnon

In Greek mythology, Agamemnon was the son of King Atreus and Queen Aerope of Mycenae, the brother of Menelaus, the husband of Clytemnestra and the father of Iphigenia, Electra or Laodike, Orestes and Chrysothemis.

HMS *Agamemnon*

Five ships of the Royal Navy were named HMS *Agamemnon*, the first being a 64-gun vessel launched in 1781 which took part in the Battle of Trafalgar. The last being an ex 'Blue Funnel Line' ship (launched 1929) which was requisitioned by the Royal Navy (Pennant No M10) and converted to a minelayer. That vessel served the Second World War. After a 1944 re-fit the vessel joined the Royal Fleet Auxiliary and thereafter was returned to 'Blue Funnel Line'.

At the time of writing an 'Astute-class' nuclear powered submarine (Pennant No S124) to be named HMS *Agamemnon* was currently under construction.

The auxiliary minelayer *HMS Agamemnon*, moored at a minelaying base on the Kyle of Lochalsh, circa 1935. *Royal Navy Photographer*

45691 ORION (LMS 5691) built Crewe Works entered traffic March 1936, Lot No 121-Works No 289 and was withdrawn by BR in December 1962 and cut up at Crewe Works in May 1963.

'Jubilee' class BR No 45691 is seen passing Dalry Road depot circa1955. The smartly turned out locomotive is in charge of a 5–coach local service in this busy railway scene typical of the era. *David Anderson*

45692 CYCLOPS (LMS 5692) built Crewe Works entered traffic March 1936, Lot No 121-Works No 290 and was withdrawn by BR in December 1962 and cut up at Campbells Airdrie in December 1963.

'Jubilee' class BR No 45692 CYCLOPS rumbles off the Forth Bridge into Dalmeny station with an unidentified van train, 15 June 1957. The iconic Forth Railway Bridge was completed in March 1890 having taken just over 7 years to build. The double track deck is 1.5 miles long and over 4000 men worked on its construction with approximately 55,000 tons of steel and some 6,500,000 rivets were used. *David Anderson*

45693 AGAMEMNON (LMS 5693) built Crewe Works entered traffic March 1936, Lot No 121-Works No 291 and was withdrawn by BR in December 1962 and cut up at Campbells Airdrie in December 1963.

45694 BELLEROPHON (LMS 5694) built Crewe Works entered traffic March 1936, Lot No 121-Works No 292 and was withdrawn by BR in January 1967 and cut up at Drapers, Hull in June 1967.

'Jubilee' class BR No 45694 BELLEROPHON is seen at Cricklewood depot after servicing, having brought a train load of fans to London for the Rugby League Challenge Cup Final on 9 May 1964. The Wembley final was contested between Wigan and Hunslet with Wigan being 20-16 winners. *Mike Morant Collection*

45695 MINOTAUR (LMS 5695) built Crewe Works entered traffic March 1936, Lot No 129-Works No 293 and was withdrawn by BR in February 1964 and cut up at J.S. Parker, Broadheath in July 1964.

'Jubilee' class BR No 45695 MINOTAUR with a 3,500 gallon/7 ton Fowler tender is seen at Diggle with a train for Manchester, circa 1955, note the then busy signal box controlling the junction. *Norman Preedy Collection*

45696 ARETHUSA (LMS 5696) built Crewe Works entered traffic April 1936, Lot No 129-Works No 294 and was withdrawn by BR in August 1964 and cut up at Connels, Calder in January 1964.

'Jubilee' class BR No 45696 ARETHUSA with a Fowler tender, note the coal rails (greedy bars) is seen with a parcels train at Penrith station during August 1961. *RCTS Archive*

Bellerophon

A hero of Greek mythology. He was said to be the greatest hero and slayer of monsters and his greatest feat was killing the Chimera, a monster that Homer depicted with a lion's head, a goat's body, and a serpent's tail.

HMS *Bellerophon*

Four ships of the Royal Navy and a shore establishment have been named HMS *Bellerophon*, the first being a 74-gun vessel launched in 1786. The fourth was a 'Bellerophon-class' battleship launched in 1907 which was present at the Battle of Jutland (1916). She served throughout the First World War and sustained no battle damage and was scrapped in 1921.

HMS *Bellerophon* was a former Royal Navy shore establishment in Portsmouth, UK.

HMS *Bellerophon* seen underway in 1909.

Minotaur

In Greek mythology, the Minotaur is a mythical creature portrayed in Classical times with the head of a bull and the body of a man or, as described by Roman poet Ovid, as being 'part man and part bull'.

HMS *Minotaur*

Six ships of the Royal Navy have been named HMS *Minotaur*, the first of which a 74-gun vessel launched in 1793 fought at the Battles of Trafalgar and Nile. In 1863 the third such named vessel launched was an 'Ironclad' battleship which spent the majority of her active career as flag ship of the Channel Fleet.

The fourth launched in 1906 was a 'Minotaur-class' armoured cruiser which took part in the First World War and was in attendance at the Battle of

'Ironclad' HMS *Minotaur* as Channel Fleet flagship.

Jutland, but in that engagement never fired her weapons, she was scrapped in 1920. The sixth vessel was a light cruiser launched in 1943 which was transferred to the Royal Canadian Navy in 1944 and renamed HMCS *Ontario*, the vessel was scrapped in 1960.

Arethusa

In Greek mythology, she was a nymph and daughter of Nereus who fled from her home in Arcadia beneath the sea and came up as a fresh water fountain on the Island of Ortygia in Syracuse, Sicily.

HMS *Arethusa*

Eight Royal Navy ships were named HMS *Arethusa,* and one vessel HMS *Arethuse,* the first a 32-gun vessel captured from the French Navy in 1759 and renamed. The sixth vessel was an 'Arethusa-class' light cruiser launched in 1913 which took part in the Battle of Heligoland Bight (28 August 1914) and also fought in 1915 at Dogger Bank and was wrecked after being damaged by a naval mine whilst under tow off Felixstowe on 11 February 1916. The seventh vessel was also an 'Arethusa-class' light cruiser launched in 1934 (Pennant No 26) which served throughout World War Two and was scrapped in 1950. The last being a 'Leander-class' frigate launched 1963 and sunk as a target in 1991.

A tug is seen alongside the wreck of HMS *Arethusa* after she was damaged by a mine in 1916.

Achilles

In Greek mythology Achilles was a Greek hero of the Trojan War and the central character and greatest warrior of Homer's Iliad. Achilles' most notable feat during the Trojan War was the slaying of the Trojan hero Hector outside the gates of Troy.

HMS *Achilles*

There were six Royal Navy ships named HMS *Achilles,* the first being an 8-gun schooner launched in 1747. Importantly the third was an 'Ironclad' frigate launched in 1863. In 1932 the fifth vessel was launched and was a 'Leander-class' light cruiser (Pennant No 70) which was transferred to the Royal New Zealand Navy in 1941, and subsequently came back to the Royal Navy in 1946. In 1948 she was transferred to the Royal Indian Navy eventually becoming *INS Delhi,* she was scrapped in 1978. The final vessel was launched in 1968 (Pennant No F12) a 'Leander-class' frigate which was sold to Chile in 1990.

Achilles statue in Hyde Park, London.
Len Mills

Mars

Mars is the fourth planet from the Sun and the second-smallest planet in the Solar System after Mercury. Mars was the Roman god of war, and second only to Jupiter in the Roman pantheon.

HMS *Mars*

Seven ships of the Royal Navy were called HMS *Mars,* the first being a 50-gun vessel captured in the Second Anglo-Dutch War in 1665. In 1794 the fifth a 74-gun vessel was launched and that vessel was associated with the Spithead Mutiny (1797) and also took part in the Battle of Trafalgar (1805). The seventh was a 'Majestic-class' battleship launched in 1896 which served as a guardship and transport throughout World War One.

Galatea

Galatea is a name popularly applied to the statue carved of ivory by Pygmalion of Cyprus, which then came to life, in Greek mythology; in modern English the name usually alludes to that story.

HMS *Galatea*

Eight ships of the Royal Navy were named HMS *Galatea,* the first being a 20-gun vessel launched in 1776.

Part of a restored statue of Mars, in Rome.

In 1914 the 6th vessel was launched and that was an 'Arethusa-class' light cruiser which served throughout World War One and was the flagship of the 1st Light Cruiser Squadron at the time of the Battle of Jutland. In the Second World War the seventh vessel launched in 1934 (Pennant No 71), was torpedoed and sunk by German submarine U-557 off Alexandria, Egypt with a loss of 470 souls. Approximately 100 members of the crew were rescued by the destroyers HMS *Griffin* and HMS *Hotspur,* and less than 48 hours after the attack U-557 was mistakenly rammed by the Italian torpedo boat *Orione* and sunk with the loss of all hands. Reportedly the Italian commander observed a submarine heading in a northerly direction and having no knowledge of a German vessel being in the area decided to ram it, assuming that it was a British vessel. The eighth vessel was a 'Leander-class' frigate launched in 1963 (Pennant No F18) and decommissioned in 1987.

The 1914 launched 'Arethusa-class' light cruiser HMS *Galatea* is seen at sea during WWI.

45697 ACHILLES (LMS 5697) built Crewe Works entered traffic April 1936, Lot No 129-Works No 295 and was withdrawn by BR in September 1967 and cut up at Cashmores, Great Bridge in May 1968.

'Jubilee' class LMS No 5697 ACHILLES is seen on the turntable at Blackpool North depot, in 1937. Note the tower! *Rail Photoprints Collection*

45698 MARS (LMS 5698) built Crewe Works entered traffic April 1936, Lot No 129-Works No 296 and was withdrawn by BR in November 1965 and cut up at Wards, Beighton in February 1966.

'Jubilee' class BR No 45698 MARS is seen heading towards Shap summit with an up train in August 1965. *RCTS Archive*

45699 GALATEA (LMS 5699) built Crewe Works entered traffic April 1936, Lot No 129-Works No 297 and was withdrawn by BR in November 1964 and saved for preservation. **P**

Now preserved 'Jubilee' class BR No 45699 GALATEA with a Stanier tender, is seen on the 'Lickey Incline', approaching Bromsgrove with a northbound service, in 1959. *Rail Photoprints Collection*

'Jubilee' class BR No 45699 GALATEA is seen with the 8:30 Liverpool – Euston express whilst passing Tamworth on 21 June 1959. *RCTS Archive*

Preserved 'Jubilee' class BR No 45699 GALATEA in maroon livery is almost on former home turf as it runs through Newton Meadows with its support coach, having worked 1Z46 from Paddington to the West Somerset Railway. GALATEA was a Bristol Barrow Road allocated engine from 1948 to 1961 during which time it appeared at Bath Green Park on several occasions via Mangotsfield and the Midland Line. *John Chalcraft/Rail Photoprints*

Preserved 'Jubilee' class BR No 45699 GALATEA in maroon livery is seen leaving Carnforth with the Carnforth-Carlisle leg of a Coventry-Carlisle working on 17 February 2016. The locomotive's exhaust further blackens the already darkening winter sky. *Fred Kerr*

GALATEA was rescued in April 1980 from Woodham Brothers scrapyard in Barry, South Wales by the late Brian Oliver and was moved to The Severn Valley Railway originally to provide a spare boiler for preserved sister engine BR No 45690 LEANDER. BR No 45699 was at Tyseley Locomotive Works until 2002 when it was sold to the West Coast Railway Company and moved to Steamtown Carnforth where it underwent a complete rebuild. Interestingly that work also included the manufacturing of a new middle driving wheel, after the original was cut through following a shunting accident at Barry Island. The locomotive returned to steam in April 2013 completing test runs around the Hellifield circle. Galatea made her railtour debut on 19 May 2013 working a private charter from King's Lynn to Norwich. At the time of writing the engine was still operational and certified in order to work on the main line.

The impressively restored 'Jubilee' class locomotive is carrying a 10A Carnforth shedplate representing the location of the West Coast Railway Company's main base. Under British Railways post 1948, the 1936 LMS built locomotive was allocated to 22A Bristol Barrow Road depot on 29/05/1948 and thereafter to 89A (formerly 84G) Shrewsbury depot on 07/10/1961. Preserved 'Jubilee' class BR No 45699 GALATEA in maroon livery is seen at the stunning location of Hellifield Green with a Carnforth-Hellifield–Preston–Carnforth with a West Coast Railways Ltd driver training working on 16 November 2016. *Fred Kerr*

45700 AMETHYST (LMS 5700) built Crewe Works entered traffic April 1936 as BRITANNIA and was renamed September 1951, Lot No 129 – Works No 298. It was withdrawn by BR in July 1964 and cut up at Crewe Works in September 1964.

'Jubilee' class BR No 45700 AMETHYST is seen departing from Manchester Victoria station, circa 1961. *Steve Armitage Archive – Photographer Jim R. Carter/ Rail Photoprints*

45701 CONQUEROR (LMS 5701) built Crewe Works entered traffic April 1936, Lot No 129 – Works No 299 and was withdrawn by BR in February 1963 and cut up at Crewe Works in May 1963.

'Jubilee' class BR No 45701 CONQUEROR is seen whilst taking water on Dillicar Troughs, circa 1952. *Norman Preedy Collection*

45702 COLOSSUS (LMS 5702) built Crewe Works entered traffic May 1936, Lot No 129 – Works No 300 and was withdrawn by BR in April 1963 and cut up at Crewe Works in August 1963.

Amethyst

Amethyst is a violet variety of quartz often used in jewellery.

HMS *Amethyst*

Six ships of the Royal Navy were named HMS *Amethyst,* the first being a 36-gun vessel launched in 1790 which was a captured French ship *Perie.* Perhaps the most famous was the sixth vessel, a modified 'Black Swan-class' sloop launched in 1943 (Pennant No U16 later No F116). The 'Yangtze Incident' was a historic event which involved HMS *Amethyst* being trapped on the Yangtze River for three months during the Chinese Civil War in the summer of 1949. A British film starring Richard Todd and released in 1957 tells the fascinating story.

HMS *Conqueror*

Nine ships of the Royal Navy were named HMS *Conqueror* the first was an 8-gun fireship, captured from the French in 1745. During World War One the eighth an 'Orion-class' battleship launched May 1911 served in the 2nd Battle Squadron of the Grand Fleet and also fought at the Battle of Jutland. She was decommissioned in 1921.

Colossus

A word derived from the Ancient Greek meaning a giant statue.

HMS *Colossus*

Six ships of the Royal Navy were named HMS *Colossus* the first was a 74-gun vessel launched in 1787. The second vessel (also a 74-gun warship) launched in 1803 fought at the Battle of Trafalgar (1805). The fifth vessel was a 'Colossus-class' dreadnought battleship launched in 1910 which fought during World War One and with distinction at the Battle of Jutland.

The sixth vessel was a 'Colossus-class' light aircraft carrier launched in 1943 and loaned to France in 1946. Renamed *Arromanches,* and subsequently bought by France in 1951.

HMS *Amethyst* is seen during WWII. *Royal Naval Photographer*

'Jubilee' class BR No 45702 COLOSSUS is seen hard at work on Beattock Bank during 1960. *David Anderson*

Thunderer

The name may refer to Thor, Norse God of Thunder.

HMS *Thunderer*

Five ships of the Royal Navy and one shore establishment were named HMS *Thunderer*. The first warship being a 74-gun vessel launched in 1760 and the second also a 74-gun vessel launched in 1783 fought at the Battle of Trafalgar. Interestingly the fourth vessel launched in 1872 was a 'Devastation-class' ironclad, the world's first mastless battleships. The fifth was an 'Orion-class' battleship launched in 1911 which fought throughout the First World War including the Battle of Jutland, during which she suffered no damage.

HMS *Thunderer* was also the name given to the Royal Naval Engineering College, located initially at Keyham, and later Manadon. The college was founded in 1880, later commissioned as HMS *Thunderer* in 1946, and finally paid off in 1995.

Four 'Orion-class' battleships in line ahead formation, circa 1916. *Surgeon Oscar Parkes*

Leviathan

Leviathan is a sea monster referenced in the Hebrew Bible.

HMS *Leviathan*

The Royal Navy allocated the name HMS *Leviathan* to four warships, but in the event only three were completed and put into service. The first was a 70-gun vessel launched in 1750 as HMS *Northumberland* and renamed in 1777. The second, a 74-gun vessel launched in 1790 fought at the Battle of Trafalgar. During World War One the third vessel, a 'Drake-class' armoured cruiser launched in 1903 served as flag ship of the 1st Cruiser Squadron before in early 1915 being transferred to the 6th Cruiser Squadron and becoming flagship of the North America and West Indies Station. The fourth vessel, a 'Majestic-class' aircraft carrier was launched in 1945 but construction was never completed, that hulk was scrapped in 1968.

Seahorse

Seahorse is the name given to 54 species of small marine fishes in the genus Hippocampus.

HMS *Seahorse*

Eleven ships of the Royal Navy were named HMS *Seahorse* the first being a captured vessel in 1626.

In 1880 Laird Brothers of Birkenhead launched a fast sea tug which also served as a survey ship throughout the First World War, and that was the tenth vessel. The eleventh was an 'S-class' submarine, launched in November 1932 (Pennant No 98S). The submarine HMS *Seahorse* was never heard from after sailing from Blyth on 26 December 1939 for her fifth war patrol and to navigate to a sea area off western Jutland. Her operational area was to be initially off Heligoland then move to the mouth of the Elbe on 30 December, and due to return to Blyth on 9 January 1940. No definite details exist but a post war examination of German naval records would suggest that she was most likely sunk, with the loss of all 38 submariners. HMS *Seahorse* was in all probability attacked and depth charged by ships from the German 1st Minesweeping Flotilla, on 7 January 1940 at a position approximately 15 nautical miles north-west of Heligoland.

HMS *Seahorse* leaving Portsmouth for sea trials on 13 October 1933.

45703 THUNDERER (LMS 5703) built Crewe Works entered traffic May 1936, Lot No 129 – Works No 301 and was withdrawn by BR in November 1964 and cut up at Wards, Killamarsh in April 1965.

'Jubilee' class BR No 45703 THUNDERER is seen passing Carpenders Park with the down 'Midlander' on 26 May 1953. 'The Midlander' Euston -Wolverhampton High Level first ran on 25 September 1950 and the last titled run took place on 11 September 1959. *Dave Cobbe Collection/Rail Photoprints*

45704 LEVIATHAN (LMS 5704) built Crewe Works entered traffic May 1936, Lot No 129 – Works No 302 and was withdrawn by BR in January 1965 and cut up at Cashmores, Great Bridge in April 1965.

'Jubilee' class LMS No 5704 LEVIATHAN is seen on shed at Cricklewood on 5 June 1937. *Rail Photoprints Collection*

45705 SEAHORSE (LMS 5705) built Crewe Works entered traffic May 1936, Lot No 129 – Works No 303 and was withdrawn by BR in November 1965 and cut up at Cashmores, Great Bridge in February 1966.

'Jubilee' class BR No 45705 SEAHORSE is seen at Carstairs on 3 October 1964 whilst receiving attention to the leading driving wheel set. A yellow stripe on the cabside indicated that the locomotive was prohibited from working south of Crewe, under the then electrified overhead cables. *Norman Preedy Collection*

45706 EXPRESS (LMS 5706) built Crewe Works entered traffic May 1936, Lot No 129 – Works No 304 and was withdrawn by BR in September 1963 and cut up at Crewe Works in October 1963.

'Jubilee' class BR No 45706 EXPRESS is seen passing Watford with relief C903 on 3 May 1958. *RCTS Archive*

45707 VALIANT (LMS 5707) built Crewe Works entered traffic May 1936, Lot No 129 – Works No 305 and was withdrawn by BR in December 1962 and cut up at Campbells, Airdrie in December 1963.

45708 RESOLUTION (LMS 5708) built Crewe Works entered traffic June 1936, Lot No 129 – Works No 306 and was withdrawn by BR in March 1964 and cut up at Crewe Works in April 1964.

'Jubilee' class BR No 45708 is seen at Manchester Exchange station during the summer of 1961 when about to leave with a Trans-Pennine service. Note that in this view there are a lot of 'number takers' in attendance. Were you one of them? *Alan H. Bryant ARPS/Rail Photoprints*

Express

Eight vessels of the Royal Navy were named HMS *Express* or *Express* the first of them being a 6-gun 'advice boat' launched in 1695. Five more vessels were launched between 1800 and 1896. In 1934 an 'E-class' destroyer was launched (Pennant No H61). During the early part of the Second World War HMS *Express* was employed laying minefields and also participated in the evacuation of allied soldiers from Dunkirk. On 31 August 1940 she struck a German mine losing her entire bow up to the bridge, with a loss of 58 crew members. The damaged ship limped to Hull docks and was later sent to Chatham Dockyard for repair. During 1943 she was converted into an escort

HMS *Express* is seen in a damaged state on 1 September 1940. Lt. C.J. *Ware RN Photographer*

destroyer and subsequently transferred to the Royal Canadian Navy and renamed RCN *Gatineau*. She was paid off in 1946 and scuttled as part of a breakwater on the coast of British Columbia in 1948.

An 'Archer-class' P2000 type patrol boat commissioned in 1988 (Pennant No P163) was the last to carry the name.

Valiant

Five vessels of the Royal Navy were named HMS *Valiant* the first being a 74-gun warship launched in 1759 and served throughout the Seven Years' War. A 'Hector-class' ironclad battleship launched in 1863 was the third to carry the name. HMS *Valiant* was hulked in 1897 as part of the stoker training school HMS *Indus* before becoming a storeship for kite balloons during the First World War. The ship was converted to a floating oil tank in 1926 and served in that role until sold for scrap in 1956. The fourth HMS *Valiant* was a 'Queen Elizabeth-class' battleship launched in November 1914. She participated in the Battle of Jutland during the First World War as part of the Grand

HMS *Valiant* a 'Queen Elizabeth-class' battleship seen circa 1930. *US Navy*

Fleet. Her service during the war generally consisted of routine patrols and training in the North Sea. She saw further action during the Second World War in both the Mediterranean and Far East. The vessel was taken out of service in 1948 and sold for scrap. The last vessel to carry the name was a nuclear-powered submarine launched in December 1963 and decommissioned in 1994.

Resolution

Eleven vessels of the Royal Navy have carried the name HMS *Resolution,* the first being a 50-gun warship named in 1660. Notably the seventh vessel was a sloop, converted merchantman collier purchased by the navy (1771) which they originally named HMS *Drake* but in order not to upset the Spanish it was renamed.

It was this vessel aboard which Captain James Cook made his second and third voyages of exploration in the Pacific. She impressed him enough that he called her 'the ship of my choice', and 'the fittest for service of any I have seen.' The tenth HMS *Resolution* (Pennant No 09) was one of five 'Revenge-class' battleships built for the Royal Navy during World War I. Completed after the Battle of Jutland

'Revenge-class' battleship HMS *Resolution* seen in late 1930s. *Royal Navy Photographer*

in 1916, she saw no combat during the war. The future First Sea Lord John H. D. Cunningham served aboard her as Flag Captain to Admiral Sir William Fisher, the commander-in-chief of the Mediterranean Fleet. On the outbreak of the Second World War, HMS *Resolution* was part of the Home Fleet and carried out convoy escort duties in the Atlantic during which time she suffered damage from a German torpedo, in addition she served in the Indian Ocean.

Returning to Great Britain in September 1943 she then became a stokers' training ship in 1944 as part of the establishment HMS *Imperieuse*. HMS *Resolution* was sold for scrap on 5 May 1948. One of the warships 15-inch guns is on display at the Imperial War Museum in London.

'Jubilee' class BR No 45707 is seen leaving Hellifield north-bound on 15 June 1957. The locomotive is coupled to a Fowler style tender.
Norman Preedy Collection

The station is 36¼ miles (58 km) north-west of Leeds on the Leeds to Morecambe Line towards Carlisle and Morecambe. The Ribble Valley Line from Blackburn also joins the Leeds to Morecambe Line at Hellifield station. The metals at Hellifield are in the current era frequently visited by steam hauled charter trains, the location is a popular one with railway enthusiasts and photographers.

Implacable

Three vessels of the Royal Navy were named HMS *Implacable,* the first being a 74-gun warship captured from the French and renamed in 1805. The second vessel was 'Formidable-class' battleship launched in 1899 which served in the Dardanelles Campaign (19/02/1915-18/03/1915) and throughout World War One and was decommissioned in 1919. The third vessel was an 'Implacable-class' aircraft carrier launched in 1942 (Pennant No 86) and commissioned in May 1944 which served during the latter part of World War Two. The ship was used to repatriate liberated Allied prisoners of war and soldiers after the Japanese surrender. Implacable returned home in 1946 and became the Home Fleet's deck-landing training carrier until 1950 and was decommissioned in September 1954.

Irresistible

Four vessels of the Royal Navy were named HMS *Irresistible,* the first a 74-gun warship launched in 1782.

The fourth vessel was a 'Formidable-class' battleship launched in 1898 which served in the Dardanelles Campaign and in World War One until 18 March 1915. On that date she was hit by Turkish artillery and then struck a mine off Canakkale Province, Turkey. The vessel sustained severe damage which resulted in the loss of 150 crew members. The remaining crew members were evacuated by the destroyer HMS *Wear* and the vessel eventually sunk after being unsuccessfully put under tow by HMS *Ocean.* Subsequently HMS *Ocean* struck a mine and sank, but nearly all the crews of both ships were saved.

Courageous

Five vessels of the Royal Navy were named HMS *Courageous,* the first three of which (1761, 1799 and 1800) were named HMS *Courageux,* the first two being captured French vessels. The fourth warship was a 'Courageous-class' battle cruiser (Pennant No 50) launched in 1916 and it

British battleship HMS *Implacable*, with awning rigged aft, is seen anchored at Spithead, in June 1909.

British battleship HMS *Irresistible* abandoned and sinking, 18 March 1915, during the Battle of Gallipoli.

served throughout World War One, including the Second Battle of Heligoland Bight. After being decommissioned at the end of the war she was rebuilt as an aircraft carrier capable of carrying 48 aircraft.

During 17 September 1939, the carrier was on patrol off the coast of Ireland. Two of her four escorting destroyers had been sent to help a merchant ship under attack and all her aircraft had returned from patrols. During this time, HMS *Courageous* was stalked by the German submarine U-29. As the carrier turned into the wind to launch her aircraft the submarine fired torpedoes which struck the ship on her port side, knocking out all electrical power. She capsized and sank within 20 minutes with the loss of 519 of her crew. Some survived, being rescued by the Dutch ocean liner *Veendam* and the British freighter *Collingworth.* The two escorting destroyers counter attacked U-29, but the submarine escaped.

The fifth vessel was a 'Churchill-class' nuclear powered submarine, launched in 1970 and decommissioned in 1992 but preserved and on display at Devonport Naval Heritage Centre, Plymouth.

HMS *Courageous* as an aircraft carrier seen in 1935. *Royal Navy Photographer*

45709 IMPLACABLE (LMS 5709) built Crewe Works entered traffic June 1936, Lot No 129 – Works No 307 and was withdrawn by BR in November 1963 and cut up at Cashmores, Great Bridge in August 1964.

'Jubilee' class BR No 45709 IMPLACABLE is seen taking water on Bushey Troughs with an up express for Euston, circa 1957. C. R. L. Coles. *(Dave Cobbe Collection)/Rail Photoprints)*

Bushey Troughs in Hertfordshire were located between all four lines, 'down slow' 503.5 yards long, 'down fast' 501.5 yards long, 'up fast' 502.5 yards long and 'up slow' 502.5 yards long. All were taken out of use by the end of 1956.

45710 IRRESISTIBLE (LMS 5710) built Crewe Works entered traffic June 1936, Lot No 129 – Works No 308 and was withdrawn by BR in June 1964 and cut up at Central Wagon Co, Wigan in February 1965.

'Jubilee' class BR No 45710 IRRESISTIBLE is seen leaving Preston with a relief service for Birmingham in July 1961. *Mike Stokes Archive*

45711 COURAGEOUS (LMS 5711) built Crewe Works entered traffic June 1936, Lot No 129 – Works No 309 and was withdrawn by BR in December 1962 and cut up at Campbells, Airdrie in December 1963.

'Jubilee' class BR No 45711 COURAGEOUS is seen on Beattock Bank with a Glasgow–Liverpool/Manchester service on 19 April 1958. *David Anderson*

45712 VICTORY (LMS 5712) built Crewe Works entered traffic June 1936, Lot No 129 – Works No 310 and was withdrawn by BR in November 1963 and cut up at Crewe Works in January 1964.

'Jubilee' class BR No 45712 VICTORY is seen at Disley with an up express in October 1960. *Alan H. Bryant ARPS/Rail Photoprints*

45713 RENOWN (LMS 5713) built Crewe Works entered traffic June 1936, Lot No 129 – Works No 311 and was withdrawn by BR in October 1962 and cut up at Cowlairs Works in January 1963.

'Jubilee' class BR No 45713 RENOWN is seen on shed at Dumfries in June 1960. *Norman Preedy Collection*

Note the 'wheel tapper' to the right of the locomotive. They tapped wheels with a long-handled hammer and the sound made determines the integrity of the wheel; cracked wheels, like cracked bells, do not sound the same as their intact counterparts (they do not 'ring true').

45714 REVENGE (LMS 5714) built Crewe Works entered traffic June 1936, Lot No 129 – Works No 312 and was withdrawn by BR in July 1963 and cut up at Cowlairs Works in August 1963.

'Jubilee' class BR No 45714 REVENGE is seen at Beattock summit (WCML) with an up freight. Note Black Five class BR No 44969 with a train of mixed vans, which is in the 'dead end' refuge siding. When cleared to do so the Black Five will reverse its train past the signal box in order to regain the up mainline. *David Anderson*

Victory

Six vessels of the Royal Navy were named HMS *Victory* the first being a 42-gun warship launched in 1569. The most famous being the last a 100-gun ship of the line launched in 1765. She served in the American War of Independence, the French Revolutionary Wars and the Napoleonic Wars. She was Keppel's flagship at Ushant, Jervis's flagship at Cape St. Vincent and Nelson's flagship at Trafalgar. She served as a harbour ship after 1824 and was moved to a dry dock at Portsmouth in 1922, where she has been the flagship of the Second Sea Lord (until 2012) and the First Sea Lord (presently) and is preserved as a museum ship. In addition, a number of shore establishments were named HMS *Victory* (as many as 8 during World War One). See also https://www.hms-victory.com/

HMS *Victory* is depicted at Portsmouth circa 1900 in this superb picture by an unknown artist.

Renown

Eight vessels of the Royal Navy were named HMS *Renown* the first being a 20-gun fireship captured from the French in 1651 (*Renommée*). A pre-dreadnought battleship built for the Royal Navy in the early 1890s carried the name and the ship served as the flagship of the North America and West Indies Station and the Mediterranean Fleet early in her career. *Renown* became a royal yacht and had all of her secondary armament removed to make her more suitable for that duty. She later became a stoker's training ship in 1909 and was sold for scrap in early 1914. A battlecruiser commissioned in 1916 (after the Battle of Jutland) served for two years during World War One, reportedly never firing a shot in anger.

The 'Renown-class' comprised a pair of battlecruisers HMS *Renown* and HMS *Repulse* which on completion were the world's fastest capital ships. The last to carry the name was a 'Resolution-class' submarine launched in 1967 (Pennant No S26). She was paid off in 1996 and is currently awaiting disposal.

President Harry S. Truman (centre) and King George VI (second from the left) on the quarterdeck of HMS *Renown* where the President had lunch with the King. Truman is preparing to leave England on the USS *Augusta*, visible in the background, after attending the Potsdam Conference in Germany. *U.S. National Archives and Records Administration*

Revenge

Thirteen vessels of the Royal Navy were named HMS *Revenge* the first being a 46-gun galleon launched in 1577 which fought against the Spanish Armada in 1588, was captured but sunk whilst under tow. A battleship launched in 1915 (Pennant No 06) was the lead ship of the 'Revenge-class' battleships built for the Royal Navy during World War I. She was commissioned in 1916 and took part in the Battle of Jutland. In 1919, at Scapa Flow, Admiral Ludwig von Reuter issued the order to scuttle the German High Seas Fleet of 74 ships. After the incident, von Reuter was brought to the quarterdeck of HMS *Revenge*, flagship of Vice-Admiral Sydney Fremantle and accused of breaching naval honour. Von Reuter replied to the accusation, 'I am convinced that any English naval officer, placed as I was, would have acted in the same way.' No charges were brought against him. The vessel was scrapped in 1948 having also served throughout World War Two. Some of the ships gun turret rack and pinion gearing was re-used in the 76-metre (249 ft) diameter 'Mark I' radio telescope built at Jodrell Bank, Cheshire, in the mid-1950s.

Scrubbing the decks of HMS *Revenge*, circa 1940. *Lt. H.W. Tomlin*

Invincible

Seven vessels of the Royal Navy were named HMS *Invincible*, the first being a renamed captured French 74-gun ship of the line in 1747. The sixth HMS *Invincible* (launched 1907) was the lead ship of her class of three battlecruisers built during the first decade of the twentieth century, and the first battlecruiser to be built by any country in the world. During World War One she participated in the Battle of Heligoland Bight, but in only a minor role as she was the oldest and slowest of the British battlecruisers present. The ship engaged the German light cruiser *Cöln* but did not land any hits on the German vessel before *Cöln* was sunk by the battlecruiser HMS *Lion*. During the Battle of the Falkland Islands, together with her sister ship HMS *Inflexible*, she sank the armoured cruisers *Scharnhorst* and *Gneisenau* almost without loss to themselves, despite numerous hits by the German ships. She was the flagship of the 3rd Battlecruiser Squadron during the Battle of Jutland in 1916. On 31 May 1916 she was destroyed following a magazine explosion, after one of her gun turret's armour was penetrated by a German shell. As a result, there was a loss of 1,026 souls with only six survivors, who were rescued by HMS *Badger*. The last vessel to carry the name was a light aircraft carrier launched in 1977 (Pennant No R05) and decommissioned in 2005.

HMS Invincible anchored at Spithead, circa 1909.

Swiftsure

According to records the Royal Navy has had ten vessels which carried the name HMS *Swiftsure* since 1573, although some were later renamed. Notably a 74-gun vessel launched in 1804 which took part in the Battle of Trafalgar and also the lead ship from a class of pre-dreadnought battleships which was launched in 1903 and served in the Mediterranean during World War One. In 1943 a 'Minotaur-class' light cruiser was launched (Pennant No 08) and that vessel served throughout World War Two. The last to carry the name was the lead ship of a class of nuclear submarines launched in 1971 (Pennant No S126) which was decommissioned in 1992.

Pre-dreadnought battleship *HMS Swiftsure* seen circa 1908.

Dauntless

Five vessels and one shore establishment of the Royal Navy were named HMS *Dauntless* the first being an 18-gun sloop launched in 1804. The fourth vessel was a 'Danae-class' light cruiser completed too late to see action in World War One, she was assigned to operate in the Baltic Sea against the Bolshevik revolutionaries in Russia during 1919. HMS *Dauntless* was a member of the Cruise of the Special Service Squadron, also known as the 'Empire Cruise', of 1923/24. Following this tour, she went with the squadron to the Mediterranean for the next few years. In May 1928 she was recommissioned and assigned to the North America and West Indies Station. She ran aground on 2 July 1928 on the Thrum Cap Shoal, 5 nautical miles (9.3 km) off Halifax, Nova

British light cruiser *HMS Dauntless* seen underway, circa 1927. *Royal Navy Photographer*

Scotia, Canada, and was badly damaged, suffering the breach of her engine room and of one of her boiler rooms. She was abandoned by most of her 462 crew, the officers remaining on board. Subsequently all of her guns and torpedo tubes and much of her other equipment had to be removed to lighten her. She was finally re-floated on 11 July 1928 and towed off by HMS *Despatch* and tugs. She was repaired throughout 1929 and thereafter served until being paid off into the reserve in 1935 and broken up in 1946. The last vessel to carry the name was a 'Type-45' air defence destroyer launched 2007 (Pennant No D33). HMS *Dauntless* was also a WRNS training establishment at Burghfield, Berkshire from 1947 until 1981.

45715 INVINCIBLE (LMS 5715) built Crewe Works entered traffic July 1936, Lot No 129 – Works No 313 and was withdrawn by BR in December 1962 and cut up at Cowlairs Works in April 1963.

45716 SWIFTSURE (LMS 5716) built Crewe Works entered traffic July 1936, Lot No 129 – Works No 314 and was withdrawn by BR in September 1964 and cut up at Crewe Works in September 1964.

'Jubilee' class BR No 45716 SWIFTSURE is seen at Carstairs passing under the impressive signal gantry with a Glasgow-Carlisle stopping service on 17 September 1956. *David Anderson*

45717 DAUNTLESS (LMS 5717) built Crewe Works entered traffic July 1936, Lot No 129 – Works No 315 and was withdrawn by BR in November 1963 and cut up at Cowlairs Works in February 1964.

'Jubilee' class BR No 45717 DAUNTLESS is seen nearing Beattock Summit with a Liverpool/Manchester-Glasgow express on 8 July 1959. Note the exhaust from the banking engine. *David Anderson*

45718 DREADNOUGHT (LMS 5718) built Crewe Works entered traffic August 1936, Lot No 129 – Works No 316 and was withdrawn by BR in October 1962 and cut up at Cowlairs Works in December 1963.

'Jubilee' class BR No 45718 DREADNOUGHT is seen at speed near Thankerton (WCML), the fireman is bending his back. *David Anderson*

45719 GLORIOUS (LMS 5719) built Crewe Works entered traffic August 1936, Lot No 129 – Works No 317 and was withdrawn by BR in March 1963 and cut up at Horwich Works in June 1963.

'Jubilee' class BR No 45719 GLORIOUS is seen at Scout Green with Glasgow-Liverpool services. Left in 1955 with a Fowler style tender and early BR crest, and right in 1959 with a Stanier style tender and later BR logo. *Both images Norman Preedy Collection*

45720 INDOMITABLE (LMS 5720) built Crewe Works entered traffic August 1936, Lot No 129 – Works No 318 and was withdrawn by BR in December 1962 and cut up at Campbells, Shieldhall in December 1963.

'Jubilee' class BR No 45720 INDOMITABLE is seen stored 'out of use' at Corkerhill depot on 22 April 1962. *Paul Claxton/Rail Photoprints Collection*

128

Dreadnought

Eight ships and one submarine of the Royal Navy have borne the name HMS *Dreadnought* in the expectation that they would 'dread naught', i.e. 'fear nothing'. The first of which being a 40-gun warship launched in 1553. The sixth a ship launched in 1906 was one of the Royal Navy's most famous vessels; battleships built after her were referred to as 'dreadnoughts', and earlier battleships became known as pre-dreadnoughts. *Dreadnought*'s entry into service represented such an advance in naval technology that its name came to be associated with an entire generation of battleships. HMS *Dreadnought* was the first battleship of her era to have a uniform main battery, rather than having a few large guns complemented by a heavy secondary armament of smaller guns. Notably she was the first capital ship to be powered by steam turbines, then making her the fastest battleship in the world. Paradoxically for a vessel designed to engage enemy

HMS Dreadnought seen circa 1915.

battleships, her only noteworthy action was the ramming and sinking of German submarine '*SM U-29*'. The ship was reduced to reserve in 1919 and sold for scrap two years later. The seventh HMS *Dreadnought* was the United Kingdom's first nuclear-powered submarine, built by Vickers Armstrongs at Barrow-in-Furness. Launched by Queen Elizabeth II on Trafalgar Day 1960 and commissioned into service with the Royal Navy in April 1963, she continued in service until 1980.

Glorious

HMS *Glorious* was the second of the three 'Courageous-class' battlecruisers built for the Royal Navy during World War One. HMS *Glorious* was completed in late 1916 (Pennant No 77) and spent the war patrolling the North Sea. She participated in the Second Battle of Heligoland Bight in November 1917 and was present when the German High Seas Fleet surrendered a year later. The ship was paid off after the war but was then rebuilt as an aircraft carrier, during the late 1920s. After re-commissioning in 1930, she spent most her career operating in the Mediterranean Sea. After the start of World War Two, the carrier spent the rest of 1939 unsuccessfully hunting for the commerce-raiding German cruiser *Admiral Graf Spee* in the Indian Ocean before returning to the Mediterranean. She was recalled home in April 1940 to support operations in Norway. Tragically whilst evacuating British aircraft from Norway in June, the ship was sunk by the German battleships *Scharnhorst* and *Gneisenau* in the North Sea with the loss of over 1,200 souls. See also the entry for Bulleid Pacific locomotive BR No 34074 46 SQUADRON in the Southern Railway section of Military Connections.

Indomitable

Two vessels of the Royal Navy were named HMS *Indomitable* the first being a vessel described as 'the first battlecruiser in the world', launched in 1907. Immediately after commissioning, HMS *Indomitable* embarked the Prince of Wales (soon to be King George V) for the City of Quebec Tercentenary celebration. On her return voyage, the average speed was a fraction below 25 knots, almost equalling the record for an Atlantic crossing of 25.08 knots, set by the liner *RMS Lusitania*. The 'Invincible-class' battlecruiser served throughout World War One and was taken out of service in February 1919. She was one of three Invincible-class battlecruisers built for the Royal Navy before World War One, HMS *Indomitable* had an active career during that war. She helped to sink the German armoured cruiser *Blücher* during the Battle of Dogger Bank in 1915 and towed the damaged British battlecruiser HMS *Lion* to safety after the battle. She damaged the German battlecruisers *Seydlitz* and *Derfflinger* during the Battle of Jutland in mid-1916 and was present when her sister ship HMS *Invincible* exploded.

The 'Invincible-class' battlecruiser HMS Indomitable, seen during the City of Quebec Tercentenary celebration in 1908.

The second vessel was a modified 'Illustrious-class' aircraft carrier launched in 1940 (Pennant No 92). She served in several theatres of war and during Operation Pedestal (the supply convoy to Malta 3–15 August 1942) the British carrier was hit by two bombs causing damage that required her to withdraw for repairs. She sailed to the United States, where repairs were completed in February 1943, after which she immediately returned to the Mediterranean. During the build-up to the invasion of Sicily she was again damaged by enemy attack and repaired in the USA. HMS *Indomitable* was sold for scrap in 1955.

Impregnable

Two vessels of the Royal Navy were named HMS *Impregnable* the first being a 98-gun ship of the line launched in 1786 and wrecked in 1799, off Spithead. In 1794 the vessel served as Rear-Admiral Benjamin Caldwell's flagship and took part in the battle later described as the 'Glorious First of June'. That action was the first and largest fleet action of the naval conflict between Great Britain and the First French Republic, during the French Revolutionary Wars. The second vessel was a 98-gun ship of the line launched in 1810 which became a school ship in 1862 and was first renamed HMS *Kent* in 1888 and HMS *Caledonia* in 1891. The vessel was sold out of service in 1906.

Two training establishments were named HMS *Impregnable*, the first in Devonport in 1862 which was active until 1929 and the second was established at Plymouth in 1935 and served until 1947/48.

The quarterdeck of HMS Impregnable, circa 1853. *NGA USA*

Defence

Four vessels of the Royal Navy were named HMS *Defence* the first was a 74-gun ship of the line launched in 1763 and that vessel took part in the aforementioned 'Glorious First of June' naval battle. In 1811 she was wrecked off the coast of Jutland with the loss of 583 souls and 14 survivors. The second vessel was also a 74-gun ship of the line launched in 1815 and broken up in 1857. The third HMS *Defence* launched in 1861 was the lead ship of the 'Defence class' ironclad armoured frigates which were ordered by the Royal Navy in 1859 and was scrapped in 1935.

The fourth vessel was a 'Minotaur class' armoured cruiser launched in 1907 and the last of that type built for the Royal Navy. The vessel was sunk on 31 May 1916 during the 'Battle of Jutland' when she was attacked by the German fleet. A direct hit detonated the ammunition stored in the vessel's rear magazine and a subsequent fire caused the explosion of the ships secondary magazine with catastrophic effect. The vessel quickly sunk resulting in total loss of the approximate 900 crew members.

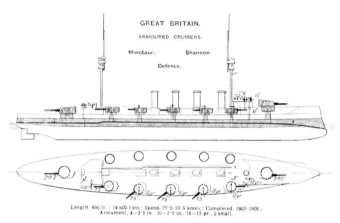

Drawings from *Brassey's Naval Annual* 1912.

In 1945 the building of a light cruiser to be named HMS *Defence* commenced but was then suspended until 1954 with the resultant vessel being named HMS *Lion*.

Fearless

Seven vessels of the Royal Navy were named HMS *Fearless* the first was a 12-gun vessel launched 1794 and wrecked in 1804. There followed a 12-gun brig launched in 1804 and wrecked in 1812. A wooden paddlewheel survey vessel acquired by the RN in 1837 which served until 1875. A torpedo cruiser launched in 1886 and taken out of service in 1905. An 'Active class' scout cruiser launched in 1912 and scrapped in 1921. An 'F class' destroyer launched in 1934 and damaged by a torpedo launched from an Italian aircraft, whilst escorting Malta convoys in the Mediterranean. That action led to the vessel being scuttled on 23 July 1941, after her crew were taken off by a sister ship. In more recent times the seventh HMS *Fearless* was launched in 1963, a 'Fearless class' (L10) landing platform dock, which saw action in the Falklands conflict (1982) and also the Gulf War (1990/91). She was decommissioned in 2002 having been the last steam powered warship to serve the Royal Navy.

On 31 January 1918 the 'Active class' scout cruiser HMS *Fearless* accidentally rammed and sank HMS *K17* a British 'K class' submarine and that vessel is seen in drydock awaiting repairs. Tragically the submarine sank with the loss of all hands.

45721 IMPREGNABLE (LMS 5721) built Crewe Works entered traffic August 1936, Lot No 129 – Works No 319 and was withdrawn by BR in October 1965 and cut up at Cashmores, Great Bridge in March 1966.

Jubilee class BR No 45721 IMPREGNABLE is seen at the head of the Locomotive Club of Great Britain 'The North Countryman. railtour (1X46), the 08:10 from London St. Pancras on Saturday 6 June 1964. The Jubilee locomotive took the railtour as far as Whitehall Junction, Leeds. *Gordon Edgar Collection/Rail Photoprints*

45722 DEFENCE (LMS 5722) built Crewe Works entered traffic August 1936, Lot No 129 – Works No 320 and was withdrawn by BR in November 1962 and cut up at Crewe Works in July 1963.

45723 FEARLESS (LMS 5723) built Crewe Works entered traffic August 1936, Lot No 129 – Works No 321 and was withdrawn by BR in August 1964 and cut up at Birds, Morriston in January 1965.

Jubilee class BR No 45723 FEARLESS is seen at Crewe in 1946 as LMS No 5723. *Rail Photoprints Collection*

45724 WARSPITE (LMS 5724) built Crewe Works entered traffic September 1936, Lot No 129 – Works No 322 and was withdrawn by BR in October 1962 and cut up at Cowlairs Works in June 1963.

Jubilee class BR No 45724 WARSPITE, with a Fowler tender is seen at Carlisle Kingmoor in 1957. *Rail Photoprints Collection*

45725 REPULSE (LMS 5725) built Crewe Works entered traffic September 1936, Lot No 129 – Works No 323 and was withdrawn by BR in December 1962 and cut up at Crewe Works in March 1964.

Jubilee class BR No 45725 REPULSE is seen at Sheffield Midland station circa 1960. *RCTS Archive*

45726 VINDICTIVE (LMS 5726) built Crewe Works entered traffic October 1936, Lot No 129 – Works No 324 and was withdrawn by BR in March 1965 and cut up at Wards, Beighton in June 1965.

Jubilee class BR No 45726 VINDICTIVE is seen heading north from Bletchley with a lengthy down freight, on 27 July 1963. *David Anderson*

Warspite

Seven vessels of the Royal Navy were named HMS *Warspite,* the first launched in 1596 was a 29-gun galleon which was originally named *Warspight* and was sold out of service in 1649. A second vessel launched in 1666 was a 70-gun ship of the line which was renamed HMS *Edinburgh* in 1721 and after being rebuilt three times was broken up in 1771. The third vessel, a 74-gun example launched in 1758 was also renamed becoming HMS *Arundel* in 1800 and was broken up in 1801. In 1807 a 76-gun vessel became the fourth HMS *Warspite* and that ship was 'razeed' in 1840 and paid off in 1846. The naval term 'razeed' was used to describe a sailing ship that has been cut down to reduce the number of decks. In 1884 an 'Imperieuse class' armoured cruiser was launched as the fifth in the series and that vessel was scrapped in 1905. Perhaps the most famous was the sixth, a 'Queen Elizabeth class' battleship launched in 1913. That

The 'Queen Elizabeth class' battle ship HMS *Warspite* is seen underway in the Indian Ocean during 1942. At that time the vessel was the Flagship of Admiral Sir James Sommerville.

vessel served throughout both World Wars and in doing so she earned the most battle honours of any Royal Navy ship. The ship ran aground in 1947 whilst being towed to the breakers and was eventually scrapped in 1950.

In 1965 a 'Valiant class' nuclear powered submarine was also given the name and that vessel was decommissioned in 1991.

Repulse

Twelve vessels of the Royal Navy were named HMS *Repulse* the first being a 50-gun galleon which was launched in 1595 and scrapped circa 1645. Seven other vessels with that name were launched or purchased between 1759 and 1855. In 1868 an ironclad ship was launched and that vessel was sold out of service in 1889. That vessel was followed by a 'Royal Sovereign class' battleship which was launched in 1892 and sold out of service 1911. In 1916 a 'Renown class' battle cruiser was launched during World War 1 and was taken into service after the Battle of Jutland (31 May – 1 June) thereafter seeing combat in the Second Battle of Heligoland Bight on 17 November 1917. The ship spent the first months of the Second World War hunting for German raiders and blockade runners. She then participated in the Norwegian Campaign of April–June 1940 and joined

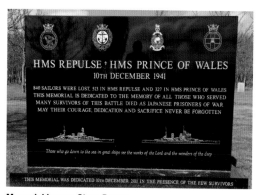

Memorial image. *Steve Bowen*

in the search for the German battleship *Bismarck* in 1941. HMS *Repulse* escorted a troop convoy around the Cape of Good Hope from August to October 1941 and was transferred to East Indies Command. She was assigned in November to Force Z a battle group intended to deter Japanese aggression against British possessions in the Far East. Whilst carrying out those duties HMS *Repulse* and the accompanying 'King George V class' battleship HMS *Prince of Wales* were sunk

by torpedoes and bombs dropped by Japanese aircraft on 10 December 1941, off the east coast of Malaya (South China Sea). During that action there was a reported loss of 840 lives. However, almost 1000 survivors were rescued. On 10 December 2011 a memorial was dedicated at The National Memorial Arboretum at Alrewas, Staffordshire, U.K. in the presence of the few surviving former crews of the ships.

Vindictive

Five vessels of the Royal Navy carried the name HMS *Vindictive* the first being a 6-gun galley captured from the Georgia Navy on the Savannah River in 1779 (American Revolution), and sold in 1786. The second vessel was also a battle capture from the Dutch Navy in 1796 and broken up in 1816. The third vessel was a 74-gun ship of the line launched in 1813 and sold in 1871. In 1897 an 'Arrogant class' cruiser was launched and that vessel played a prominent part in the First World War Zeebrugge Raid of 23 April 1918, and then sunk as a blockship at Ostend in 1918. In 1918 a vessel originally designed as a 'Hawkins class' cruiser (HMS *Cavendish*) was converted to an aircraft carrier during construction and appropriately renamed. That vessel was later returned to a cruiser configuration in 1924 and was scrapped in 1946.

The raised bow section of HMS *Vindictive* is displayed at Ostend Harbour as a memorial of the Zeebrugge Raid. *Marc Ryckaert*

Inflexible

Five vessels of the Royal Navy carried the name HMS *Inflexible* the first being a 180-ton sloop of war which was launched in 1776 and fought at the Battle of Valcour Island on 11 October 1776, after which her fate is unknown. The second vessel was a 64-gun 'Inflexible class' ship of the line launched in 1780 which was also used as a storeship and a troopship, she was broken up in 1820. The third such vessel was a wooden screw sloop which was launched in 1845 and sold out of service in 1864. In 1876 the fourth vessel an ironclad battleship was launched and it saw service in the Mediterranean before being sold out of service in 1903. The final vessel was an 'Invincible class' battlecruiser

'Invincible class' battlecruiser HMS *Inflexible* which was launched in 1907 is seen during a visit to New York, USA circa 1909. *USN*

launched in 1907 which saw service in World War 1. That action included taking part in the Battle of the Falklands on 8 December 1914, when together with her sister ship HMS *Invincible,* sank the German armoured cruisers *SMS Scharnhorst* and *SMS Gneisenau*. During the Battle of Jutland (31 May – 1June 1916) and after successfully shelling the German battlecruiser *SMS Lützow* she witnessed the fatal explosion of HMS *Invincible*. Deemed to be obsolete after the war the vessel was scrapped in 1922.

Defiance

Twelve vessels and two Shore Establishments of the Royal Navy carried the name HMS *Defiance* the first being a pinnace 8-gun launched in 1588 which took part in the action against the Spanish Armada. Between 1590 until 1794 a further ten vessels with the name were launched. Notably a 91-gun screw propelled vessel launched in 1861 (which was the RN's last wooden line-of-battle ship) became the Royal Navy's 'Torpedo School' ship in 1884 and served in that position until 1931 when it was sold out of service.

HMS *Defiance* (shore establishment 1884) was the Royal Navy's torpedo school, established in 1884 in the aforementioned HMS *Defiance*, and in subsequent ships that were renamed HMS *Defiance*.

The original HMS *Defiance* training ship is seen whilst being moved, positioned between a pair of paddle wheel steam powered tug boats circa 1900.

These included:

HMS *Defiance* the original school ship from 1884 until 1931.
HMS *Perseus* was HMS *Defiance II* from 1904 until 1931.
HMS *Spartan* was HMS *Defiance II* from 1921 until 1931.
HMS *Cleopatra* was HMS *Defiance III* from 1922 until 1931.
HMS *Inconstant* was HMS *Defiance IV* from 1922 until 1930 and HMS *Defiance II* from 1930 until 1956.
HMS *Andromeda* was HMS *Defiance* from 1931 until 1956.
HMS *Vulcan* was HMS *Defiance III* from 1931 until 1955.

The school moved ashore at Portsmouth in 1955, becoming a stone frigate. It was paid off in 1959.

HMS *Defiance* (shore establishment 1970) was the Fleet Maintenance Base at HMNB Devonport between 1972 and 1979, and again between 1981 and 1994 when it was absorbed into the main base.

One ship was renamed HMS *Defiance* whilst serving as the establishment's depot ship. HMS *Forth* was HMS *Defiance* from 1972 until 1978.

45727 INFLEXIBLE (LMS 5727) built Crewe Works entered traffic October 1936, Lot No 129 – Works No 325 and was withdrawn by BR in December 1962 and cut up at Campbells, Airdrie in December 1963.

Jubilee class BR No 45727 INFLEXIBLE then a Carlisle Kingmoor allocated locomotive, is seen at the head of a Perth service. Note the imposing backdrop to Edinburgh Waverley station, on 1 June 1957. *Gordon Edgar Collection/Rail Photoprints*

45728 DEFIANCE (LMS 5728) built Crewe Works entered traffic October 1936, Lot No 129 – Works No 326 and was withdrawn by BR in October 1962 and cut up at Cowlairs Works in November 1963.

Jubilee class BR No 45728 DEFIANCE is seen on shed at Carstairs on 19 June 1960. *Norman Preedy Collection*

45729 FURIOUS (LMS 5729) built Crewe Works entered traffic October 1936, Lot No 129 – Works No 327 and was withdrawn by BR in October 1962 and cut up at Cowlairs Works in September 1963.

Jubilee class BR No 45729 FURIOUS is seen on shed at Carlisle Kingmoor in 1947. Note the sheet of metal on top of the steam dome. *Rail Photoprints Collection*

45730 OCEAN (LMS 5730) built Crewe Works entered traffic October 1936, Lot No 129 – Works No 328 and was withdrawn by BR in October 1963 and cut up at Wards, Beighton in March 1965.

Jubilee class BR No 45730 OCEAN is seen after failing to stop at a signal and almost demolishing the Dock Junction signal box just outside St. Pancras station, on 20 July 1959. The signalman, his supervisor and other colleagues are surveying the extent of the damage. As a result, trains had to be hand signalled in and out of the station for several days. *RCTS Archive*

Furious

Five vessels of the Royal Navy carried the name HMS *Furious* the first being a 120-gun 'Courser class' gun brig launched in 1797 and sold out of service in 1802. In 1804 the second vessel was 12-gun 'Archer class' gun brig which in 1815 was also sold out of service. A wooden hulled paddle frigate became the third vessel when launched in 1850. That vessel was hulked in 1867 and sold out of service in 1884. The fourth vessel launched in 1896 was an 'Arrogant class' protected cruiser which was hulked in 1915 and renamed HMS *Forte* and sold out of service in 1923. The last HMS *Furious* was a modified 'Courageous class' battlecruiser launched in 1916 which was converted to a flush-deck aircraft carrier between 1921 and 1925.

After the new aircraft carrier HMS *Ark Royal* came into service HMS *Furious* was used extensively as a training carrier.

During World War 2 the vessel carried out Atlantic convoy protection work also during the Norwegian Campaign her aircraft provided air support to British troops and in addition attacked German shipping. Later in the war the vessel made a number of attacks against the German 'Bismarck class' battleship *Tirpitz*. She was decommissioned in April 1945 and sold for scrap in 1948.

British aircraft carrier HMS *Furious* with naval airship (SSZ – Sea Scout Zero) on the after-flight deck, circa 1918.

Ocean

Six vessels of the Royal Navy carried the name HMS *Ocean* the first being so named was a 90-gun ship of the line launched in 1761. The second vessel was a 98-gun ship launched in 1805 which was active during the Napoleonic Wars (1803–1815). The third to carry the name was originally ordered to be built as a 'Bulwark-class' wooden screw line-of-battle ship intended to carry 91 guns. However, the order was changed and she was eventually launched in 1863 as a 'Prince Consort-class' ironclad of 24 guns. In the late 1860s she served as flagship to the Commander in Chief of the China Station and after a short active life was paid off in 1872. The fourth launched in 1898 was a 'Canopus-class' pre-dreadnought battleship which was sunk by a mine in 1915, her crew were taken off by escorting destroyers.

The crew of the carrier HMS *Ocean* are seen on the flight deck for inspection by Field Marshal Earl Alexander, 14 June 1952. *USN*

The fifth vessel was a 'Colossus-class' aircraft carrier completed in 1945, which served in the Korean War as an aircraft carrier, and the Suez Crisis as a helicopter platform. She was scrapped in 1962.

In more recent times the sixth and last vessel was a Landing Platform, Helicopter (LPH) launched in 1995 and decommissioned in March 2018, after which she was sold to the Brazilian Navy who renamed her *Atlântico*.

Other Jubilee locomotives

BR Number/Name	Loco Period in Service	HMS – Date Launched / Date Established
45553 CANADA	06/1934–11/1964	4 ships 1765 to 1913
45554 ONTARIO	06/1934–11/1964	1 ship 1780
45555 QUEBEC	06/1934–08/1963	3 ships 1760 to 1782 / 1 Shore establishment 1940/46
45556 NOVA SCOTIA	06/1934–09/1964	1 Ship 1812
45563 AUSTRALIA	08/1934–11/1965	1 Ship 1886 + 1 Ship HMAS 1911
45564 VICTORIA	08/1934–01/1967	4 Ships 1839 to 1887
45569 TASMANIA	08/1934–05/1964	1 Ship HMAS 1918
45570 NEW ZEALAND	08/1934–12/1962	2 Ships 1904, 1911,
45573 NEWFOUNDLAND	09/1934–09/1965	1 Ship 1941
45585 HYDERABAD	12/1934–05/1964	1 Ship 1941
45588 KASMIR	12/1934–05/1965	1 Ship 1939
45596 BAHAMAS	01/1935–07/1966	1 Ship 1943
45597 BARBADOS	01/1935–01/1965	1 Ship 1943
45600 BERMUDA	02/1935–12/1965	8 Ships 1795 to 1941
45604 CEYLON	03/1935–07/1965	2 Ships 1793, 1942
45607 FIJI	06/1934–11/1962	1 Ship 1939
45608 GIBRALTAR	07/1934–09/1965	6 Ships 1711 to 1892,
45612 JAMAICA	08/1934–04/1964	6 Ships 1710 to 1940
45613 KENYA	08/1934–09/1964	1 Ship 1939
45617 MAURITIUS	09/1934–11/1964	1 Ship 1939 / Shore Establishment 1962/75
45619 NIGERIA	10/1934–08/1961	1 Ship 1939
45622 NYASALAND	10/1934–09/1964	1 Ship 1943
45625 SARAWAK	10/1934–08/1963	1 Ship 1943
45626 SEYCHELLES	11/1934–11/1965	1 Ship 1943
45628 SOMALILAND	11/1934–12/1962	1 Ship 1943
45634 TRINIDAD	11/1934–05/1963	1 Ship 1941
45635 TOBAGO	11/1934–09/1964	4 Ships 1779 to 1944
45636 UGANDA	12/1934–12/1962	1 Ship 1941
45638 ZANZIBAR	12/1934–03/1964	1 Ship 1943
45731 PERSEVERANCE	10/1936–11/1963	3 Ships 1781 to 1854
45732 SANSPAREIL	10/1936–08/1964	3 Ships 1794 to 1887
45734 METEOR	11/1936–04/1964	9 Ships 1797 to 1941
45735 COMET	11/1936–01/1965	16 Ships 1695 to 1944
45736 PHOENIX	11/1936–01/1965	16 Ships 1546 to 1929 / 2 Shore Establishments 1941/46
45737 ATLAS	11/1936–06/1964	2 Ships 1782, 1860
45738 SAMPSON	12/1936–12/1963	6 Ships 1643 to 1844
45739 ULSTER	12/1936–06/1967	2 Ships 1917 and 1942
45740 MUNSTER	12/1936–12/1963	1 Ship 1915

The 'Jubilee class' listings have included names which are commonly accepted to have been selected by the LMS naming committee because of their obvious military connection i.e. Admiral, Battle, Warship etc. However, other locomotives of the class have names which could be linked to the military for a secondary reason. For example, they were of a country, region or celebrated pioneer locomotive, with various names in those categories having associations with British/Allied naval vessels. Those details are listed in this table.

The nameplate of the preserved locomotive BR No 45596.

'Jubilee' class BR No 45563 AUSTRALIA is seen leaving Chester with a train of vans for Holyhead in the spring of 1965. Note that the backing plate remains but the nameplate has been removed. *Keith Langston Collection*

Rebuilt Jubilee class BR No 45736 PHOENIX is seen passing Grayrigg with a down parcels service, on 1 August 1964. Two locomotives of the class were rebuilt with Type 2A boilers and double exhausts in 1942 (BR 45735 and 45736). In this image BR No 45736 is also fitted with smoke deflectors and has the look of a rebuilt 'Royal Scot' class engine. *Paul Claxton – Steve Armitage Collection/Rail Photoprints*

Jubilee class BR No 45737 ATLAS is seen as LMS No 5737 passing Tring Summit, with a Euston–Birmingham service in 1939. *C.R.L Coles/Dave Cobbe Collection*

LMS Fowler/Stanier 4-6-0 'Royal Scot' class

In 1927 the LMS found itself in urgent need of powerful express locomotives to replace the ageing and somewhat underpowered Claughton Class on its heavier Anglo-Scottish services. Having been impressed with a GWR 4-6-0 'Castle Class' locomotive (No 5000 Launceston Castle) during a 1926 locomotive exchange, the London Midland & Scottish Railways Chief Mechanical Engineer Sir Henry Fowler (1925-1931) allegedly asked Swindon to build 50 'Castle' types for the LMS.

History has it that the GWR chiefs declined to accept the order and even put a block on Swindon lending the Derby design office a set of 'King' class drawings! Thus, the only alternative open to Fowler was to design his own three-cylinder 4-6-0. Maunsell of the Southern

Royal Scot class LMS No 6100 ROYAL SCOT (in reality sister locomotive LMS No 6152) is seen at Crewe Works being prepared for the 1933 trip to North America. Note the smokebox mounted train name board and the electric headlamp. The locomotive was also coupled to a new non-standard tender, with roller bearing axleboxes. *The Metcalfe Collection*

Railway lent a hand and sanctioned the loan of a set of 'Lord Nelson' class drawings to Derby and whether the drawings were useful or not is open to debate. The LMS were from several accounts impressed with the performance of the four-cylinder 'Nelsons' but in the event decided to proceed with their original plans to build a three-cylinder parallel boiler class of locomotives. Hence the 'Royal Scot' class was born.

After the completion of the design work at Derby the order for the first 50 locomotives were constructed, not by an LMS works but by the contractors North British Locomotive Co Ltd of Glasgow. Thereafter a further 21 examples were built at Derby. All of those 71 locomotives were named (with numerous name changes) and all passed into BR ownership in 1948.

Enthusiasts at the time were a little bemused by the goings on at NBL, as they eagerly awaited sight of the first new engine. Every effort was made to ensure that one engine was completed as soon as possible and that was the first engine produced at NBL Queens Park, LMS No 6100. However, the first completed NBL Hyde Park engine LMS No 6125 was painted in shop grey, complemented by an LMSR crest on the cab side, the number 6100 in large numerals on the tender side and then used for the official photograph.

In October 1927 LMS No 6100 was named ROYAL SCOT after the train service with which it became associated. The rest of the class received an assortment of names, some from long scrapped LNWR engines, and the remainder received names of a direct military/regimental origin except the last three which were named respectively THE GIRL GUIDE, THE BOY SCOUT and BRITISH LEGION.

The original 'Scots' were by all accounts fine engines which under difficult conditions turned in some memorable performances. The 'Royal Scot' service itself was inaugurated on 26 September 1927 a scheduled London Euston-Glasgow Central service which included a non-stop run from Euston to Carlisle with a heavy 15-coach train.

Interestingly the nameplates were all cast at either Crewe or Derby. You could easily identify which works made some of the nameplates (at least that is those with a comma in the name) e.g. The Derby cast plates had an apostrophe with a square top (left), while the Crewe castings (right) featured one with a round top. *Both images David Anderson*

It has been well documented that in 1933 locomotive LMS No 6152 THE KING'S DRAGOON GUARDSMAN swapped name and number with the 'first built' LMS No 6100 and went to Canada and the USA as ROYAL SCOT in order to tour and then attend the 'Century of Progress Exhibition' in Chicago. That locomotive completed a tour of North America clocking up some 11,194 miles in the process, including crossing the Rocky Mountains. The two locomotives never reverted back to their old identities.

For some time after returning to the UK the locomotive then numbered 6100 carried a bell in commemoration of the stateside trip. No 6100 ROYAL SCOT still carrying the aforementioned bell was recorded as being in Crewe Works for repair during July 1934, and there is photographic evidence to that effect. David Jenkinson presents solid evidence that the identities of LMS Nos 6100 and 6152 were not swapped back after the Chicago trip, in his excellent publication '*The Power of the Royal Scots*'.

Two examples of the class survived into preservation and at the time of writing both restored engines were mainline certified and are rebuilt Royal Scot tapered boiler locomotives. Those engines are BR No 46100 ROYAL SCOT (actually LMS No 6152) and BR No 46115 SCOTS GUARDSMAN.

The Royal Scot class were rebuilt at Derby to an earlier Stanier design between 1943 and 1955. William Stanier (knighted 1943) actually ceased to work at the LMS after 1942 having taken a government post connected with wartime production, although his official resignation from the LMS did not take place until 1944. Thus the 'Scot' rebuilding programme was effectively supervised by his successors, firstly by Charles Fairburn (LMS CME 1944–45) and then by the last CME of the LMS H.G. Ivatt (1945-47).

No 6100 with bell. *Crewe Archive*

The rebuilding using Crewe top feed tapered LMS 2A type boilers, new cylinders, new frames (on most of the class) and incorporating very necessary mechanical modifications served to ensure that the engines would spend another 10 to 20 years in top-link service. The Stanier tapered boiler and double chimney gave the 'new' locomotives a completely different look, the later addition of 'curved to the boiler' profile 'sloping front' smoke deflectors, added to what many described as the 'new loco look'.

Tenders

When the Royal Scot class locomotives first entered into traffic various examples were coupled to LMS small standard Midland Railway style tenders, with a coal capacity of 5 tons and a water capacity of 3,500 gallons. Later the addition of coal rails to those tenders meant that with careful loading 5½ tons of coal could be carried. Those Midland 6-wheel tenders (similar to those coupled with other LMS locomotives) were noticeably narrower than the engine's footplate. In order to better suit the jobs rostered to the Royal Scot class the small tenders were gradually replaced by the LMS with a Stanier designed 6-wheel high sided curved top tender, with a coal capacity of 9-tons and a water capacity of 4,000 gallons.

For the trip to North America the locomotive designated as LMS 6100 was coupled to a specially built tender with roller bearing axleboxes similar to those intended for use with the pioneer Stanier 'Princess Royal' class locomotives.

A genuine preserved wooden Royal Scot class style nameplate. The LMS was known to fix such plates to new locomotives in order to gather opinions etc. It is thought that LMS No 6100 may once have temporarily been fitted with this nameplate. *John Magnall*

ROYAL SCOT

PRIOR TO CONVERSION
THIS LOCOMOTIVE WITH THE ROYAL SCOT TRAIN WAS EXHIBITED AT THE CENTURY OF PROGRESS EXPOSITION. CHICAGO, 1933, AND MADE A TOUR OF THE DOMINION OF CANADA AND THE UNITED STATES OF AMERICA. THE ENGINE AND TRAIN COVERED 11,194 MILES OVER THE RAILROADS OF THE NORTH AMERICAN CONTINENT AND WAS INSPECTED BY 3,021,601 PEOPLE.
W. GILBERTSON. • DRIVER. • • T. BLACKETT. — FIREMAN.
J. JACKSON. • FIREMAN. • W. C. WOODS. • FITTER.

46100 ROYAL SCOT (LMS 6100) built Derby Works, entered traffic July 1930 as LMS 5971 Lot/Works No 073. Identity swopped with 46152 in 1933. Rebuilt June 1950. Thus, retaining a parallel boiler throughout the LMS period. Withdrawn by BR in April 1965 (first of the class withdrawn) and saved for preservation. **P**

Rebuilt Royal Scot class then known as BR No 46100 ROYAL SCOT (actually LMS No 6152 with a Derby designed motion bracket behind the valve spindle) is seen in pristine condition (but minus a shedplate) at Crewe Works in 1950. *Norman Preedy Collection*

The Royal Scots (The Royal Regiment), once known as the Royal Regiment of Foot, was the oldest and most senior infantry regiment of the line of the British Army, having been raised in 1633 during the reign of Charles I of Scotland. The regiment existed continuously until 2006, when it amalgamated with the King's Own Scottish Borderers to become the Royal Scots Borderers, which merged with the Royal Highland Fusiliers (Princess Margaret's Own Glasgow and Ayrshire Regiment), the Black Watch, the Highlanders (Seaforth, Gordons and Camerons) and the Argyll and Sutherland Highlanders to form the Royal Regiment of Scotland.

The Royal Scots Regimental window at Canongate Kirk (Edinburgh). *Kim Traynor*

Preserved Rebuilt Royal Scot class BR No 46100 ROYAL SCOT is seen exiting the tunnel at Whiteball with the 'Torbay Express' on 3 July 2016. *Pete Skelton*

Preservation

After being withdrawn from service BR No 46100 was sold to the holiday camp mogul Billy Butlin (later Sir) in 1962 and was cosmetically restored at Crewe Works. It was painted in LMS Crimson Lake livery, which although the original livery applied to the parallel boilered engine, BR No 46100 never carried that livery after its rebuild. Thereafter the locomotive was set on a plinth at Butlins Holiday Camp, Skegness. On the 16 March 1971 the locomotive moved to Bressingham Steam Museum where it was returned to steam in 1972. It ran until 1978 when it again became a static exhibit. During 2005/6, following a National Lottery Heritage Grant restoration to mainline condition began at Southall. In 2009 the locomotive was moved to LNWR Heritage Ltd, Crewe for that work to be completed, after which it visited the Llangollen and West Somerset railways as a working locomotive. Following the sale to Royal Scot Locomotive and General Trust (RSL&GT) in April 2009, the locomotive was completely rebuilt to mainline standard. It is part of the *Icons of Steam* preserved locomotive fleet. For more information visit http://www.iconsofsteam.com/

Preserved rebuilt Royal Scot class BR No 46100 ROYAL SCOT at Orchard Farm Crossing SVR on 19 September 2015 whilst working the 13.28 Bridgnorth-Kidderminster service. *Fred Kerr*

46101 ROYAL SCOTS GREY (LMS 6101) built North British Locomotive Works (NBL), entered traffic in August 1927. Lot No L833, Works No 23596. Rebuilt November 1945. Withdrawn by BR in August 1963 and cut up by Slag Reduction Co Ltd, Ickles Rotherham in April 1964.

Royal Scot class LMS No 6101 ROYAL SCOTS GREY is seen at Camden depot in 1931. Note the NBL design motion bracket. *Rail Photoprints Collection*

Rebuilt Royal Scot class BR No 46101 ROYAL SCOTS GREY is seen at Harthope WCML with a down express for Glasgow Central, on 15 August 1955. *David Anderson*

The Royal Scots Greys was a cavalry regiment of the British Army from 1707 until 1971, when they amalgamated with the 3rd Carabiniers (Prince of Wales's Dragoon Guards) to form The Royal Scots Dragoon Guards (Carabiniers and Greys). The regiment's history began in 1678, when three independent troops of Scots Dragoons were raised. In 1681, these troops were regimented to form The Royal Regiment of Scots Dragoons, numbered the 4th Dragoons in 1694. They were already mounted on grey horses by this stage and were already being referred to as the Grey Dragoons. They were often referred to, during the first Jacobite uprising, as Portmore's Dragoons. In 1877, their nickname was made official when the regiment became the 2nd Dragoons (Royal Scots Greys), which was inverted in 1921 to The Royal Scots Greys (2nd Dragoons).

The Royal Scots Greys Memorial, Princes Street Gardens, Edinburgh. *Kim Traynor*

46102 BLACK WATCH (LMS 6102) built North British Locomotive Works (NBL), entered traffic in August 1927. Lot No L833, Works No 23597. The name was bestowed in March 1928 and an official naming ceremony took place on 15 October 1930. Rebuilt October 1949. Thus, retaining a parallel boiler throughout the LMS period. Withdrawn by BR in December 1962 and cut up by J McWilliams, Shettleston in May 1964.

Rebuilt Royal Scot class BR No 46102 BLACK WATCH departs Glasgow (Buchanan Street) station with a Glasgow – Manchester express on 16 October 1960. *J & J Collection – Sid Rickard/Rail Photoprints.* The locomotive nameplate was complemented by a regimental plaque, but in this instance the plaque, at the request of the regimental officials, was placed below the nameplate and as a consequence was fixed to the splasher. *David Anderson*

The Black Watch, 3rd Battalion, Royal Regiment of Scotland (3 SCOTS) is an infantry battalion of the Royal Regiment of Scotland. The regiment was created as part of the Childers Reforms in 1881, when the 42nd (Royal Highland) Regiment of Foot (The Black Watch) was amalgamated with the 73rd (Perthshire) Regiment of Foot. It was known as The Black Watch (Royal Highlanders) from 1881 to 1931 and The Black Watch (Royal Highland Regiment) from 1931 to 2006. Part of the Scottish Division for administrative purposes from 1967, it was the senior Highland regiment. It has been part of the Scottish, Welsh and Irish Division for administrative purposes from 2017.

The source of the regiment's name is uncertain. In 1725, following the Jacobite rebellion of 1715, General George Wade was authorised by George I to form six 'watch' companies to patrol the Highlands of Scotland, three from Clan Campbell, one from Clan Fraser of Lovat, one from Clan Munro and one from Clan Grant. These were to be 'employed in disarming the Highlanders, preventing depredations, bringing criminals to justice, and hindering rebels and attainted persons from inhabiting that part of the kingdom.' The force was known in Gaelic as Am Freiceadan Dubh, 'the dark' or 'black watch'.

The Royal Regiment of Scotland is the senior and only Scottish line infantry regiment of the British Army Infantry. It consists of four regular and two reserve battalions, plus an incremental company, each formerly an individual regiment (with the exception of the first battalion, which is an amalgamation of two regiments). However, each battalion maintains its former regimental pipes and drums to carry on the traditions of their antecedent regiments.

The picture 'A Black Watch sentry at ease' from 1892, by Harry Payne. *Anne S. K. Brown Military Collection*

Rebuilt Royal Scot class BR No 46103 ROYAL SCOTS FUSILIER seen with Jubilee BR No 45568 WESTERN AUSTRALIA. The location is Leeds City station and the date was 5 October 1962. Both locomotives are carrying 55A Leeds Holbeck shed plates. *Keith Langston Collection*

46103 ROYAL SCOTS FUSILIER (LMS 6103) built North British Locomotive Works (NBL), entered traffic in August 1927. Lot No L833, Works No 23598. The name was bestowed in April 1928 and an official naming ceremony took place on 2 August 1935. Rebuilt June 1943. Withdrawn by BR in December 1962 and cut up at Crewe Works in September 1963.

The ROYAL SCOTS FUSILIER nameplate is complemented by a regimental badge with a thistle and motto. The motto originates from the Royal Stuart dynasty of Scotland from the reign of James V1. Latin – *Nemo me impune lascessit*, translation 'no one attacks me with impunity'. *David Anderson*

The Royal Scots Fusiliers cap badge.

The Royal Scots Fusiliers was a line infantry regiment of the British Army that existed from 1678 until 1959 when it was amalgamated with the Highland Light Infantry (City of Glasgow Regiment) to form the Royal Highland Fusiliers (Princess Margaret's Own Glasgow and Ayrshire Regiment) which was later itself merged with the Royal Scots Borderers, the Black Watch (Royal Highland Regiment), the Argyll and Sutherland Highlanders and the Highlanders (Seaforth, Gordons and Camerons) to form a new large regiment, the Royal Regiment of Scotland.

Rebuilt Royal Scot class BR No 46103 ROYAL SCOTS FUSILIER is seen at Saltley on 17 June 1962 at the head of a line of locomotives, all awaiting disposal. The backing plate remains in place but the nameplate (and shedplate) have already been removed. *Pete Skelton*

46104 SCOTTISH BORDERER (LMS 6104) built North British Locomotive Works (NBL), entered traffic in August 1927. Lot No L833, Works No 23599. Rebuilt March 1946. Withdrawn by BR in December 1962 and cut up by J McWilliams, Shettleston in May 1964.

Rebuilt Royal Scot class BR No 46104 SCOTTISH BORDERER is seen approaching Carstairs Junction station with an overnight sleeping car express from London Euston on 13 September 1958. *David Anderson*

Memorial to soldiers of the King's Own Scottish Borderers who died in the South African War, 1900-1902. North Bridge Edinburgh. *Katie Chan*

The King's Own **Scottish Borderers** was a line infantry regiment of the British Army, part of the Scottish Division. The regiment was raised on 18 March 1689 by David Melville, 3rd Earl of Leven to defend Edinburgh against the Jacobite forces of King James II. It's claimed that 800 men were recruited within the space of two hours.

On 28 March 2006 the regiment was amalgamated with the Royal Scots, the Royal Highland Fusiliers (Princess Margaret's Own Glasgow and Ayrshire Regiment), the Black Watch (Royal Highland Regiment), the Highlanders (Seaforth, Gordons and Camerons) and the Argyll and Sutherland Highlanders to form the Royal Regiment of Scotland, becoming the 1st Battalion of the new regiment.

46105 CAMERON HIGHLANDER (LMS 6105) built North British Locomotive Works (NBL), entered traffic in August 1927. Lot No L833, Works No 23600. Rebuilt May 1948. Thus, retaining a parallel boiler throughout the LMS period. Withdrawn by BR in December 1962 and cut up by J McWilliams, Shettleston in May 1964.

Rebuilt Royal Scot class BR No 46105 CAMERON HIGHLANDER is seen on Beattock Bank with a down relief passenger train in June 1958. *David Anderson*

The Queen's Own **Cameron Highlanders** or 79th (The Queen's Own Cameron Highlanders) Regiment of Foot was a line infantry regiment of the British Army, raised in 1793. It amalgamated with the Seaforth Highlanders (Ross-shire Buffs, The Duke of Albany's) to form the Queen's Own Highlanders in 1961. The regiment was raised as the 79th Regiment of Foot (Cameronian Volunteers) on 17 August 1793 at Fort William from among the members of the Clan Cameron by Sir Alan Cameron of Erracht.

This image is of an extremely rare (one of three known) original belt-plate, of the 79th Cameron Highlanders from the year of their formation (1793). Due to a War Department clerical error they were erroneously designated as the 'Cameronian' Volunteers, a mistake later perpetuated when they were renamed the 'Cameronian Highlanders'. This was not corrected until 1804 after repeated petitions from both the Cameron regiment and the original Cameronian regiment, originally founded in 1689 by James Douglas, the Earl of Angus, as a Covenanter guard unit, later becoming the 26th Regiment of Foot, and then the Scottish Rifles.

Men of the 1st Battalion Queen's Own Cameron Highlanders digging trenches at Aix, France, November 1939. *War Department image*

46106 GORDON HIGHLANDER (LMS 6106) built North British Locomotive Works (NBL), entered traffic in August 1927. Lot No L833, Works No 23601. Rebuilt September 1949. Thus, retaining a parallel boiler throughout the LMS period. Withdrawn by BR in December 1962 and cut up at Crewe Works in April 1963.

See also LNER BR No 62277 (49)

Rebuilt Royal Scot class BR No 46106 GORDON HIGHLANDER is seen between turns at Dalry Road depot Edinburgh on 6 February 1955. The smartly turned out locomotive is coupled to a high sided tender and is fitted with BR Standard type smoke deflectors. *Norman Preedy Collection*

The Gordon Highlanders was a line infantry regiment of the British Army that existed for 113 years, from 1881 until 1994, when it was amalgamated with the Queen's Own Highlanders (Seaforth and Camerons) to form the Highlanders (Seaforth, Gordons and Camerons).

The regiment was formed on 1 July 1881 instigated under the Childers Reforms. The new two-battalion regiment was formed out of the 75th (Stirlingshire) Regiment of Foot, which became the 1st Battalion of the new regiment, and the 92nd (Gordon Highlanders) Regiment of Foot, which became the 2nd Battalion.

Gordon Highlanders cap badge.

Men of the 2nd Battalion, Gordon Highlanders are seen during the assault on Tilburg in October 1944.

46107 ARGYLL AND SUTHERLAND HIGHLANDER (LMS 6107) built North British Locomotive Works (NBL), entered traffic in September 1927. Lot No L833, Works No 23602. Named April 1928. Rebuilt February 1950. Thus, retaining a parallel boiler throughout the LMS period. Withdrawn by BR in December 1962 and cut up by J McWilliams, Shettleston in May 1964.

Rebuilt Royal Scot class BR No 46107 ARGYLL AND SUTHERLAND HIGHLANDER is seen after being serviced at Glasgow Polmadie depot in March 1958. *Norman Preedy Collection*

The nameplate of BR No 46107 was complemented by a regimental crest above. The plaque is a representation of the cap badge. *David Anderson*

The Argyll and Sutherland Highlanders (Princess Louise's) was a line infantry regiment of the British Army that existed from 1881 until amalgamation into the Royal Regiment of Scotland on 28 March 2006, from when it became a single battalion therein. The regiment was created under the Childers Reforms in 1881, as the Princess Louise's (Sutherland and Argyll Highlanders), by the amalgamation of the 91st (Argyllshire Highlanders) Regiment of Foot and 93rd (Sutherland Highlanders) Regiment of Foot, amended the following year to reverse the order of the 'Argyll' and 'Sutherland' sub-titles. In July 2012 the 5th Battalion was reduced to a single public duties company called Balaklava Company, 5th Battalion, Royal Regiment of Scotland, (Argyll and Sutherland Highlanders).

Boer War Memorial, Stirling Castle. Erected by the Argyll and Sutherland Highlanders, in memory of their comrades who gave their lives in the South African War, 1899-1902. *Andrew Smith*

46108 SEAFORTH HIGHLANDER (LMS 6108) built North British Locomotive Works (NBL), entered traffic in September 1927. Lot No L833, Works No 23603. Rebuilt August 1943. Withdrawn by BR in January 1963 and cut up at Crewe Works in May 1963.

Rebuilt Royal Scot class BR No 46108 SEAFORTH HIGHLANDER is seen with a down local service whilst passing Minsull Vernon station (closed March 1942) on 26 May 1958. The signal box was closed in the early 1960s. The site was cleared and the buildings demolished just prior to the electrification of the WCML. *Norman Preedy Collection*

The **Seaforth Highlanders** (Ross-shire Buffs, The Duke of Albany's) was a historic line infantry regiment of the British Army, mainly associated with large areas of the northern Highlands of Scotland. The regiment existed from 1881 to 1961, and saw service in World War I and World War II, along with many numerous smaller conflicts. The regiment was created through the amalgamation of the 72nd (Duke of Albany's Own Highlanders) Regiment of Foot and the 78th (Highlanders) (Ross-shire Buffs) Regiment of Foot, as part of the Childers Reforms of the British Army in 1881. It was named after Kenneth Mackenzie, 1st Earl of Seaforth, who had originally raised the 72nd Regiment. In 1961 the regiment was amalgamated with others as part of the Royal Regiment of Scotland.

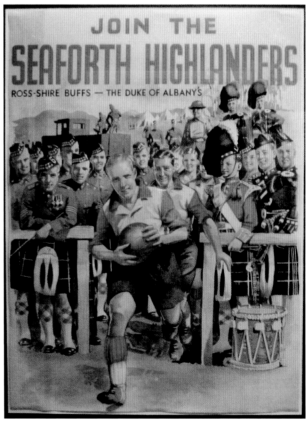

Recruiting poster on display in the Scottish National War Museum, Edinburgh Castle. *Kim Traynor*

153

46109 ROYAL ENGINEER (LMS 6109) built North British Locomotive Works (NBL), entered traffic in September 1927. Lot No L833, Works No 23604. Named April 1928, naming ceremony 17 June 1933. Rebuilt July 1943. Withdrawn by BR in December 1962 and cut up at Crewe Works in December 1963.

Rebuilt Royal Scot class BR No 46109 ROYAL ENGINEER is seen during a 1950s visit to Crewe Works. *Norman Preedy Collection*

ROYAL ENGINEER nameplate with regimental crest above. Latin *Ubique*, translation 'everywhere'. *David Anderson*   Royal Engineer's badge.

The Corps of Royal Engineers, usually just called the **Royal Engineers**, and commonly known as the Sappers, is one of the corps of the British Army. The Royal Engineers trace their origins back to the military engineers brought to England by William the Conqueror, specifically Bishop Gundulf of Rochester Cathedral, and claim over 900 years of unbroken service to the Crown. Engineers have always served in the armies of the Crown; however, the origins of the modern corps, along with those of the Royal Artillery, lie in the Board of Ordnance established in the 15th century. The corps provides military engineering and other technical support to the British Armed Forces and is headed by the Chief Royal Engineer. The Regimental Headquarters and the Royal School of Military Engineering are in Chatham, Kent. The corps is divided into several regiments, based at various locations in the United Kingdom and worldwide.

Royal Engineers recruitment poster est. 1901 or later.

46110 GRENADIER GUARDSMAN (LMS 6110) built North British Locomotive Works (NBL), entered traffic in September 1927. Lot No L833, Works No 23605. Rebuilt January 1953. Thus, retaining a parallel boiler throughout the LMS period. Withdrawn by BR in February 1964 and cut up by J McWilliams, Shettleston in December 1964.

Rebuilt Royal Scot class BR No 46110 GRENADIER GUARDSMAN is seen at Birmingham New Street station. The locomotive is about to double head a train south and a railwayman can be seen between the Royal Scot and an unidentified Black Five, circa 1959. At that time the WCML electrification from Crewe to Manchester was underway, accordingly the locomotives are affixed with overhead power warning plates. The Birmingham line electrification took place in the mid 1960s. *Norman Preedy Collection*

Grenadier Guards cap badge.

The **Grenadier Guards** (GREN GDS) is an infantry regiment of the British Army. It is the most senior regiment of the Guards Division and, as such, is the most senior regiment of infantry. It is not, however, the most senior regiment of the Army, this position being attributed to the Life Guards. Although the Coldstream Guards were formed before the Grenadier Guards, the regiment is ranked after the Grenadiers in seniority as, having been a regiment of the New Model Army, the Coldstream Guards served the Crown for four fewer years than the Grenadiers (the Grenadiers having formed as a Royalist regiment in exile in 1656 and the Coldstream Guards having sworn allegiance to the Crown upon the Restoration in 1660).

Their uniform white belt ('Buff Belt') with brass clasps carries the Royal Cypher. Modern Grenadier Guardsmen wear a cap badge of a 'grenade fired proper' with seventeen flames. This cap badge has to be cleaned twice a day – once in the morning, and once in the afternoon. A tarnished grenade is severely frowned upon and can be punished by disciplinary action within the Regiment.

Grenadier Guardsman on sentry duty outside Buckingham Palace. *Len Mills*

46111 ROYAL FUSILIER (LMS 6111) built North British Locomotive Works (NBL), entered traffic in September 1927. Lot No L833, Works No 23606. Rebuilt October 1947. Withdrawn by BR in September 1963 and cut up at Crewe Works in December 1964.

Rebuilt Royal Scot class BR No 46111 ROYAL FUSILIER is seen at Huddersfield with a Liverpool–Newcastle service in September 1963. *Mike Morant Collection*

The Royal Fusiliers (City of London Regiment) was a line infantry regiment of the British Army in continuous existence for 283 years. It was known as the 7th Regiment of Foot until the Childers Reforms of 1881. The regiment served in many wars and conflicts throughout its long existence, including the Second Boer War, the First World War and the Second World War.

In 1968, the regiment was amalgamated with the other regiments of the Fusilier Brigade – the Royal Northumberland Fusiliers, the Royal Warwickshire Fusiliers and the Lancashire Fusiliers – to form a new large regiment, the Royal Regiment of Fusiliers.

The Royal Fusiliers War Memorial, dedicated to the almost 22,000 Royal Fusiliers who died during World War 1, stands on Holborn in the City of London. *Len Mills*

Royal Fusiliers cap badge.

46112 SHERWOOD FORESTER (LMS 6112) built North British Locomotive Works (NBL), entered traffic in September 1927. Named April 1928, naming ceremony 16 June 1933. Lot No L833, Works No 23607. Rebuilt September 1943. Withdrawn by BR in May 1964 and cut up by Cashmores, Great Bridge in September 1964.

Rebuilt Royal Scot class BR No 46112 SHERWOOD FORESTER is seen at Crewe North shed on a rainy day in March 1946 whilst awaiting servicing. At that time the rebuilt locomotive carried a 6P power rating and was not fitted with smoke deflectors. *Rail Photoprints Collection*

Men of 'D' Company, 2nd Sherwood Foresters, 1st Division, in a forward trench near Roches, 1 April 1940. Lance Corporal L J Harris has a shave while other men keep watch, one armed with a 2-inch mortar. *Lt. E.A. Taylor, Official War Photographer*

The Sherwood Foresters (Nottinghamshire and Derbyshire Regiment) was a line infantry regiment of the British Army in existence for just under 90 years, from 1881 to 1970. In 1970, the regiment was amalgamated with the Worcestershire Regiment to form the Worcestershire and Sherwood Foresters Regiment, which in 2007 was amalgamated with the Cheshire Regiment and the Staffordshire Regiment (Prince of Wales's) to form the present (2019) Mercian Regiment. The lineage of the Sherwood Foresters is now continued by the 2nd Battalion, Mercian Regiment. The regiment was formed on 1 July 1881 as part of the Childers Reforms.

The nameplate for this locomotive was complemented by a regimental crest placed above the name. *David Anderson*

Interesting items of correspondence from the LMS internal mail system of the time, relating to the naming of SHERWOOD FORESTER.

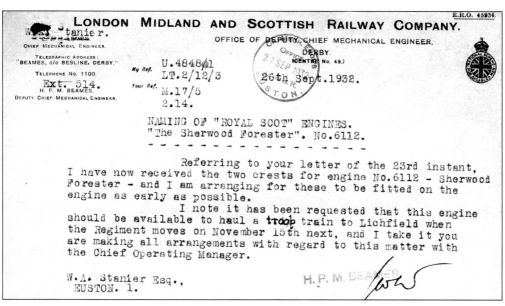

LONDON MIDLAND AND SCOTTISH RAILWAY COMPANY.

E.R.O. 45934.

W. Stanier.
CHIEF MECHANICAL ENGINEER.

OFFICE OF DEPUTY CHIEF MECHANICAL ENGINEER.
DERBY.
(CENTRE No. 49.)

Telegraphic Address:
"BEAMES, c/o BESLINE, DERBY."

Telephone No. 1100.
Ext. 514.
H. P. M. BEAMES,
DEPUTY CHIEF MECHANICAL ENGINEER.

My Ref. U.4848/1
LT.2/12/3

Your Ref. M.17/5
2.14.

26th Sept.1932.

NAMING OF "ROYAL SCOT" ENGINES.
"The Sherwood Forester". No.6112.
- - - - - - - - - - - - - - - - - -

            Referring to your letter of the 23rd instant,
I have now received the two crests for engine No.6112 - Sherwood
Forester - and I am arranging for these to be fitted on the
engine as early as possible.
            I note it has been requested that this engine
should be available to haul a troop train to Lichfield when
the Regiment moves on November 15th next, and I take it you
are making all arrangements with regard to this matter with
the Chief Operating Manager.

W.A. Stanier Esq.,
EUSTON. 1.   H. P. M. BEAMES

26 September 1932.

LONDON MIDLAND AND SCOTTISH RAILWAY COMPANY.

Telegraphic Address—
"BEAMES, c/o
BESLINE, DERBY."

Telephone No. 1100.
Ext.513.

OFFICE OF DEPUTY CHIEF MECHANICAL ENGINEER,

DERBY,——27th October,——19 32
(Centre No. 49.)

OUR REFERENCE.
U.4848
LT.1/10-3

YOUR REFERENCE.
M/.17/5/6-14

NAMING OF "ROYAL SCOT" ENGINES.
"SHERWOOD FORESTER" No.6112.
                    ————————

            Further to my letter to you of the 24th October,
will you please note that the above engine was turned off
Crewe Works this morning after the service repair, and sent
to Crewe North Shed. Mr. Anderson has been notified accordingly.
            I shall be glad to hear from you early in reply to
the penultimate paragraph of my letter of the 24th October.

W.A. Stanier, Esq.,
EUSTON. 1.

27 October 1932.

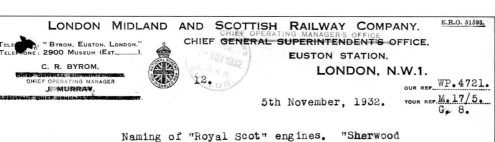

LONDON MIDLAND AND SCOTTISH RAILWAY COMPANY.

E.R.O. 51593.

CHIEF OPERATING MANAGER'S OFFICE.
CHIEF GENERAL SUPERINTENDENT'S OFFICE,
EUSTON STATION,
LONDON, N.W.1.

TELEGRAMS: "BYROM, EUSTON, LONDON."
TELEPHONE: 2900 MUSEUM (EXT.____).

C. R. BYROM,
CHIEF GENERAL SUPERINTENDENT.
CHIEF OPERATING MANAGER
J. MURRAY,
ASSISTANT CHIEF GENERAL SUPERINTENDENT.

5th November, 1932.

OUR REF. WP.4721.

YOUR REF. M.17/5.
G. 8.

Naming of "Royal Scot" engines. "Sherwood
            Forester", No.6112.
————————————————————————————

            In reply to your letter of 31st ultimo;
engine No.6112 will be at Camden Shed during the night
of the 14th instant and will leave there "light" for
Willesden about 11.0am. on the 15th instant.

                        for C.R.Byrom,

W.A.Stanier Esq.,
            EUSTON.

5 November 1932.

46113 CAMERONIAN (LMS 6113) built North British Locomotive Works (NBL), entered traffic in September 1927. Named March 1928, naming ceremony 16 March 1936. Lot No L833, Works No 23608. Rebuilt December 1950. Thus, retaining a parallel boiler throughout the LMS period Withdrawn by BR in December 1962 and cut up at Crewe Works in June 1963.

Cameronian's Memorial plaque, Douglas, Lanarkshire. *Kim Traynor*

Royal Scot class BR No 46113 CAMERONIAN, seen as LMS No 6113 at Carlisle Kingmoor depot on 10 June 1930. Note that the power rating indication is alongside the cab side window. This locomotive's nameplate was complemented by a regimental crest located above the name. The crest was a representation of the regimental cap badge. *Rail Photoprints Collection*

The Cameronians (Scottish Rifles) was a rifle regiment of the British Army, the only regiment of rifles amongst the Scottish regiments of infantry. It was formed in 1881 under the Childers Reforms by the amalgamation of the 26th Cameronian Regiment and the 90th Perthshire Light Infantry. In 1968, when reductions were required, the regiment chose to be disbanded rather than amalgamated with another regiment, one of only two infantry regiments in the British Army to do so, with the other being the York and Lancaster Regiment. It can trace its roots to that of the Cameronians, later the 26th of Foot, who were raised in 1689. The 1881 amalgamation coincided with the Cameronian's selection to become the new Scottish Rifles. After the amalgamation, the 1st Battalion preferred to be known as 'Cameronians' while the 2nd preferred to be known as 'The Scottish Rifles'.

46114 COLDSTREAM GUARDSMAN (LMS 6114) built North British Locomotive Works (NBL), entered traffic in September 1927. Lot No L833, Works No 23609. Rebuilt June 1946. Withdrawn by BR in September 1963 and cut up by Slag Reduction Co. Ltd. Ickles, Rotherham in April 1964.

Rebuilt Royal Scot class BR No 46114 COLDSTREAM GUARDSMAN is seen with 'The Comet' London- Manchester express whilst approaching Cheadle Hulme on 8 September 1953. *Norman Preedy Collection*

The Coldstream Guards is a part of the Guards Division, Foot Guards regiments of the British Army. It is the oldest regiment in the Regular Army in continuous active service, originating in Coldstream, Scotland in 1650 when General George Monck founded the regiment. It is one of two regiments of the Household Division that can trace its lineage to the New Model Army, the other being the Blues and Royals (Royal Horse Guards and 1st Dragoons). The origin of The Coldstream Guards lies in the English Civil War when Oliver Cromwell gave Colonel George Monck permission to form his own regiment as part of the New Model Army. Monck took men from the regiments of George Fenwick and Sir Arthur Haselrig, five companies each, and on 13 August 1650 formed Monck's Regiment of Foot.

Crimean War. Coldstream Guards Joseph Numa, John Potter and James Deal. *Windsor Collection*

A soldier with the Regimental Colours of No7 Company Coldstream Guards prior to the start of the ceremonial season. *Sgt. Dan Harmer*

46115 SCOTS GUARDSMAN (LMS 6115) built North British Locomotive Works (NBL), entered traffic in September 1927. Lot No L833, Works No 23610. Rebuilt August 1947. The last engine to be withdrawn by BR in January 1966, and saved for preservation. **P**

Rebuilt Royal Scot class BR No 46115 SCOTS GUARDSMAN is seen at Crewe prior to working the RCTS railtour to Carlisle on 13 March 1965. Note the overhead power warning plates on the smoke deflector, boiler barrel, Belpaire firebox and also inside the cab on the tender bulkhead. *Hugh Ballantyne/Rail Photoprints*

SCOTS GUARDSMAN under guard! At MOSI Manchester in 1980. *Keith Langston Collection*

LMS No 6115 was named SCOTS GUARDSMAN in 1928. After receiving smoke deflectors, it starred in the 1936 film *Night Mail.* It was the first of the rebuilt engines to receive smoke deflectors and the only one to run with them as an LMS engine. It was renumbered 46115 by British Railways in 1948. In May 1969 it was bought by the late Bob Bill and moved to the Keighley & Worth Valley Railway. Later the locomotive moved to the now defunct Dinting Railway Centre, where restoration took place. In 1978 BR No 46115 ran two mainline railtours before being withdrawn in need of major boiler repairs. In 1989 it was transferred to the Birmingham Railway Museum in Tylesely, but the 'hoped for' restoration did not take place. BR No 46115 was later purchased by David Smith (West Coast Railway Company) and in 2008, it was restored to main-line running standard. Its first test run from Carnforth to Hellifield was completed in June 2008. It then hauled its first railtour called 'The Settle-Carlisle Venturer' between Hellifield and Carlisle. The locomotive carried the Olympic torch in 2012 in place of FLYING SCOTSMAN. In 2019 SCOTS GUARDSMAN was main line certified and was normally based at WCRC, Carnforth.

The Scots Guards, part of the Guards Division, is one of the Foot Guards regiments of the British Army. Their origins lie in the personal bodyguard of King Charles I of England and Scotland. Its lineage can be traced back to 1642, although it was only placed on the English Establishment (part of what is now the British Army) in 1686. The Regiment is the oldest formed Regiment in the Regular Army in service today. On the order of King Charles I the regiment was raised by Archibald Campbell, 1st Marquess of Argyll for service in Ireland, and was then known as the Marquis of Argyll's Royal Regiment.

Scots Guards badge.

Preserved Rebuilt Royal Scot class BR No 46115 SCOTS GUARDSMAN is seen at York station with the 'Scarborough Spa Express' on 19 July 2012, York-Scarborough and reverse.

Preserved Rebuilt Royal Scot class BR No 46115 SCOTS GUARDSMAN is seen at Carlisle station on 1 August 2017 with 'The Fellsman' charter, Lancaster-Carlisle and reverse. *Both images Phil Brown*

Rebuilt Royal Scot class BR No 46116 IRISH GUARDSMAN is seen in the environs of Stafford, circa 1962. *Norman Preedy*

The nameplate of the locomotive had a small representation of the regimental badge below it. Latin Quis Separabit, translation 'who shall separate'. *The Hon. Joshua Wood*

IRISH GUARDSMAM seen as LMS No 6116 circa 1930. Note the Midland Railway style two colour front buffer beam. *Mike Stokes Archive/BR*

The Irish Guards, as a part of the Guards Division, is one of the Foot Guards regiments of the British Army and, together with the Royal Irish Regiment is one of the two Irish infantry regiments. The Irish Guards recruit in Northern Ireland and the Irish neighbourhoods of major British cities. The Irish Guards regiment was formed on 1 April 1900 by order of Queen Victoria, to commemorate the Irishmen who fought in the Second Boer War for the British Empire

One way to distinguish between the five regiments of Foot Guards is the spacing of the buttons on their tunics. The Irish Guards have buttons arranged in groups of four as they were the fourth Foot Guards regiment to be founded. They also have a prominent St. Patrick's blue plume on the right side of their bearskins.

A modern bronze Memorial to the Irish Guards overlooking the High Street in Windsor, Berkshire. *Len Mills*

46117 WELSH GUARDSMAN (LMS 6117) built North British Locomotive Works (NBL), entered traffic in October 1927. Lot No L833, Works No 23612. Rebuilt December 1943. Withdrawn by BR in November 1962 and cut up at Crewe Works December 1963.

Rebuilt Royal Scot class BR No 46117 WELSH GUARDSMAN is seen climbing Ais Gill with 'The Thames -Clyde Express' in February 1962. 'The Thames Clyde Express' ran between London St. Pancras and Glasgow St. Enoch (after the closure of St. Enoch Glasgow Central). The first titled run took place on 26 September 1927 and the last 3 May 1975 (with a break during WW2). *Norman Preedy Collection*

The Welsh Guards (Gwarchodlu Cymreig), part of the Guards Division, is one of the Foot Guards regiments of the British Army. The regiment came into existence on 26 February 1915 by Royal Warrant of George V in order to include Wales in the national component to the Foot Guards, (although the order to raise the regiment had actually been given by King George V to Earl Kitchener, the then Secretary of State for War, on 6 February 1915.They were the last of the Guards to be created, with the Irish Guards coming into being in 1900. Just three days after they came into existence the 1st Battalion Welsh Guards mounted its first King's Guard at Buckingham Palace, on 1 March 1915 – St David's Day.

Welsh Guards cap badge.

Welsh Guardsman in full dress are distinguished by the white/ green/white plume on their bearskin hats. *Ronnie Macdonald*

46118 ROYAL WELCH FUSILIER (LMS 6118) built North British Locomotive Works (NBL), entered traffic in October 1927.Lot No L833, Works No 23613. Named April 1928, official naming ceremony April 1929.Rebuilt December 1946. Withdrawn by BR in June 1964 and cut up by Connels of Calder, Coatbridge December 1964.

Rebuilt Royal Scot class BR No 46118 ROYAL WELCH FUSILIER is seen with a down train at Lamington WCML 5 July 1958. The nameplate is complemented by a crest displaying a Dragon which is fixed on the splasher below the name. *David Anderson*

The Colour of the Royal Welch Fusiliers, as publicly displayed at the Royal Welch Fusiliers Museum, within Caernarfon Castle, Wales. Listed on it are the names of the regiment's major battles/campaigns, as well as motifs related to the regiment, the British Army, and the United Kingdom, such as the Royal heraldic badges of the UK. *Len Mills*

The end of a Royal Scot. BR No 46118 is seen being cut up at the yard of Connels of Calder in December 1964. Suprisingly a smokebox number plate is still in place. *David Anderson*

The Royal Welch Fusiliers was a line infantry regiment of the British Army, part of the Prince of Wales' Division. It was founded in 1689 to oppose James II and to take part in the imminent war with France.

The regiment was numbered as the 23rd Regiment of Foot, though it was one of the first regiments to be granted the honour of a fusilier title and so was known as The Welch Regiment of Fusiliers from 1702. The 'Royal' accolade was earned fighting in the War of the Spanish Succession in 1713.

It was one of the oldest infantry regiments in the British Army, hence the continued use of the archaic spelling of the word Welch instead of Welsh, and also historically Fuzileers instead of Fusiliers; these archaic spellings were engraved on swords the regiment carried during Napoleonic times.

46119 LANCASHIRE FUSILIER (LMS 6119) built North British Locomotive Works (NBL), entered traffic in October 1927. Lot No L833, Works No 23614. Rebuilt September 1944. Withdrawn by BR in November 1963 and cut up at Crewe Works November 1963.

Rebuilt Royal Scot class BR No 46119 LANCASHIRE FUSILIER is seen in the roundhouse at Willesden in the company of 'Black Five' class BR No 45391 and 'Jubilee' class BR No 45625 SARAWAK in August 1959. *Keith Langston Collection*

The Lancashire Fusiliers was a line infantry regiment of the British Army that saw distinguished service through many centuries and wars, including the Second Boer War, World War I and World War II, and had many different titles throughout its 280 years of existence. In 1968 the regiment was amalgamated with the other regiments of the Fusilier Brigade–the Royal Northumberland Fusiliers, Royal Warwickshire Fusiliers and the Royal Fusiliers (City of London Regiment)–to form the current Royal Regiment of Fusiliers.

Lancashire Fusiliers cap badge.

A Lancashire Fusiliers Memorial, St. Mary's Cathedral, Madras, India. *Wikipedia*

Rebuilt Royal Scot class BR No 46120 ROYAL INNISKILLING FUSILIER is seen departing Manchester London Road station with a London express service on 9 April 1954. Plenty of railway men in this image but not a hi-vis jacket to be seen. The nameplate is complemented by a regimental crest on the splasher below the name. *Norman Preedy*

The Royal Inniskilling Fusiliers was an Irish line infantry regiment of the British Army in existence from 1881 until 1968. The regiment was formed in 1881 by the amalgamation of the 27th (Inniskilling) Regiment of Foot and the 108th Regiment of Foot. On 1 July 1881 the 27th (Inniskilling) Regiment of Foot and the 108th Regiment of Foot were redesignated as the 1st and 2nd Battalions, The Royal Inniskilling Fusiliers, respectively. In 1903 the Regiment was granted a grey hackle for their fusilier raccoon-skin hats to commemorate the original grey uniforms of the Inniskilling Regiment. The regimental district comprised the City of Londonderry and the counties of Donegal, Londonderry, Tyrone and Fermanagh in Ireland, with its garrison depot located at St Lucia Barracks in Omagh.

Detail of the stained-glass window in the fifth bay of the north aisle, depicting the insignia of the Royal Inniskilling Fusiliers, displaying the Inniskilling Castle with the flag of Saint George flying. St. Macartin's Cathedral, Enniskillen, County Fermanagh, Northern Ireland. *Andreas F. Borchert*

46121 H.L.I. (LMS 6121) built North British Locomotive Works (NBL), entered traffic in October 1927. Lot No L833, Works No 23616. Name changed to **HIGHLAND LIGHT INFANTRY THE CITY OF GLASGOW REGIMENT** and a renaming ceremony was held 22 January 1949. Rebuilt August 1946. Withdrawn by BR in December 1962 and cut up by J. McWilliams of Shettleston May 1964.

Royal Scot class BR No 46121 H.L.I. is seen at Cricklewood in 1929 as LMS No 6121, then with the abbreviated form of the regimental nameplate. Note the North British Locomotive Co Queens Park diamond pattern works plate on the smoke box barrel. NBL built Royal Scot locomotives LMS Nos 6100 – 6124 were Queens Park built engines whilst LMS Nos 6125 – 6149 with circular works plates were Hyde Park built engines. *Norman Preedy Collection*

Highland Light Infantry Badge. ASSAYE is a village in Western India and was the location of The Battle of Assaye fought in 1803 between the Maratha Empire and the British East India Company.

The nameplate as fitted to BR No 46121. *David Anderson*

Highland Light Infantry memorial located in Kelvingrove Park, Glasgow. The memorial commemorates the Officers, Non-Commissioned Officers and men who fell during the South African War 1899-1900/2. The statue was commissioned by comrades and friends and depicts a soldier sitting on a rock wearing a traditional pith helmet and puttees. *Len Mills*

The Highland Light Infantry was a light infantry regiment of the British Army formed as part of the Childers Reforms in 1881. The regiment insisted on being classified as a non-kilted Highland regiment which recruited mainly from the city of Glasgow and Lowland Scotland. In 1959 it was amalgamated with the Royal Scots Fusiliers and others to form the Royal Regiment of Scotland, becoming the 2nd Battalion of the new regiment.

46122 ROYAL ULSTER RIFLEMEN (LMS 6122) built North British Locomotive Works (NBL), entered traffic in October 1927. Lot No L833, Works No 23617. Date of naming April 1928 followed by an official ceremony later in that year. Rebuilt September 1945. Withdrawn by BR in October 1964 and cut up by Drapers of Hull February 1965.

Rebuilt Royal Scot class BR No 46122 ROYAL ULSTER RIFLEMAN is seen at Bristol Temple Meads station with a postal train on 4 July 1961. *Rail Photoprints Collection*

The nameplate was complemented by a regimental crest located below it and mounted on the splasher. *David Anderson*

Regimental crest/badge.

The Royal Irish Rifles (which became the Royal Ulster Rifles from 1 January 1921) was an infantry rifle regiment of the British Army, first created in 1881 by the amalgamation of the 83rd (County of Dublin) Regiment of Foot and the 86th (Royal County Down) Regiment of Foot (Childers Reforms). It was then one of eight regiments raised and garrisoned in Ireland. In 1968 the Royal Ulster Rifles was amalgamated with the other regiments of the North Irish Brigade, the Royal Irish Fusiliers (Princess Victoria's) and the Royal Inniskilling Fusiliers to create the Royal Irish Rangers.

Regimental Monument, Belfast City Hall. *Peter Clarke.*

46123 ROYAL IRISH FUSILIER (LMS 6123) built North British Locomotive Works (NBL), entered traffic in October 1927. Lot No L833, Works No 23618. Date of naming April 1928 followed by an official ceremony 21 June 1930. Rebuilt May 1949. Thus, still with parallel boiler at the end of LMS period. Withdrawn by BR in November 1962 and cut up at Crewe Works May 1963.

Rebuilt Royal Scot class BR No 46123 ROYAL IRISH FUSILIER is seen in the environs of Gloucester on 28 October 1961. *Norman Preedy Collection.* The nameplate was complemented by a regimental crest located below it and mounted on the splasher. Enscribed 'Faugh- a-Ballagh', translation 'Clear the Way'. *David Anderson*

The Royal Irish Fusiliers (Princess Victoria's) was an Irish line infantry regiment of the British Army, formed by the amalgamation of the 87th (Prince of Wales's Irish) Regiment of Foot and the 89th (Princess Victoria's) Regiment of Foot in 1881, as part of the Childers Reforms. The regiment's first title in 1881 was Princess Victoria's (Royal Irish Fusiliers), changed in 1920 to the Royal Irish Fusiliers (Princess Victoria's). In 1968, the Royal Irish Fusiliers (Princess Victoria's) was amalgamated with the other regiments of the North Irish Brigade, the Royal Inniskilling Fusiliers and the Royal Ulster Rifles, to become the Royal Irish Rangers.

Men of the Royal Irish Fusiliers are seen in the trenches on the southern section of Gallipoli Peninsula during World War I. *Ernest Brooks*

46124 LONDON SCOTTISH (LMS 6124) built North British Locomotive Works (NBL), entered traffic in November 1927. Lot No L833, Works No 23619. Date of naming April 1928 followed by an official ceremony 11 July 1937. Rebuilt December 1943. Withdrawn by BR in December 1962 and cut up at Crewe Works April 1963.

Rebuilt Royal Scot BR No 46124 LONDON SCOTTISH without smoke deflectors is seen near Sutton Weaver (WCML) with an up Liverpool express, in 1949. Note the regimental crest above the nameplate and also that the tender still shows LMS branding. *R.A. Whitfield/Rail Photoprints Collection*

A 3.7-inch AA gun of 97th Heavy Anti-Aircraft Regiment (London Scottish) bombarding enemy positions on the Gothic Line, 2 September 1944. *Sgt Dawson Army Film and Photographic Unit*

The London Scottish was a Volunteer infantry regiment of the British Army. The regiment was founded on the formation of the Volunteer Force in 1860. It was originally a part of the Volunteer Force sponsored by *The Highland Society of London* and *The Caledonian Society of London*, a group of individual Scots raised The London Scottish Rifle Volunteers under the command of Lt Col Lord Elcho, later The Earl of Wemyss and March. The regiment became the 7th (London Scottish) Middlesex Volunteer Rifle Corps and then, in 1908, the 14th (County of London) Battalion, London Regiment (London Scottish).

London Scottish cap badge.

46125 LANCASHIRE WITCH (LMS 6125) built North British Locomotive Works (NBL), entered traffic in September 1927. Lot No L834, Works No 23620. Renamed 3RD CARABINIER in September 1935 followed by an official ceremony 30 June 1936. Rebuilt August 1943. Withdrawn by BR in October 1964 and cut up by Cashmores of Great Bridge January 1965.

Rebuilt Royal Scot BR No 46125 3RD CARABINIER is seen at Crewe station, facing south and adjacent to the North Bridge, circa 1960. *Norman Preedy Collection*

The 3rd Carabiniers (Prince of Wales's Dragoon Guards) was a cavalry regiment of the British Army. It was formed in 1922 as part of a reduction in the army's cavalry by the amalgamation of the 3rd Dragoon Guards (Prince of Wales's) and the Carabiniers (6th Dragoon Guards), to form the 3rd/6th Dragoon Guards. It was renamed the 3rd Carabiniers (Prince of Wales's Dragoon Guards) in 1928 and amalgamated with the Royal Scots Greys (2nd Dragoons), forming the Royal Scots Dragoon Guards (Carabiniers and Greys) in 1971.

The Carabiniers South Africa War memorial situated on the Chelsea Embankment, London. *Len Mills*

The nameplate was complemented by a regimental crest located above it in the form of the heraldic badge of the Prince of Wales, which consists of three white ostrich feathers emerging from a gold coronet. A ribbon below that is inscribed 'Ich Dien', translation 'I Serve'. The abbreviated form of number proceeding the word Carabinier is shown in smaller upper-case letters aligned with the top of the figure 3. That is not the case with the official regimental web sites and other publications which normally show the name thus, 3rd Carabiniers. *David Anderson*

L. M. S. INTERNAL CORRESPONDENCE. 20/5

OUR REFERENCE. C.O.261/15/1

YOUR REFERENCE. M.17/2 G.3.D.

FROM OFFICE OF VICE-PRESIDENT,

W.A.Stanier, Esq.,

EUSTON.

(Centre No.)

CH. MECH. ENGR'S OFFICE 10 MAY 1935 L.M.S.R. EUSTON

EUSTON STATION.
(Centre No. 1).
E.R.O. 1019
1/10/VIII 33

8th May 1935

NAMING OF ENGINES

With reference to your letter of the 3rd instant; as regards the last paragraph thereof, I see no reason why, after all Empire and Colonial names have been exhausted, the names of well-known engines taken off "Royal Scots" to give place to regimental names, should not be utilised for the "Jubilee" Class.

H. Hartley

Mr Riddles spoke to Mr Smith (Mr E J H Lemon office) re last of Empire & colonial name 14/5

This copy of an LMS item of internal mail sent 8 May 1935 to the office of Mr. Stanier (Chief Mechanical Engineer) from the office of the railway's Vice Presidents and signed by Sir Harold Hartley is self-explanatory. Of course, not all the 25 names concerned were transferred to 'Jubilee' class locomotives but some notable ones were. The hand-written additional to the note informs Stanier that Mr. Riddles (Stanier's Principal Assistant) wrote to Mr. Smith, of Mr. Lemon's office (Ernest Lemon was an ex CME and one of four Vice Presidents), regarding the allocation of the last of Empire and Colonial names on 14 May 1935. *LMS*

46126 SANSPAREIL (LMS 6126) built North British Locomotive Works (NBL), entered traffic in September 1927. Lot No L834, Works No 23621. Renamed ROYAL ARMY SERVICE CORPS in August 1935 followed by an official ceremony 14 January 1936. Rebuilt June 1945. Withdrawn by BR in October 1963 and cut up at Crewe Works November 1963.

Rebuilt Royal Scot BR No 46126 ROYAL ARMY SERVICE CORPS is seen at Euston Station, circa 1961. *Mike Morant Collection*

LMS No 6126 is seen as SANSPAREIL at complemented by a regimental crest mounted above. *Collection David Anderson*

1915 Recruiting Poster.

The Royal Army Service Corps nameplate was Polmadie depot in 1930. *Norman Preedy*

Regimental badge.

The Royal Army Service Corps was a corps of the British Army responsible for land, coastal and lake transport, air despatch, barracks administration, the Army Fire Service, staffing headquarters' units, supply of food, water, fuel and domestic materials such as clothing, furniture and stationery and the supply of technical and military equipment. In 1965 its functions were divided between other Corps (RCT and RAOC) and the RASC ceased to exist; subsequently, in 1993, they in their turn (with some functions of the Royal Engineers) became the 'Forming Corps' of the Royal Logistic Corps.

175

46127 NOVELTY (LMS 6127) built North British Locomotive Works (NBL), entered traffic in September 1927. Lot No L834, Works No 23622. Renamed, THE OLD CONTEMPTIBLE, nameplate fitted (covered), 11 December 1935. Second renaming as OLD CONTEMPTIBLES on 26 November 1936 (badge fitted), official ceremony 28 November 1936. Rebuilt August 1944. Withdrawn by BR in December 1962 and cut up at Crewe Works May 1963.

Rebuilt Royal Scot BR No 46127 is seen at Willesden depot on 28 October 1956. *Norman Preedy Collection*

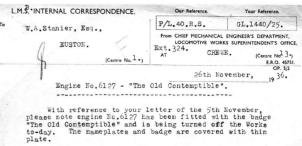

As previously noted in this publication Mr. Stanier was not in favour of this name being used. However, nameplates with the indefinite article and without the plural of the name being used, were produced (see image). LMS records show that those were fitted to the locomotive and covered up with steel plate(s), with LMS No 6127 returning to traffic on 11 December 1935. Those nameplates remained in situ for almost a year until being replaced two days before the November 1936 naming ceremony. LMS correspondence, November 1936 refers to the fitting of a badge described as 'The Old Contemptible', note indefinite article and no letter 's', That memo also mentions a 'nameplate' (possibly incorrectly). The description of the name on that document was also incorrect, as the design of the badge(s), which replaced the nameplate(s), no doubt with the approval of Mr. Stanier, was taken from the logo of the Old Contemptibles Association. It was without an indefinite article but plural, and was cast in copper/bronze.

Badge in place of nameplate.

Both badges survive one as part of the national collection, also one of the reportedly original nameplates was saved for preservation, and that is part of a private collection.

The origin of the title **'Old Contemptibles'** is a reference to the British Expeditionary Force (BEF) which was sent to France in 1914. The term 'British Expeditionary Force' is often used to refer only to the forces present in France prior to the end of the First Battle of Ypres on 22 November 1914. By the end of 1914, and after the battles of Mons, Le Cateau, the Aisne and Ypres the old Regular Army had been decimated, although it did manage to help stop the German advance. An alternative endpoint of the BEF was 26 December 1914, when it was divided into the First and Second Armies (a Third, Fourth and Fifth being created later in the war). BEF remained the official name of the British armies in France and Flanders throughout World War I. Emperor Wilhelm II of Germany, who was famously dismissive of the BEF, allegedly issued an order on 19 August 1914 to 'exterminate the treacherous English and walk over General French's contemptible little army'. Hence, in later years, the survivors of the regular army dubbed themselves 'The Old Contemptibles'.

A Memorial to 'The Old Contemptibles' which is located in the west cloister of Westminster Abbey. It is made of limestone and Welsh blue slate and as can be seen it was unveiled on 15 July 1993, by H.M. Queen Elizabeth, The Queen Mother. *Len Mills*

Royal Scot BR No 46128 with a very full tender of coal is seen in original condition as LMS No 6128 METEOR, at Polmadie depot in June 1930. Note the 6P power rating on the cabside window mullion and NBL circular Hyde Park works makers plate on the smoke box. *Rail Photoprints Collection*

Rebuilt Royal Scot BR No 46128 THE LOVAT SCOUTS is posed on the turntable at Crewe North depot, circa 1960. From the various members of the public seen in this image it can be assumed that it was taken at an Open Day event. The 7P power rating can be seen above the cabside number. The nameplate is complemented by a regimental crest located above. *Norman Preedy Collection*

The Lovat Scouts was a British Army unit first formed during the Second Boer War as a Scottish Highland yeomanry regiment of the British Army. In 1916 they formally became the British Army's first sniper unit, then known as sharpshooters.

In modern times it forms A Company (The Lovat Scouts) within the 2nd Battalion, 51st Highland Volunteers. Recruited initially from gamekeepers on Highland estates, the unit was commanded by an American, Major Frederick Russell Burnham, the British Army Chief of Scouts under Lord Roberts, who fittingly described Lovat Scouts as 'half wolf and half jackrabbit'. They were well practised in the arts of marksmanship, field craft, and military tactics, they were also phenomenal woodsmen always ready to tempt fate. Lovat Scouts have the distinction of being the first military unit to wear a Ghillie suit.

Lovat Scouts mortar officer and rangefinder operator seen during an exercise in the Faroe Islands, June 1941. *Lt. Taylor, War Office Official Photographer*

46129 COMET (LMS 6129) built North British Locomotive Works (NBL), entered traffic in September 1927. Lot No L834, Works No 23624. Renamed **THE SCOTTISH HORSE** in December 1935. Rebuilt December 1944. Withdrawn by BR in June 1964 and cut up by Central Wagon Co., Wigan November 1964.

Rebuilt Royal Scot BR No 46129 THE SCOTTISH HORSE is seen on the depot at Patricroft, Manchester in November 1961. The nameplate was complemented by a regimental crest, placed above the name. The depot image was taken by the accomplished photographer known as the 'Footplate Cameraman'. *Jim Carter* Nameplate image. *David Anderson*

The Scottish Horse was a Yeomanry regiment of the British Army's Territorial Army raised in 1900 for service in the Second Boer War. In late 1900, the Marquess of Tullibardine was asked by Lord Kitchener, whom he had served under on the Omdurman Campaign, to raise a regiment of Scotsmen in South Africa, called The Scottish Horse. It amalgamated with the Fife and Forfar Yeomanry to form the Fife and Forfar Yeomanry/Scottish Horse in 1956. The lineage was maintained by 'C' Fife and Forfar Yeomanry/Scottish Horse Squadron of The Scottish and North Irish Yeomanry based in Cupar in Fife.

The Scottish Horse Imperial Yeomanry Badge as worn during the Boer War.

The Scottish Horse memorial located on Edinburgh Castle Esplanade. *Elmarie Malherbe*

46130 LIVERPOOL (LMS 6130) built North British Locomotive Works (NBL), entered traffic in September 1927. Lot No L834, Works No 23625. Renamed **THE WEST YORKSHIRE REGIMENT** in March 1935, naming ceremony 24 June 1935. Rebuilt December 1949. Thus, still with parallel boiler at the end of LMS period. Withdrawn by BR in December 1962 and cut up at Crewe Works October 1963.

Royal Scot BR No 46130 is seen when first named THE WEST YORKSHIRE REGIMENT as LMS No 6130, in this official LMS image. The nameplate was complemented by a regimental crest above the name. *David Anderson Collection*

Rebuilt Royal Scot BR No 46130 THE WEST YORKSHIRE REGIMENT is seen at Ducie Street goods yard Manchester in this 1955 image. *Norman Preedy Collection*

The West Yorkshire Regiment (Prince of Wales's Own) (14th Foot) was an infantry regiment of the British Army. The regiment was raised by Sir Edward Hales in 1685, by order of King James II. One of the nine new regiments of foot, raised to meet the Monmouth Rebellion it was termed Hales's Regiment. In 1958 it amalgamated with the East Yorkshire Regiment (15th Foot) to form the Prince of Wales's Own Regiment of Yorkshire which was, on 6 June 2006, amalgamated with the Green Howards and the Duke of Wellington's Regiment (West Riding) to form the Yorkshire Regiment (14th/15th, 19th and 33rd/76th Foot).

Regimental colours 1845.

Regimental Badge.

46131 PLANET (LMS 6131) built North British Locomotive Works (NBL), entered traffic in September 1927. Lot No L834, Works No 23626. Renamed **THE ROYAL WARWICKSHIRE REGIMENT** in November 1936, naming ceremony 20 June 1938. Rebuilt October 1944. Withdrawn by BR in November 1962 and cut up at Crewe Works November 1962.

The nameplate was complemented by a regimental crest above. *David Anderson*

Royal Scot class locomotive LMS No 6131 is seen at Birmingham New Street station on 20 June 1938 and after the unveiling of the nameplates. William Stanier (CME LMS) is pictured standing on the extreme left of the front of the engine. He is with regimental dignitaries and with top hat in hand, the Lord Mayor of Birmingham. *John Magnall Collection*

Rebuilt Royal Scot BR No 46131 THE ROYAL WARWICKSHIRE REGIMENT is seen passing Duffield with 'The Palatine' in March 1958. The Palatine ran between London St. Pancras and Manchester Central between 4 July 1938 and 9 September 1939 and 16 September 1957 and 13 June 1964. *Bernard Brown*

The Royal Warwickshire Regiment, previously titled the 6th Regiment of Foot, was a line infantry regiment of the British Army in continuous existence for 283 years. On 1 May 1963, the regiment was retitled, for the final time, as the Royal Warwickshire Fusiliers and became part of the Fusilier Brigade. In 1968, and by then reduced to a single 'Regular' battalion, the regiment was amalgamated with the other regiments in the Fusilier Brigade – the Royal Northumberland Fusiliers, the Royal Fusiliers (City of London Regiment) and the Lancashire Fusiliers. Thus, becoming part of a new infantry regiment, to be known as the Royal Regiment of Fusiliers, it became the 2nd Battalion of that new regiment.

Troops of the 2nd Battalion, Royal Warwickshire Regiment dug in with a Bren gun along a hedge near Venray, the Netherlands, 17 October 1944. *No 5 Army Film & Photographic Unit, Sgt. Norris*

46132 PHEONIX (LMS 6132) built North British Locomotive Works (NBL), entered traffic in September 1927. Lot No L834, Works No 23627. Renamed THE KING'S REGIMENT LIVERPOOL in April 1936, naming ceremony 9 May 1937. Rebuilt November 1943. Withdrawn by BR in February 1964 and cut up by Arnott Young, Troon April 1965.

Rebuilt Royal Scot BR No 46132 THE KING'S REGIMENT LIVERPOOL is seen at Saltley on 17 June 1962. Although some 2 years before officially being withdrawn the locomotive is already minus nameplates. *Pete Skelton.* The nameplate was complemented by a regimental crest above. *David Anderson*

An imposing monument in honour of the King's Regiment Liverpool, created by Sir William Goscombe John in 1905, stands in St. Johns Gardens, Liverpool. *Len Mills*

The King's Regiment (Liverpool) was one of the oldest line infantry regiments of the British Army, having been formed in 1685 and numbered as the 8th (The King's) Regiment of Foot in 1751. Unlike most British Army infantry regiments, which were associated with a county, the King's represented the city of Liverpool, one of only four regiments affiliated to a city in the British Army. After 273 years of continuous existence, the regiment was amalgamated with the Manchester Regiment in 1958 to form the King's Regiment (Liverpool and Manchester), which was later amalgamated with the King's Own Royal Border Regiment and the Queen's Lancashire Regiment to form the Duke of Lancaster's Regiment (King's, Lancashire and Border).

46133 VULCAN (LMS 6133) built North British Locomotive Works (NBL), entered traffic in September 1927. Lot No L834, Works No 23628. Renamed THE GREEN HOWARDS in SEPTEMBER 1936, naming/dedication ceremony 13 December 1946. Rebuilt July 1944. Withdrawn by BR in February 1963 and cut up at Crewe Works May 1963.

Rebuilt Royal Scot BR No 46133 THE GREEN HOWARDS is seen at Leeds City station circa 1949, and without smoke deflectors. The nameplate was complemented by a regimental crest above. *Mike Morant Collection*

The Green Howards (Alexandra, Princess of Wales's Own Yorkshire Regiment), frequently known as the Yorkshire Regiment until the 1920s, was a line infantry regiment of the British Army, in the King's Division. It was raised in 1688 and was known as the Green Howards from 1744. At that time, regiments were known by the name of their colonel. The 19th regiment's colonel was Hon. Sir Charles Howard. However, at the same time, the 3rd Regiment of Foot had been commanded by its colonel Thomas Howard, since 1737. To tell them apart (since they both would have been known as 'Howard's Regiment of Foot'), the colours of their uniform facings were used to distinguish them. In this way, one became 'Howard's Buffs' (eventually simply The Buffs), while the other became the Green Howards. In June 2006 the regiment was amalgamated with the Prince of Wales's Own Regiment of Yorkshire and the Duke of Wellington's Regiment (West Riding), all Yorkshire-based regiments in the King's Division, to form the Yorkshire Regiment (14th/15th, 19th and 33rd/76th Foot) on 6 June 2006.

A memorial to the Green Howards in the village of Crépon in the Normandy Region of France. *Len Mills Collection*

46134 ATLAS (LMS 6134) built North British Locomotive Works (NBL), entered traffic in September 1927. Lot No L834, Works No 23629. Renamed **THE CHESHIRE REGIMENT** in August 1936, naming/dedication ceremony 14 May 1947. Rebuilt December 1954. Thus, still with parallel boiler at the end of LMS period. Withdrawn by BR in December 1962 and cut up at Crewe Works April 1963.

Royal Scot BR No 46134 THE CHESHIRE REGIMENT is seen at Euston station circa 1949, note early BRITISH RAILWAYS name style on the tender. *Mike Morant Collection*

LMS No 6134 ATLAS is seen at Polmadie, April 1928. *Keith Langston Collection*

The nameplate was complemented by a Regimental crest above. *David Anderson*

The Cheshire Regiment was a line infantry regiment of the British Army, part of the Prince of Wales' Division. The 22nd Regiment of Foot was raised by the Duke of Norfolk in 1689 and was able to boast an independent existence of over 300 years. The regiment was expanded in 1881 as part of the Childers Reforms by the linking of the 22nd (Cheshire) Regiment of Foot and the militia and rifle volunteers of Cheshire. The title 22nd (Cheshire) Regiment continued to be used within the regiment. On 1 September 2007, the Cheshire Regiment was merged with the Worcestershire and Sherwood Foresters Regiment (29th/45th Foot) and the Staffordshire Regiment (Prince of Wales's) to form a new large regiment, the Mercian Regiment, becoming the 1st Battalion, Mercian Regiment.

Cheshire's Queen's Colour – Regimental Colour.

46135 SAMSON (LMS 6135) built North British Locomotive Works (NBL), entered traffic in September 1927. Lot No L834, Works No 23630. Renamed **THE EAST LANCASHIRE REGIMENT** in May 1936, naming/dedication ceremony 28 May 1947. Rebuilt January 1947. Withdrawn by BR in December 1962 and cut up at Crewe Works April 1963.

Rebuilt Royal Scot BR No 46135 THE EAST LANCASHIRE REGIMENT is seen with a fully fitted train of vans circa 1956, whilst passing Standish Junction, Lancashire. *Norman Preedy Collection.* The nameplate was complemented by a regimental badge above. *David Anderson*

The East Lancashire Regiment was, from 1881 to 1958, a line infantry regiment of the British Army. Under the Childers Reforms it was amalgamated with the 30th (Cambridgeshire) Regiment of Foot and 59th (2nd Nottinghamshire) Regiment of Foot, the militia and rifle volunteer units of eastern Lancashire.

In 1958 the regiment was amalgamated with the South Lancashire Regiment to form the Lancashire Regiment. In 1970, it merged with the Loyal Regiment (North Lancashire) to form the Queen's Lancashire Regiment. In 2006, the Queen's Lancashire was amalgamated with the King's Own Royal Border Regiment and the King's Regiment (Liverpool and Manchester) to form Duke of Lancaster's Regiment (King's, Lancashire and Border).

The Memorial is dedicated to the memory of all members of 'The Accrington Pals', 11th (Service) Battalion East Lancashire Regiment who fought and fell in that location during the Battle of the Somme. Built in Accrington red brick, it stands in Sheffield Memorial Park, Serre, Somme France. It is located in the south east corner of the wood in the position of the 1 July 1916 British front line where the 11th East Lancashire Regiment began their attack on that day. *Len Mills Collection*

46136 GOLIATH (LMS 6136) built North British Locomotive Works (NBL), entered traffic in September 1927. Lot No L834, Works No 23631. Renamed **THE BORDER REGIMENT** in April 1936, naming ceremony 6 June 1946. Rebuilt March 1950. Thus, still with parallel boiler at the end of LMS period. Withdrawn by BR in March 1964 and cut up at Crewe Works April 1964.

Rebuilt Royal Scot BR No 46136 THE BORDER REGIMENT is seen at Crewe North, in 1957. *Rail Photoprints Collection*

Royal Scot BR No 46136 THE BORDER REGIMENT is seen in fine external condition as LMS No 6136 at Carlisle Upperby 10 June 1936. Note that the nameplate was complemented by a regimental badge above. *Rail Photoprints Collection*

The Border Regiment was a line infantry regiment of the British Army, which was formed in 1881 under the Childers Reforms by the amalgamation of the 34th (Cumberland) Regiment of Foot and the 55th (Westmorland) Regiment of Foot. In 1959 the regiment was amalgamated with the King's Own Royal Regiment (Lancaster) into the King's Own Royal Border Regiment, which was later merged with the King's Regiment (Liverpool and Manchester) and the Queen's Lancashire Regiment to form the present Duke of Lancaster's Regiment (King's, Lancashire and Border), which continued the lineage of the Border Regiment.

Cap Badge of the Border Regiment.

46137 VESTA (LMS 6137) built North British Locomotive Works (NBL), entered traffic in September 1927. Lot No L834, Works No 23632. Renamed **THE PRINCE OF WALES'S VOLUNTEERS SOUTH LANCASHIRE** in October 1936, naming ceremony 14 October 1947. The last engine to be rebuilt, March 1955. Thus, still with parallel boiler at the end of LMS period. Withdrawn by BR in November 1962 and cut up at Crewe Works May 1963.

Royal Scot BR No 46137 THE PRINCE OF WALES'S VOLUNTEERS SOUTH LANCASHIRE is seen passing Hartford Station (WCML) with a southbound express service from Liverpool on 31 July 1953. *Norman Preedy Collection*

Nameplate BR No 46137. *David Anderson*

Regimental Cap Badge.

The South Lancashire Regiment was a line infantry regiment of the British Army in existence from 1881 to 1958. The regiment recruited primarily from the South Lancashire area, was created during the Childers Reforms as the Prince of Wales's Volunteers (South Lancashire Regiment) by the amalgamation of the 40th (the 2nd Somersetshire) Regiment of Foot and the 82nd Regiment of Foot (Prince of Wales's Volunteers). In 1938, it was renamed the South Lancashire Regiment (The Prince of Wales's Volunteers) and on 1 July 1958 the regiment was amalgamated with the East Lancashire Regiment to form the Lancashire Regiment (Prince

> T. F. Coleman, Esq.,
>
> DERBY.
>
> 49   Ext. 813D.
>
> 2nd July,   36.
>
> Naming of "Royal Scot" class Engines.
>
> ───────────────────────────
>
> With reference to your letter of the 26th June, I am in receipt of the drawing and cannot understand why you have put the words "South Lancashire" in the same size lettering as the main portion of the name. The words in question are meant to be supplementary to the name to indicate to which county the regiment belongs and should have been in letters half the size of the actual regimental name as has been done with other engine's nameplates. Since in this particular instance the nameplate has already been cast I am not proposing to alter it, but should be glad if you would arrange in future for all words supplementary to the main name to be put in letters half the size of the main name.

This copy of an official LMS internal memorandum dated 2 July 1936 tells its own interesting story in regards to the double row nameplate with crest cast for THE PRINCE OF WALES'S VOLUNTEERS SOUTH LANCASHIRE. The missive was between Euston (presumably the office of Mr. Stanier) and the Derby office of MR. T.F. Coleman, who was Technical Assistant and Chief Draughtsman of the LMS during that period.

of Wales's Volunteers) which was later amalgamated with the Loyal Regiment (North Lancashire) to form the Queen's Lancashire Regiment, which was later merged with the King's Regiment (Liverpool and Manchester), the King's Own Royal Border Regiment to form the Duke of Lancaster's Regiment (King's, Lancashire and Border) in 2007.

46138 FURY (LMS 6138) built North British Locomotive Works (NBL), entered traffic in September 1927. Lot No L834, Works No 23633. Renamed **THE LONDON IRISH RIFLEMAN** in October 1929, naming ceremony 23 October 1929. Rebuilt June 1944. Withdrawn by BR in February 1963 and cut up at Crewe Works May 1963.

Royal Scot BR No 46138 THE LONDON IRISH RIFLEMAN is seen as LMS 6138 at Carlisle Kingmoor depot, circa 1930. *Norman Preedy Collection*

BR No 46138 is seen at Shap Wells (WCML) on 3 July 1954. *Norman Preedy Collection*

BR No 46138 nameplate with regimental crest below. Note, that the small oil box has been relocated. *David Anderson*

The London Irish Rifles was a volunteer rifle regiment of the British Army. The regiment was originally formed in 1859 during the Victorian Volunteer Movement, and named 28th Middlesex (London Irish) Rifle Volunteer Corps. In 1908, the London Irish was transferred to the Territorial Force and renamed the 18th (County of London) Battalion, the London Regiment (London Irish Rifles). Since 1993 the London Irish Rifles was incorporated as 'D' (London Irish Rifles) Company of the London Regiment as a part of the Army Reserve.

16th Middlesex Rifle Volunteers (London Irish). Taken from Col C Cooper-King, *The British Army and Auxiliary Forces*, published by Cassell and Company Ltd, London, c1895.

46139 AJAX (LMS 6139) built North British Locomotive Works (NBL), entered traffic in October 1927. Lot No L834, Works No 23634. Renamed **THE WELCH REGIMENT** in 1936. Rebuilt November 1946. Withdrawn by BR in October 1962 and cut up at Crewe Works May 1963.

Rebuilt Royal Scot BR No 46139 THE WELCH REGIMENT is seen passing Standish Junction with a down express service on 1 May 1954. Note that the backing plates associated with BR No 46139s nameplates were configured to accommodate a badge or crest which were never fitted. *Norman Preedy Collection*

The Welch Regiment (Welch, note the archaic spelling of 'Welsh') was an infantry regiment of the line of the British Army in existence from 1881 until 1969. The regiment was created in 1881 under the Childers Reforms by the amalgamation of the 41st (Welch) Regiment of Foot and 69th (South Lincolnshire) Regiment of Foot to form the Welsh Regiment, by which it was known until 1920 when it was renamed the Welch Regiment. In 1969 the regiment was amalgamated with the South Wales Borderers to form the Royal Regiment of Wales.

Welch Regiment Cenotaph designed by Sir Edwin Lutyens and located in Maindy Barracks Cardiff. *Len Mills Collection*

Regimental cap badge.

46140 HECTOR (LMS 6140) built North British Locomotive Works (NBL), entered traffic in October 1927. Lot No L834, Works No 23635. Renamed **THE KINGS ROYAL RIFLE CORPS** in 1936. Rebuilt May 1952. Thus, still with parallel boiler at the end of LMS period. Withdrawn by BR in November 1965 and cut up by J. McWilliams, Shettleston March 1966.

Rebuilt Royal Scot BR No 46140 THE KINGS ROYAL RIFLE CORPS is seen in the company of 'Jubilee' class BR No 45669 FISHER with both locomotives in ex works condition at Crewe, June 1961. Note that the backing plates associated with BR No 46140s nameplates were configured to accommodate a badge or crest which were never fitted. *Jim Carter/Rail Photoprints*

The King's Royal Rifle Corps was an infantry rifle regiment of the British Army that was originally raised in British North America as the Royal American Regiment (also known as the Royal Americans) in the Seven Years War and for Loyalist service in the American Revolutionary War. Later, ranked as the 60th Regiment of Foot. In 1958, the regiment joined the Oxfordshire and Buckinghamshire Light Infantry and the Rifle Brigade in the Green Jackets Brigade, and in 1966 those three regiments were formally amalgamated to become the Royal Green Jackets. The Kings Royal Rifle Corps became the 2nd Battalion Royal Green Jackets. On the disbandment of 1/Royal Green Jackets in 1992, the Royal Green Jackets King's Royal Rifle Corps battalion was redesignated as 1/Royal Green Jackets, eventually becoming 2/Rifles in 2007.

The King's Royal Rifle Corps are seen setting up 3" mortars beside a farm building in Italy, January 1945. *Sgt. Bowman, No 2 Army Film and Photographic Unit*

189

46141 CALEDONIAN (LMS 6141) built North British Locomotive Works (NBL), entered traffic in October 1927. Lot No L834, Works No 23636. Renamed **THE NORTH STAFFORDSHIRE REGIMENT** in an official ceremony 13 May 1935. Rebuilt October 1950. Thus, still with parallel boiler at the end of LMS period. Withdrawn by BR in April 1964 and cut up at Crewe Works July 1964.

Royal Scot BR No 46141 THE NORTH STAFFORDSHIRE REGIMENT is seen whilst receiving the attention of the fitters as LMS No 6141 CALEDONIAN at Derby in June 1928. The locomotive is fitted with an experimental smoke deflector device fitted behind and partially to the side of the chimney, which were often referred to as 'Gladstone Collars'. Note also the locomotive number on the non-coal railed tender and the LMS insignia of the cabside. *Norman Preedy Collection.* The North Staffordshire Regiment nameplate was complemented by a regimental crest above. *David Anderson*

The North Staffordshire Regiment (Prince of Wales's) was a line infantry regiment of the British Army, which was in existence between 1881 and 1959. The 64th (2nd Staffordshire) Regiment of Foot was created on 21 April 1758 from the 2nd Battalion of the 11th Regiment of Foot. In 1881, under the Childers Reforms, the 64th Regiment of Foot was merged with the 98th (Prince of Wales's) Regiment of Foot (originally raised in 1824) to form the Prince of Wales's (North Staffordshire Regiment). In 1921 the regimental title was altered to the North Staffordshire Regiment (Prince of Wales's). In 1959 the North Staffordshire Regiment (then a single regular battalion) was amalgamated with the South Staffordshire Regiment to form the Staffordshire Regiment (Prince of Wales's) which was, in 2006, amalgamated with the Cheshire Regiment and the Worcestershire and Sherwood Foresters Regiment (29th/45th Foot) to form the Mercian Regiment.

Royal Tank Regiment 'Matilda' tanks operate with infantry of 2nd Battalion North Staffordshire Regiment during an exercise near Hebuterne, France during January 1940. A large number of the charmingly named 'Matilda' tanks were built under contract for the government by the famous locomotive builders Vulcan Foundry, Newton le Willows.

46142 LION (LMS 6142) built North British Locomotive Works (NBL), entered traffic in October 1927. Lot No L834, Works No 23637. Renamed **THE YORK AND LANCASTER REGIMENT** 1935/36. Rebuilt February 1951. Thus, still with parallel boiler at the end of LMS period. Withdrawn by BR in January 1964 and cut up at Crewe Works January 1964.

Royal Scot BR No 46142 THE YORK AND LANCASTER REGIMENT is seen as LMS No 6142 at Edge Hill, Liverpool, circa 1929. Note the locomotive number on the non-coal railed narrow tender and the LMS insignia on the cabside. *Norman Preedy Collection*

Rebuilt Royal Scot BR No 46142 THE YORK AND LANCASTER REGIMENT is seen at Trafford Park circa 1960. Note that the backing plates associated with BR No 46142's nameplates were configured to accommodate a badge or crest which were never fitted. *Norman Preedy Collection*

The York and Lancaster Regiment was a line infantry regiment of the British Army that existed from 1881 until 1968. The regiment was created in the Childers Reforms of 1881 by the amalgamation of the 65th (2nd Yorkshire, North Riding) Regiment of Foot and the 84th (York and Lancaster). In 1968, the regiment chose to be disbanded rather than amalgamated with another regiment, one of only two infantry regiments in the British Army to do so, the other being the Cameronians (Scottish Rifles).

Men of the 2nd Battalion, York and Lancaster Regiment rest while on a patrol in Burma, July 1944.

46143 MAIL (LMS 6143) built North British Locomotive Works (NBL), entered traffic in October 1927. Lot No L834, Works No 23638. Renamed **THE SOUTH STAFFORDSHIRE REGIMENT** 1935/36. Rebuilt June 1949. Thus, still with parallel boiler at the end of LMS period. Withdrawn by BR in December 1963 and cut up at Crewe Works January 1964.

Royal Scot BR No 46143
THE SOUTH STAFFORDSHIRE
REGIMENT is seen as LMS No
6143 in this official image,
taken in 1932 after the fitting of
smokebox side smoke deflectors.
Mike Stokes Collection

Rebuilt Royal Scot BR No 46143 THE SOUTH STAFFORDSHIRE REGIMENT waits to depart north from Birmingham New Street station circa 1950, however the pair of 2-6-4T's heading the train to the left will obviously have to depart first. *Rail Photoprints Collection*

The South Staffordshire Regiment was a line infantry regiment of the British Army in existence for only 68 years. The regiment was created in 1881 under the Childers Reforms by the amalgamation of the 38th (1st Staffordshire) Regiment of Foot and the 80th (Staffordshire Volunteers). Reduced to a single Regular Army battalion after the Second World War, the regiment was amalgamated, in 1959, with the North Staffordshire Regiment (Prince of Wales's) to form the Staffordshire Regiment (Prince of Wales's) which was later, in 2007, amalgamated with the Cheshire Regiment and the Worcestershire and Sherwood Foresters Regiment to form the Mercian Regiment.

A rifleman of the 1st Battalion South Staffordshire Regiment wearing a light-coloured oversuit for camouflage against the sand dunes, during training at Mersa Matruh, Egypt in October 1940. *No 1 Army Film & Photographic Unit*

46144 OSTRICH (LMS 6144) built North British Locomotive Works (NBL), entered traffic in October 1927. Lot No L834, Works No 23639. Renamed **HONOURABLE ARTILLERY COMPANY** September 1932 official naming/dedication ceremony 18 March 1938. Rebuilt June 1945. Withdrawn by BR in January 1964 and cut up at Crewe Works January 1964.

Royal Scot BR No 46144 HONOURABLE ARTILLERY COMPANY is seen at Crewe Station as LMS No 6144 OSTRICH. Note the locomotive number on the non-coal railed narrow tender and the LMS insignia on the cabside. *Norman Preedy Collection*

Rebuilt Royal Scot BR No 46144 HONOURABLE ARTILLERY COMPANY is seen between Hockley and Uttoxeter, in April 1960. The nameplate was complemented by a regimental crest above. *Mike Stokes Collection*

Honourable Artillery Company Gunner Badge worn by Officers in No 1 Dress (Gunner) on Artillery ceremonial duties. Latin, '*Arma pacis fulcra*' – translation 'Armed Strength For Peace'.

The Honourable Artillery Company was incorporated by Royal Charter in 1537 by King Henry VIII and is considered one of the oldest military organisations in the world. In the 17th century, its members played a significant part in the formation of both the Royal Marines and the Grenadier Guards. In modern times it is a registered charity whose purpose is to attend to the 'better defence of the realm', this purpose is primarily achieved by the support of the HAC Regiment and a detachment of Special Constabulary to the City of London Police. The regiment, as part of the Army Reserve, is the oldest surviving regiment in the British Army.

46145 CONDOR (LMS 6145) built North British Locomotive Works (NBL), entered traffic in October 1927. Lot No L834, Works No 23640. Renamed **THE DUKE OF WELLINGTON'S REGT.** (WEST RIDING) in December 1935 official naming ceremony 4 October 1938. Rebuilt January 1944. Withdrawn by BR in December 1962 and cut up at Crewe Works October 1963.

The cap badge of the Duke of Wellington's Regiment. Latin '*Virtutis Fortuna Comes*' – translation, Fortune is the companion of virtue. *Richard Harvey*

The two line nameplate of Royal Scot BR No 46145. The style of this nameplate, with a regimental crest above, was the subject of a great deal of correspondence between the regiment and the LMS. A selection of which is illustrated. *David Anderson*

Men of the 1st Battalion, Duke of Wellington's Regiment march into Rome, 8 June 1944. *Sgt. Menzies No2 Photographic Unit*

The Duke of Wellington's Regiment (West Riding) was a line infantry regiment of the British Army, forming part of the King's Division. In 1702 Colonel George Hastings, 8th Earl of Huntingdon, was authorised to raise a new regiment, which he did in and around the city of Gloucester. The regiment was named Huntingdon's Regiment after its Colonel.

In 1751 regiments were given numbers, and the regiment was then officially known as the 33rd Regiment of Foot. In 1782 the regiment's title was changed to the 33rd (or First Yorkshire West Riding) Regiment, thus formalising an association with the West Riding of Yorkshire. Following the Childers Reforms, the 33rd was linked with the 76th Regiment of Foot, who shared their depot in Halifax. The 76th had first been raised in 1745, by Simon Harcourt and disbanded in 1746, re-raised in 1756 disbanded again in 1763, before being raised again in 1777, disbanded in 1784 and finally re-raised, in 1787. The two regiments became, respectively, the 1st and 2nd battalions of the Duke of Wellington's Regiment. In 1948 the 1st and 2nd battalions were amalgamated into a single battalion, the 1st Battalion. On 6 June 2006 the 'Dukes' were amalgamated with the Prince of Wales's Own Regiment of Yorkshire and the Green Howards to form the 3rd Battalion, Yorkshire Regiment (14th/15th, 19th and 33rd/76th Foot). Following further mergers, in 2012, the battalion was redesignated as the new 1st Battalion (1 Yorks) of the regiment.

A self-explanatory letter
dated 8 July 1935, from
the office of Brigadier
General P.A. Turner to
the office of William
Stanier re the naming of
LMS No 6145.

Telephone : Cambridge 1526.

Telegrams and Cables :
" Turner, Cambridge 1526."

From **Brig.-General P. A. TURNER,**
Kilsyth, Storey's Way, Cambridge.

July **8th** 1935.

W.A. Stainer, Esq.,
    Chief Mechanical Engineers' Office,
        Euston Station,
            London, N.W. 1.

Dear Sir,

I have to thank you for your letter M 1440/18. G 19/D of the
28th June referring to the naming of a Royal Scot Engine after our
Regiment. In a former letter from Sir Harold Hartley he told me that
there might be a difficulty as to getting our full title on the name
plate and I note you propose a shorter one. The full title is of course
"The Duke of Wellington's Regiment (West Riding)". If it is possible we
should like the full title on the name plate.

First of all with regard to the "The". We are very keen on this, *in our title*
I think that the feeling would be that we would rather have the "The" in
and shorten the word "Regiment" to "Regt" - or can we have the lettering
rather smaller than usual. Secondly, "(West Riding)" in brackets is the
only reference to the county of Yorkshire which is our Territorial County.
I was wondering whether it would be possible to have the name plate in the
following way

Something

I was also informed the cost of the two crests would be approximately
£10 and as I shall have to write round to the different battalions for a
subscription for the crests I should be much obliged if you would comfirm
this information.

Yours faithfully,

P A Turner Brig Genl
Colonel The Duke of Wellington's Reg

Longest existing name

6143. THE SOUTH STAFFORDSHIRE
        REGIMENT

W.A.Stanier, Esq.,
EUSTON.

(Centre No. 1.)

From CHIEF OPERATING MANAGER'S DEPARTMENT,
OFFICE OF THE SUPERINTENDENT OF MOTIVE POWER.
EUSTON.

(Centre No. 1)

E.R.O. 51605
O.P. 1

13th July, 1936.

WORKING OF ENGINE NO. 6145 "DUKE OF
WELLINGTON'S REGIMENT (WEST RIDING)
FITTED WITH 4,000 GALLON TENDER.

With reference to your letter of the 12th June
and further to my letter of the 20th idem.

Permission has now been given by the Chief
Engineer for the above engine fitted with a 4,000 gallon
tender to work between Preston and Halifax for the naming
ceremony which is to be held at Halifax Station on Sunday
October 4th, 1936.

I shall be obliged, therefore, if you will proceed
with the arrangements for this engine to be fitted with a
4,000 gallon tender and shall be glad if you will advise me
when this has been done.

The regiment had requested a naming ceremony at Halifax station as
detailed. On 21 January 1936 Mr Stanier had informed Mr G. H. Loftus Allen
to contact the operations manager about 'whether it is possible to work a
Royal Scot type engine' to that station. The 13 July 1936 correspondence
shown is the answer from the Chief Operating Manager. Note the change of
tender required, from 3,500 gallon to 4,000 gallon. *Both documents LMS*

46146 JENNY LIND (LMS 6146) built North British Locomotive Works (NBL), entered traffic in October 1927. Lot No L834, Works No 23641. Renamed **THE RIFLE BRIGADE** in May 1935. Rebuilt October 1943. Withdrawn by BR in December 1962 and cut up at Crewe Works March 1963.

Royal Scot BR No 46146 THE RIFLE BRIGADE is seen as LMS No 6146 JENNY LIND in the environs of Berkhampsted, circa 1932. *Rail Photoprints Collection*

Rebuilt Royal Scot BR No 46146 THE RIFLE BRIGADE (on the right in this 1959 image) is seen whilst being passed by sister locomotive BR 46140, outside Camden shed. *Mike Morant Collection*

THE RIFLE BRIGADE nameplate was complemented by a regimental crest above.

The Rifle Brigade (The Prince Consort's Own) was an infantry rifle regiment of the British Army formed in January 1800 and they were later renamed the 'Rifle Corps'. In January 1803, they became an established regular regiment entitled the 95th Regiment of Foot (Rifles) then renamed as the 'Rifle Brigade' in 1816. The unit was distinguished by its use of green uniforms in place of the traditional redcoat, as well as being armed with the Baker rifle which was the first British-made rifle accepted by the British Army in place of smooth-bore muskets—and the first regular infantry corps in the British Army to be so. The regiment was amalgamated with the 1st Green Jackets (43rd and 52nd) and the King's Royal Rifle Corps to form the Royal Green Jackets on 1 January 1966.

A carrier crew of 8th Rifle Brigade hands out chocolate to Dutch civilians during the advance of 11th Armoured Division in Holland, 22 September 1944. *Sgt. Laing, No5 Army Film and Photographic Unit*

46147 COURIER (LMS 6147) built North British Locomotive Works (NBL), entered traffic in October 1927. Lot No L834, Works No 23642. Renamed **THE NORTHAMPTONSHIRE REGIMENT** in July 1935, official naming ceremony 17 October 1935. Rebuilt September 1946. Withdrawn by BR in December 1962 and cut up at Crewe Works March 1963.

Royal Scot BR No 46147 is seen as LMS No 6147 passing South Kenton with a down express service, circa 1936. *Rail Photoprints Collection*

THE NORTHAMPTONSHIRE REGIMENT nameplate was complemented by a regimental crest above. *David Anderson*

Rebuilt Royal Scot BR No 46147 is seen as LMS No 6147 THE NORTHAMPTONSHIRE REGIMENT as it prepares to enter into the gloom of Liverpool Lime Street's Tunnels, on 1 July 1948. *Rail Photoprints/R. A. Whitfield*

The Northamptonshire Regiment was a line infantry regiment of the British Army in existence from 1881 until 1960, when it was amalgamated with the Royal Lincolnshire Regiment to form the 2nd East Anglian Regiment (Duchess of Gloucester's Own Royal Lincolnshire and Northamptonshire). It was then amalgamated with the 1st East Anglian Regiment (Royal Norfolk and Suffolk), the 3rd East Anglian Regiment (16th/44th Foot) and the Royal Leicestershire Regiment to form the Royal Anglian Regiment.

Troops from 2nd Battalion, The Northamptonshire Regiment wait to board landing craft at Catania, Sicily, for the invasion of Italy, 2 September 1943. *Sgt. Drennan No2 Army Film and Photographic Unit*

46148 VELOCIPEDE (LMS 6148) built North British Locomotive Works (NBL), entered traffic in November 1927. Lot No L834, Works No 23643. Renamed **THE MANCHESTER REGIMENT** in July 1935, official naming ceremony 1 October 1935. Rebuilt July 1954. Thus, still with parallel boiler at the end of LMS period. Withdrawn by BR in November 1964 and cut up by Birds, Morriston January 1965.

When first renamed the locomotive ran for a short period with a plain two-line nameplate and no regimental crest as seen in the official LMS image. Royal Scot BR No 46148 is seen at Carstairs Junction with a southbound express service in July 1953. Note that the nameplate is then complemented by a regimental crest above. *David Anderson*

Royal Scot BR No 46148 is seen at Carstairs Junction with a southbound express service in July 1953. Note that the nameplate is then complemented by a regimental crest above. *David Anderson*

Dear Sir,

In reply to your letter of 22nd July, the plaques which you have of "The Manchester Regiment" crest for attachment to engine No.6148 should be sent to -

Mr. W.A. Stanier,
Chief Mechanical Engineer,
L M S Locomotive Works,
L M S Railway, Crewe.

If you will get in touch with the local L M S Station Master, the latter will be pleased on production of this letter to arrange for the plaques if suitably packed to be despatched to Crewe "O.C.S." - i.e. without charge.

In July 1935 the regiment requested for plaques (regimental crests) to be added and LMS correspondence, a portion of which is shown, instructed the Manchester Regiment officials of the shipping details.

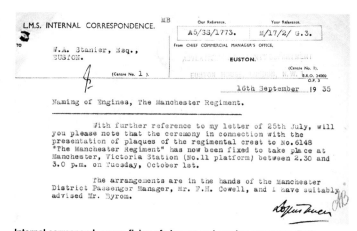

Internal correspondence re fixing of plaques and naming ceremony. *Both documents LMS*

WW1 Cap badge.

The Manchester Regiment was a line infantry regiment of the British Army in existence from 1881 until 1958. The regiment was created during the Childers Reforms by the amalgamation of the 63rd (West Suffolk) Regiment of Foot and the 96th Regiment of Foot as the 1st and 2nd battalions; the 6th Royal Lancashire Militia became the 3rd (Reserve) and 4th (Extra Reserve) battalions and the Volunteer battalions became the 5th, 6th, 7th, 8th, 9th and 10th battalions. In 1958 the Manchester Regiment was amalgamated with the King's Regiment (Liverpool) to form the King's Regiment (Manchester and Liverpool), which was, in 2006, amalgamated with the King's Own Royal Border Regiment and the Queen's Lancashire Regiment to form the Duke of Lancaster's Regiment (King's, Lancashire and Border).

WW2 Cap badge.

46149 LADY OF THE LAKE (LMS 6149) built North British Locomotive Works (NBL), entered traffic in November 1927. Lot No L834, Works No 23644. Renamed **THE MIDDLESEX REGIMENT** in 1935/36. The nameplate had a regimental plaque added 4 May 1939. Rebuilt April 1945. Withdrawn by BR in September 1963 and cut up at Crewe Works November 1963.

Rebuilt Royal Scot BR No 46149 THE MIDDLESEX REGIMENT is seen at Willesden depot on 21 September 1958, in the company of BR No 49078 a Bowen Cooke 'G2A' class 0-8-0. *RCTS Archive*

Note that the nameplate is complemented by a regimental crest above.

In almost all instances the cost of additional regimental plaques/badges was born by the regiment/association. The nameplates having been cast in house by the LMS. Contractors were employed to produce the plaque/crest etc. Firmin & Sons Ltd in this instance quoted a price of £8. 11 .0 each. *LMS*

P.&W. MacLellan, Ltd quoted less than half that amount, £4. 5. 0. each. Not surprisingly this contract went to the latter. The finished items were then forwarded to the LMS for fitting to the nameplates. *LMS*

In many instances it was arranged for locomotives to be named/dedicated during a ceremony at a specific location. Where those instances were near to the allocation date of the new name they are simply considered as naming ceremonies, in this publication. However, where a longer amount of time has elapsed between the new name allocation (in some instances years) they could be considered to be dedication ceremonies.

In the case of LMS No 6149 (BR No 46149) there is no record of an official ceremony either before or after the plaques/crests were fitted. However, an LMS memorandum dated May 1939 from Crewe Works to Euston Head Office states *'Engine No 6149 has been fitted with regimental crests and was put back into service on the 4th May'.*

The Middlesex Regiment (Duke of Cambridge's Own) was a line infantry regiment of the British Army in existence from 1881 until 1966. The regiment was formed, as the Duke of Cambridge's Own (Middlesex Regiment), in 1881 as part of the Childers Reforms when the 57th (West Middlesex) and 77th (East Middlesex) Regiments of Foot were amalgamated with the county's militia and rifle volunteer units.

On 31 December 1966 the Middlesex Regiment (Duke of Cambridge's Own) was amalgamated with the other regiments of the Home Counties Brigade, the Queen's Royal Surrey Regiment, the Queen's Own Buffs, The Royal Kent Regiment and the Royal Sussex Regiment to form the Queen's Regiment. The latter regiment was, however, short-lived and itself subject to a merger on 9 September 1992 with the Royal Hampshire Regiment to form the Princess of Wales's Royal Regiment (Queen's and Royal Hampshires).

46150 THE LIFE GUARDSMAN (LMS 6150) built at Derby Works, entered traffic May 1930. Lot No 073. Rebuilt December 1945. Withdrawn by BR in November 1963 and cut up at Crewe Works December 1963.

Rebuilt Royal Scot BR No 46150 is seen on Camden Bank with a down express service circa 1957. *Norman Preedy Collection*

The Life Guards is the senior regiment of the British Army and part of the Household Cavalry, along with the Blues and Royals. The Life Guards grew from the four troops of Horse Guards (exclusively formed of gentlemen-troopers until the transformation of the last two remaining troops into Regiments of Life Guards in 1788) raised by Charles II around the time of his restoration, plus two troops of Horse Grenadier Guards (rank and file composed of commoners), which were raised some years later.

In 1992, as part of a defence review, The Life Guards were joined together with the Blues and Royals in a 'Union', not an amalgamation, forming the Household Cavalry Regiment (armoured reconnaissance) and the Household Cavalry Mounted Regiment (ceremonial duties). However, they maintain their regimental identity, with distinct uniforms and traditions, and their own colonel. In common with the Blues and Royals, they have a peculiar non-commissioned rank structure: In brief, they lack sergeants, replacing them with multiple grades of corporal.

Mounted lifeguards wearing cloaks over full dress uniform are seen at Horse Guards Building Whitehall. *Len Mills Collection*

46151 THE ROYAL HORSE GUARDSMAN (LMS 6151) built at Derby Works, entered traffic June 1930. Lot No 073. Rebuilt April 1953. Thus, still with parallel boiler at the end of LMS period. Withdrawn by BR in December 1962 and cut up at Crewe Works August 1963.

Royal Scot BR No 46151 THE ROYAL HORSEGUARDSMAN is seen as LMS No 6151 at Crewe North depot circa 1936. *Rail Photoprints Collection*

The Royal Regiment of Horse Guards (The Blues) was a cavalry regiment of the British Army, part of the Household Cavalry.

Blues and Royals badge.

Raised in August 1650 at Newcastle upon Tyne and County Durham by Sir Arthur Haselrigge on the orders of Oliver Cromwell as a Regiment of Horse, the regiment became the Earl of Oxford's Regiment in 1660 upon the Restoration of King Charles II. As, uniquely, the regiment's coat was blue in colour at the time, it was nicknamed 'the Oxford Blues', from which was derived the nickname the 'Blues.' In 1750 the regiment became the Royal Horse Guards Blue and eventually, in 1877, the Royal Horse Guards (The Blues).

The Royal Horse Guards was amalgamated with the Royal Dragoons (1st Dragoons) to form the Blues and Royals (Royal Horse Guards and 1st Dragoons) in 1969.

A mounted lance corporal of the Household Cavalry wearing a gas mask, in 1939. His horse is also wearing a gas mask. *Capt. Console War Office Official Photographer*

46152 THE KINGS DRAGOON GUARDSMAN (LMS 6152) built by North British Locomotive Co, entered traffic July 1927. Lot No L833 23595. Swopped identity with LMS 6100 in 1933. Rebuilt August 1945. Withdrawn by BR in April 1965 and cut up at Crewe Works July 1965.

Rebuilt Royal Scot BR No 46152 THE KING'S DRAGOON GUARDSMAN is seen at Polmadie depot in May 1954. This engine started life as LMS No 6100 with which it swopped identity in 1933. See entry for 46100-6100. *Norman Preedy Collection*

Regimental cap badge.

LMS No 6152 as LMS No 6100 after the 1933 identity swop. *The Metcalf Collection*

The 1st King's Dragoon Guards was a cavalry regiment in the British Army. The regiment was raised by Sir John Lanier in 1685 as the 2nd Queen's Regiment of Horse, named in honour of Queen Mary, consort of King James II. It was renamed the 2nd King's Own Regiment of Horse in 1714 in honour of George I. The regiment attained the title 1st King's Dragoon Guards in 1751. The regiment served as horse cavalry until 1937 when it was mechanised with light tanks. The regiment became part of the Royal Armoured Corps in 1939. The regiment amalgamated with the 2nd Dragoon Guards (Queen's Bays) in 1959 to form the 1st The Queen's Dragoon Guards.

46153 THE ROYAL DRAGOON (LMS 6153) built at Derby Works, entered traffic July 1930. Lot No 073. Rebuilt August 1949. Thus, still with parallel boiler at the end of LMS period. Withdrawn by BR in December 1962 and cut up at Crewe Works May 1963.

Rebuilt Royal Scot BR No 46153 THE ROYAL DRAGOON awaits to be united with a tender after an overhaul at Crewe Works, January 1961. *Alan H. Bryant/Rail Photoprints*

Civilians ride on a Daimler armoured car of the 1st Royal Dragoons as it enters the town of Hadersleben in Denmark, 7 May 1945. *Sgt. Norris Army Film and Photographic Unit*

The Royal Dragoons (1st Dragoons) was a mounted infantry and later a heavy cavalry regiment of the British Army. The regiment was first raised as a single troop of veterans of the Parliamentary Army in 1661, shortly thereafter expanded to four troops as the Tangier Horse in 1661, taking the name from their service in Tangier. Of the four troops three were originally troops in the English Regiment of Light Horse in France attached to the French army of Louis XIV and under the command of Sir Henry Jones. In 1969 it amalgamated with the Royal Horse Guards to form The Blues and Royals.

The Royal Dragoon Guards (RDG) is a cavalry regiment of the British Army. It was formed in 1992 by the amalgamation of two other regiments: The 4th/7th Royal Dragoon Guards and the 5th Royal Inniskilling Dragoon Guards.

46154 THE HUSSAR (LMS 6154) built at Derby Works, entered traffic July 1930. Lot No 073. Rebuilt March 1948 (but withdrawn prior to rebuilding in 1947). Thus, still with parallel boiler at the end of LMS period. Withdrawn by BR in November 1962 and cut up at Crewe Works March 1963.

Rebuilt Royal Scot BR No 46154 THE HUSSAR is seen at Colwyn Bay station with a stopping train for Chester during August 1958. *Keith Langston Collection*

Traditionally the title Hussar referred to a member of a certain regiment of light cavalry and was Hungarian in origin. The hussars of the period created the tradition of sabrage, the opening of a champagne bottle with a sabre. Moustaches were universally worn by Napoleonic-era hussars and the British hussars were the only moustachioed troops in the British Army.

The 19th Royal Hussars (Queen Alexandra's Own) was a cavalry regiment of the British Army, created in 1858. In 1922 it was amalgamated with the 15th The King's Hussars to form the 15th/19th The King's Royal Hussars. The Queen's Own Hussars was a cavalry regiment of the British Army, formed from the amalgamation of the 3rd The King's Own Hussars and the 7th Queen's Own Hussars at Candahar Barracks, Tidworth in 1958. The regiment was amalgamated with the Queen's Royal Irish Hussars to form the Queen's Royal Hussars on 1 September 1993.

Cap badge.

Queens Royal Hussars (The Queens Own and Royal Irish) Memorial at the National Arboretum, Alrewas, Staffordshire. Latin '*Mente Et Manu*' translation By Mind and Hand. *Len Mills*

46155 THE LANCER (LMS 6155) built at Derby Works, entered traffic July 1930. Lot No 073. Rebuilt August 1950. Thus, still with parallel boiler at the end of LMS period. Withdrawn by BR in December 1964 and cut up by Arnott Young, Troon February 1965.

Mike Morant Collection

Norman Preedy Collection

Royal Scot BR No 46155 THE LANCER is pictured at two unknown locations circa 1949.

Traditionary the title Lancer referred to a type of cavalryman who fought with a lance.

The Royal Lancers (Queen Elizabeth's Own) is a cavalry regiment of the British Army. The regiment was formed by an amalgamation of The Queen's Royal Lancers and 9th/12th Royal Lancers (Prince of Wales's) on 2 May 2015. It serves as the Formation Reconnaissance Regiment of the 12th Armoured Infantry Brigade. The Queen's Royal Lancers was a cavalry regiment of the British Army. It was formed in 1993 and amalgamated with the 9th/12th Royal Lancers (Prince of Wales's) on 2 May 2015 to form the Royal Lancers. The Royal Lancers are the armoured cavalry regiment of 12 Armoured Infantry Brigade. The regiments famous skull and crossbones cap badge is one of the most recognisable in the British Army and represents its motto: 'Death or Glory'.

Cap Badge.

The Queen's Royal Lancers Memorial at the National Arboretum, Alrewas, Staffordshire. *Simon Hodson*

46156 THE SOUTH WALES BORDERER (LMS 6156) built at Derby Works, entered traffic July 1930. Lot No 073. Rebuilt May 1954. Thus, still with parallel boiler at the end of LMS period. Withdrawn by BR in October 1964 and cut up by Drapers, Hull February 1965.

Not so sunny perhaps for those Rhyl football supporters aboard this special train as they had just been beaten 5-1 by Carlisle United in the Football Association Cup, on 16 November 1957. Rebuilt Royal Scot BR No 46156 THE SOUTH WALES BORDERER, in charge of the football special, is seen taking water at Chester station on the return journey. *R. A. Whitfield/ Rail Photoprints*

The South Wales Borderers was a line infantry regiment of the British Army in existence for 280 years. It first became the 24th Regiment of Foot in 1689. Based at Brecon the regiment recruited from the border counties of Monmouthshire, Herefordshire and Brecknockshire, but was not called the South Wales Borderers until the Childers Reforms of 1881. In 1969 the regiment was amalgamated with the Welch Regiment to form the Royal Regiment of Wales.

The two line nameplate of Royal Scot locomotive BR No 46156. *Norman Preedy Collection*

Plaque remembering the liberation of a Normandy bridge on D-Day by the 2nd Battalion, South Wales Borderers. *Lklundin*

A 1928 South Wales Borderers recruiting poster. *National Army Museum*

46157 THE ROYAL ARTILLERYMAN (LMS 6157) built at Derby Works, entered traffic August 1930. Lot No 073. Rebuilt January 1946. Withdrawn by BR in January 1964 and cut up at Crewe Works February 1964.

Rebuilt Royal Scot BR No 46157 THE ROYAL ARTILLERYMAN on an up freight near Hartford, in March 1963. *Colin Whitfield/Rail Photoprints*

The Royal Regiment of Artillery, commonly referred to as the Royal Artillery and colloquially known as 'The Gunners', is the artillery arm of the British Army. The introduction of artillery into the English army came as early as the Battle of Crécy in 1346. Henry VIII made the army's artillery semi-permanent in the sixteenth century but the recognition of the need for a permanent body of artillery did not happen until 1716. The Royal Regiment of Artillery comprises thirteen Regular Army regiments, King's Troop Royal Horse Artillery and five Army Reserve regiments.

Royal Regiment of Artillery badge. Latin '*Ubique Quo Fas Et Gloria Ducunt*' translation – Everywhere that right and glory lead.

Gunners of the 78th Field Regiment, Royal Artillery make use of two sunshades from a cafe to keep the rain off while making a brew, Anzio, Italy, 27 February 1944. *Sgt. Dawson, No2 Army Film and Photographic Unit*

46158 THE LOYAL REGIMENT (LMS 6158) built at Derby Works, entered traffic August 1930. Lot No 073. Officially named July 1931.Rebuilt September 1952. Thus, still with parallel boiler at the end of LMS period. Withdrawn by BR in November 1963 and cut up at Crewe Works November 1963.

Royal Scot BR No 46158 THE LOYAL REGIMENT is seen as LMS No 6158 at Crewe circa 1947, after being paired with a Stanier tender. Note the regimental plaque on the splasher below the nameplate, on account of which the small oil box has been relocated. In military terms the word Loyal added to a regiment etc has deeply historical origins. This locomotive was named in 1931 thus the name would refer to the period of post 1921 regimental name change. *Rail Photoprints Collection*

Cap Badge Loyal North Lancashire Regiment.

Royal Scot LMS No 6158 THE LOYAL REGIMENT is seen under the coaling facility at Camden in 1936. Note the railwayman on top of the railed tender. *Rail Photoprints Collection*

The Loyal North Lancashire Regiment was formed in 1881. Its title changed to The Loyal Regiment (North Lancashire) in 1921. The Regiment was formed initially with two battalions, the 1st Battalion being created from the former 47th (Lancashire) Regiment of Foot, and the 2nd from the former 81st (Loyal Lincoln Volunteers). The Regiment recruited primarily from the towns of Central Lancashire, including Preston, Chorley, Bolton and Wigan. In 1970 the regiment was amalgamated with the Lancashire Regiment to form the Queen's Lancashire Regiment which was in 2006, amalgamated with The King's Own Royal Border Regiment and the King's Regiment (Liverpool and Manchester) to form the Duke of Lancaster's Regiment (King's, Lancashire and Border).

46159 THE ROYAL AIR FORCE (LMS 6159) built at Derby Works, entered traffic August 1930. Lot No 073. Rebuilt October 1945. Withdrawn by BR in November 1962 and cut up at Crewe Works February 1963.

Rebuilt Royal Scot BR No 46159 THE ROYAL AIR FORCE is seen departing Euston station on 14 August 1956. Note the burn on the smokebox door caused by ash build up. *Mike Morant Collection*

The Royal Air Force is the United Kingdom's aerial warfare force. Formed towards the end of the First World War on 1 April 1918, it is the oldest independent air force in the world. The RAF was founded by the merger of the Royal Flying Corps and the Royal Naval Air Service. Following victory over the Central Powers in 1918 the RAF emerged as, at the time, the largest air force in the world.

Famous Motto, Latin '*Per Ardua ad Astra*' translation – Through Adversity to the Stars.

Preserved RAF World War II Spitfire LF Mk 1X is seen whilst being flown by Ray Hanna during a 2005 air display. *Franck Cabrol*

46160 QUEEN VICTORIA'S RIFLEMAN (LMS 6160) built Derby Works, entered traffic in August 1930. Lot No 073. Rebuilt February 1945. Withdrawn by BR in May 1965 and cut up by Motherwell Machinery & Scrap, Wishaw July 1965.

Sadly, then running with nameplates removed, Rebuilt Royal Scot BR No 46160 QUEEN VICTORIA'S RIFLEMAN is seen at Nottingham in early 1962. Note the front end of class '25' diesel No D 7581. *Rail Photoprints Collection*

The 9th (County of London) Battalion, London Regiment (**Queen Victoria's Rifles**) was a Territorial Army infantry battalion of the British Army. The regiment was raised as the 1st (Victoria Rifle Club) Middlesex Rifle Volunteer Corps and became the 1st Middlesex Rifle Volunteer Corps on the formation of the Volunteer Force in 1860.

The London Regiment was formed in 1908 in order to regiment the various Volunteer Force battalions in the newly formed County of London, and the Queen Victoria's Rifles were one of twenty-six units brought together in this way. The Queen Victoria's Rifles could trace their origins back to the old volunteer regiments of the Napoleonic Wars when the Duke of Cumberland's Sharpshooters were formed as a Corps of Riflemen on 5 September 1803. After World War 2, the Queen Victoria's Rifles was merged with the Queen's Westminsters to form the Queen's Royal Rifles on May 1 1961.

'Hill 60' Ypres, Belgium. The Queen Victoria's Rifles Memorial. *Len Mills Collection*

46161 KING'S OWN (LMS 6161) built Derby Works, entered traffic in September 1930. Lot No 073. Official naming ceremony 7 January 1931. Rebuilt October 1946. Withdrawn by BR in November 1962 and cut up at Crewe Works December 1963.

Royal Scot BR No 46161 KING'S OWN is seen as LMS No 6161 at Crewe North depot in 1932. Originally this locomotive was named THE KING'S OWN and without a crest, as can be seen in this image the small oil box has been relocated to accommodate a plaque. Note the experimental smoke deflector device with cut away top and allied to a conical smoke box door, also the stovepipe style chimney. *Rail Photoprints Collection*

The later shortened name and lion crest mounted on the wheel splasher. Note also that the apostrophe has a square top in the

style of nameplates cast at Derby Works. Crewe Works nameplates were cast using apostrophes with a round top. *Tony Wilson Collection/David Anderson*

Original nameplate. *BR/Keith Langston Collection*

The Regiment had the unique distinctions of being known as **The King's Own** and of wearing the 'Lion of England' as its cap badge. The regiment was raised in the West Country on 13 July 1680, by the Earl of Plymouth for service in Tangiers. It became one of the oldest regiments of foot in the British Army.

The King's Own Royal Regiment was amalgamated with the 1st Battalion, The Border Regiment to form The Kings Own Royal Border Regiment. However, the Territorial Battalion of the King's Own based at Lancaster carried on the name of the Regiment until 1969 when that unit ceased to exist following the reduction of the Territorial Army. The Colours of this Battalion, the last Colours of the King's Own Royal Regiment to remain in use, were laid up in the Regimental Chapel in July, 1980, exactly three hundred years from the founding of the Regiment.

46162 QUEEN'S WESTMINSTER RIFLEMAN (LMS 6162) built Derby Works, entered traffic in September 1930. Lot No 073. Rebuilt January 1948. Thus, still with parallel boiler at the end of LMS period. Withdrawn by BR in May 1964 and cut up by Connels, Calder September 1964.

Rebuilt Royal Scot BR No 46162 QUEEN'S WESTMINSTER RIFLEMAN is seen taking water at Whitmore Troughs on 15 June 1957. Note the associated storage tank and building housing the control gear etc. *Norman Preedy Collection*

The Queen's Westminsters were an infantry regiment of the Territorial Army, part of the British Army. Originally formed from Rifle Volunteer Corps, which were established after a French invasion scare of 1859. The unit became part of the newly established London Regiment on the formation of the Territorial Force in 1908. It was subsequently amalgamated in 1921 with the Civil Service Rifles, and became a territorial Battalion of the King's Royal Rifle Corps in 1937. It ceased to exist as separate entity after it was amalgamated on 1 May 1961 with the Queen Victoria's Rifles to form the Queen's Royal Rifles.

Stained glass window in Holy Trinity Church Leverstock Green, commemorating the men of the Queen's Westminster Rifles stationed at Leverstock in 1914. The window was given by the men of the regiment to Holy Trinity Church in gratitude for the hospitality and kindness shown them by the people of Leverstock Green during World War 1. It shows St. George in one panel and St. Lois of France in the other, with the arms of the City of Westminster above. There was a similar window in Westminster Abbey, which was unfortunately destroyed during WW2. *Barbara Chapman*

Bath time 1914 style. Troops of the regiment are seen at Leverstock Green, Hertfordshire. *Jon Spence Collection*

LONDON MIDLAND AND SCOTTISH RAILWAY COMPANY.

OFFICE OF DEPUTY CHIEF MECHANICAL ENGINEER,
DERBY.
(CENTRE No. 49.)

W.A. Stanier
CHIEF MECHANICAL ENGINEER.
& H. LEMON.
TELEGRAPHIC ADDRESS:
EAMES, c/o BESLINE, DERBY."
TELEPHONE No. 1100.
Ext. 514
H. P. M. BEAMES,
DEPUTY CHIEF MECHANICAL ENGINEER.

My Ref. U.4848
Your Ref. LT.2/16-3
M.17/5
G.8.

10th August, 1932.

NAME PLATES ON "ROYAL SCOT" ENGINES.

Further to my letter of the 27th ultimo, and
with reference to conversation on the telephone between
Mr. Warburton and Mr. Chambers, as promised I send
herewith sketch R.S.1778 illustrating the arrangement
of the name plates for two "Royal Scot" engines as
follows:-

Queen's Westminster Rifleman
Civil Service Rifleman

It will be necessary to increase the width of
the splashers for this alteration.

I also enclose copy of R.S.1779 illustrating
the existing name plate for the "Sherwood Foresters"
arranged on similar lines to the above two engines. I
shall be glad to have your approval for this arrangement
so that particulars can be sent to Crewe for the material
to be prepared and the alterations to be carried out
without loss of time.

You will note that the carrying plate is provided
for a crest of 11" diameter, and no doubt you will communicate
this information to the Regiments concerned so that the crests
may be made to a suitable size.

Sketches are also being prepared for the other
name plates mentioned in your letter of the 12th ultimo,
and no doubt you will confirm in due course the last four
Regimental names which were then not definitely decided.

H. P. M. BEAMES.

W.A. Stanier, Esq.,
Euston. 1.

LONDON MIDLAND AND SCOTTISH RAILWAY COMPANY.

OFFICE OF DEPUTY CHIEF MECHANICAL ENGINEER,

DERBY, 20th September, 1932.
(Centre No. 49.)

OUR REFERENCE.
U.4848./1.
LT.1/19/3.
YOUR REFERENCE.
M.17/5. G.9

NAME PLATES ON "ROYAL SCOT" ENGINES.

Further to my letter to you of the 15th August, will you
kindly note that the name plates "Queen's Westminster Rifleman" on
Engine No. 6162 and "Civil Service Rifleman" on Engine No. 6163 were
fitted at Holyhead on the 14th instant.

I will notify you as and when the remaining six engines
have the new name plates fitted.

Beames.

Both Documents. *LMS*

213

Royal Scot class BR No 46163 CIVIL SERVICE RIFLEMAN is seen approaching Rugeley with a local service circa 1952. The dirt on the smoke box number plate partially obscures the figure 4 giving the image an LMS feel. *Norman Preedy Collection*

Nameplate of BR No 46163. *Geoff Rixon*

Rebuilt Royal Scot BR No 46163 CIVIL SERVICE RIFLEMAN is seen at Patricroft depot, during September 1961. *Jim Carter/Rail Photoprints*

A rifleman was traditionally an infantry soldier armed with a rifled long gun. By the mid-19th century, entire regiments of riflemen were formed and became the mainstay of all standard infantry, and rifleman became a generic term for any common infantryman. A rifleman regiment was formed as the Bank of England Volunteers in 1798 but was disbanded in 1814. The regiment was re-raised by Viscount Bury on the formation of the Volunteer Force as the 21st Middlesex Rifle Volunteers (**Civil Service Rifles**) in 1860. By 1880 and the re-numbering of London Rifle Volunteers the unit was titled 12th Middlesex (Civil Service) Rifle Volunteer Corps and were linked as a Volunteer Battalion of the King's Royal Rifle Corps. On formation of the Territorial Force in 1908 the Civil Service Rifles became part of the newly formed London Regiment and was titled 15th Battalion London Regiment (Civil Service Rifles). In 1921 the Civil Service Rifles were amalgamated with the 16th (County of London) Battalion, London Regiment.

The Civil Service Rifles Memorial at the Riverside Terrace, Somerset House where it was re-sited in 2002 from its original location in the courtyard of Somerset House. *Harry Mitchell*

46164 THE ARTISTS' RIFLEMAN (LMS 6164) built Derby Works, entered traffic in September 1930. Lot No 073. Rebuilt June 1951. Thus, still with parallel boiler at the end of LMS period. Withdrawn by BR in December 1962 and cut up at Crewe Works March 1963.

Rebuilt Royal Scot BR No 46164 THE ARTISTS' RIFLEMAN is seen departing Gloucester with a relief service in August 1962. *Norman Preedy Collection*

The **Artists' Rifleman** regiment was formed in 1859, part of the widespread volunteer movement which developed in the face of potential French invasion after Felice Orsini's attack on Napoleon III was linked to Britain. The group was organised in London by Edward Sterling, an art student, and comprised various professional painters, musicians, actors, architects and others involved in creative endeavours. It was established on 28 February 1860 as the 38th Middlesex (Artists) Rifle Volunteer Corps, with headquarters at Burlington House. Its first commanders were the painters Henry Wyndham Phillips and Frederic Leighton. The unit's badge, designed by William Wyon, shows the heads of the Roman gods Mars and Minerva in profile (Artists Rifles Regiment Badge). The Artists Rifles was originally Artists' Rifles until the apostrophe was officially dropped from the full title in 1937. This title is now carried by the 21st Special Air Service Regiment (Artists) (Reserve). The Artists Rifles became a reserve regiment in the Territorial Army in 1967.

TO THE GLORIOUS MEMORY OF THE 2003 MEMBERS OF THE ARTISTS RIFLES. 28th BATTALION THE LONDON REGIMENT, WHO GAVE THEIR LIVES FOR KING AND COUNTRY IN THE GREAT WAR ANNIS DOMINI 1914-1919. THEIR NAME LIVETH FOR EVERMORE

The unit's badge, designed by William Wyon, shows the heads of the Roman gods Mars and Minerva in profile.

Memorial to the Artists Rifles is located at the Royal Academy, London. *Stephen C. Dickson*

215

46165 THE RANGER (12TH LONDON REGT.) (LMS 6165) built Derby Works, entered traffic in October 1930. Lot No 073. Rebuilt June 1952. Thus, still with parallel boiler at the end of LMS period. Withdrawn by BR in November 1964 and cut up by T.W. Ward, Beighton March 1965.

Rebuilt Royal Scot BR No 46165 THE RANGER (12TH LONDON REGT.) waits to take over an up service at Carlisle Citadel station, circa 1957. *Rail Photoprints Collection*

The Rangers was a volunteer unit of the British Army, originally formed in 1860. The enthusiasm for the Volunteer movement following an invasion scare in 1859 saw the creation of many Rifle Volunteer Corps composed of part-time soldiers eager to supplement the Regular British Army in time of need. One such unit was the Central London Rifle Rangers formed in 1859 at Gray's Inn, London, from members of the legal profession. Known as 12th (County of London) Battalion, London Regiment (The Rangers). Other similar regiments were 40th Middlesex Rifle Volunteer Corps and the 22nd Middlesex Volunteer Rifle Corps (Central London Rangers).

Rangers cap badge.

RECRUITS WANTED
for the Poly Company *of the*
12th LONDON REGT.
THE RANGERS

Apply at Once to the Recruiting Sergeant in Poly Entrance Hall

Recruiting advertisment which appeared in the Polytechnic Magazine in 1916.

216

46166 LONDON RIFLE BRIGADE (LMS 6166) built Derby Works, entered traffic in October 1930. Lot No 073. Officially named November 1932. Rebuilt January 1945. Withdrawn by BR in October 1964 and cut up by Arnott Young, Troon December 1964.

Rebuilt Royal Scot BR No 46166 LONDON RIFLE BRIGADE is seen with a down express service at Shap Wells, circa 1955. *Norman Preedy Collection*

The **London Rifle Brigade** was a volunteer unit of the British Army. The regiment was first raised in the City of London on 14 December 1859 as 1st London (City of London Volunteer Rifle Brigade) Rifle Volunteer Corps, a rifle volunteer unit made up of five companies. On 1 July 1881 it was made part of the King's Royal Rifle Corps as its 9th Volunteer Battalion. In December 1891, it was renamed the 1st London Volunteer Rifle Corps (City of London Volunteer Rifle Brigade). When the volunteer and militia units were reorganised as the Territorial Force (TF) in 1908 the unit was again renamed, becoming the 5th (City of London) Battalion of the new London Regiment. On 1 April 1947 it absorbed the duplicate 8th Battalion and was renamed the London Rifle Brigade, The Rifle Brigade (Prince Consort's Own). On 1 May 1960 it amalgamated with The Rangers, becoming the London Rifle Brigade/Rangers, whose successor unit was part of the 4th (Volunteer) Battalion Royal Green Jackets. This later became G (Royal Green Jackets) Company of the London Regiment and G Company, 7th Battalion, The Rifles.

London Rifles Brigade Cap Badge.

The nameplate of the locomotive was complemented by a regimental crest/plaque. Latin *PRIMUS IN URBE*, translation 'The first in the city'. *David Anderson*

46167 THE HERTFORDSHIRE REGIMENT (LMS 6167) built Derby Works, entered traffic in October 1930. Lot No 073. Rebuilt December 1948. Thus, still with parallel boiler at the end of LMS period. Withdrawn by BR in April 1964 and cut up at Crewe Works May 1964.

Rebuilt Royal Scot class BR No 46167 THE HERTFORDSHIRE REGIMENT is seen in light steam between 'Black 5' class BR No 45449 and an unidentified 'Jinty' class tank engine at Patricroft depot, in June 1961. *Jim Carter/Steve Armitage Archive*

The Hertfordshire Regiment was a line infantry regiment, part of the British Army. These units were raised across Britain during a period of heightened Anglo-French tension resulting from the Second Italian War of Independence.

In Hertfordshire the newly formed companies of rifle volunteers were grouped into two separate administrative battalions of the Hertfordshire Rifle Volunteers. In 1880 these units were rearranged in two battalion-sized units titled 1st and 2nd Hertfordshire Rifle Volunteer Corps. As a result of the Childers Reforms, the county lost its regular regiment because the two Hertfordshire Rifle Corps were nominated to be attached to the neighbouring Bedfordshire Regiment. In 1961 the Hertfordshire Regiment (TA) was amalgamated with the 5th Battalion Bedfordshire Regiment (TA) to form the Bedfordshire and Hertfordshire Regiment (TA). In 1967 they then became the 3rd Battalion of the Royal Anglian Regiment.

Memorial honouring the fallen of the Hertfordshire Regiment during the 3rd Battle of Ypres, World War 1, stands on the field of that battle. It was unveiled 31 July 2017, 100 years after the battle. *Herts at War*

46170 BRITISH LEGION (LMS 6170) built North British Locomotive Co, entered traffic in October 1935. Lot No 23890. It was a rebuilt locomotive following the catastrophic failure of experimental Hi-Pressure engine LMS No 6399 FURY, which was built in 1929. Withdrawn by BR in December 1961 and cut up at Crewe Works January 1963.

The unique Royal Scot class BR No 46170 BRITISH LEGION is seen at Crewe in 1946 as LMS No 6170, with an LMS Type 2 tapered boiler. The later Royal Scot rebuilds incorporated 2A boilers which were 15 inch shorter and the resulting boiler overhang can be clearly seen in this image. also note the bigger steam pipe, and the top feed which was positioned further back. *Rail Photoprints Collection*

The Royal British Legion is a British charity providing financial, social and emotional support to members and veterans of the British Armed Forces, their families and dependants. The organisation was founded in 1921. The organisation is synonymous with Remembrance Day and thus the end of World War 1, on the 11th hour of the 11th day of the 11th month, 1918 and the poppy symbol. The remembrance poppy is an artificial flower that has been used since 1921 to commemorate the military personnel who have died in war, and represents a common or field poppy.

In Flanders Fields
by John McCrae May 1915

In Flanders fields the poppies blow
Between the crosses, row on row,
    That mark our place; and in the sky
    The larks, still bravely singing, fly
Scarce heard amid the guns below.

We are the Dead. Short days ago
We lived, felt dawn, saw sunset glow,
    Loved and were loved, and now we lie,
        In Flanders fields.

Take up our quarrel with the foe:
To you from failing hands we throw
    The torch; be yours to hold it high.
    If ye break faith with us who die
We shall not sleep, though poppies grow
        In Flanders fields.

Chapter 3

STANIER 8F

LMS & War Department Stanier 2-8-0 '8F' class

The London Midland & Scottish Railway (LMSR) suffered from a lack of reliable heavy freight locomotives right from the company's creation. In 1935 William A. Stanier addressed the shortage by creating a heavy freight 2-cylinder 2-8-0 design born out of his earlier introduced and proven 4-6-0 'Black Five' class. The 8F class was an immediate success being far superior to the then ageing ex L&Y and LNWR 0-8-0 locomotives it replaced. Initially the class was power rated as 7F but that was very soon uprated to 8F.

Four Stanier 8F locomotives are seen grouped around the turntable at Northwich in the early 1960s. *Keith Langston Collection*

However, the class was not just an LMS success story. With the very real threat of hostilities approaching the type was adopted for war-time use and the War Department placed orders for 240 engines to be built by the contractors, North British Locomotive Co, Beyer Peacock Ltd and the Vulcan Foundry. Those locomotives were allocated War Department numbers in the series WD 300-539, later changed to WD 70300-WD 70539. Several of those 8Fs were in service for a while with LMS numbers LMS 8226 upwards before being transferred to WD stock.

The class soon gained the collective title 'Engines of War'. All of the class built for the WD were eventually shipped overseas specifically to the Middle East together with some LMS examples, with numbers between LMS 8012 and LMS 8094 respectively. The majority of those WD 8Fs being converted to oil firing. Many of those locomotives never returned to home shores. The exploits of 8Fs working on the vital supply route linking the Persian Gulf with the Caspian Sea and into the Soviet

A driver seen on the footplate of a Stanier 8F locomotive. Can you spot the brew can? *Hugh Ballantyne/Rail Photoprints*

Union were recorded as being amongst the types most notable war time performances. Not all of those shipped to theatres of war ever turned a wheel, as a good number were lost at sea when the vessels carrying them were sunk by enemy action.

Many more 8Fs were built during the war but for use at home, something which led to a unique situation with engines of a purely LMS design being constructed in the workshops of the independent railway companies, in addition to outside contractors. None of the BR 8Fs were officially given names. In 2019 seven ex LMS/BR examples were preserved in the UK, and an eighth had been repatriated from Turkey.

In total 849 8F locomotives were built by the following companies;

North British Locomotive Co, 208.	SR Ashford Works, 14.	
LMS Crewe Works, 136.	SR Brighton Works, 93.	GWR Swindon Works, 80.
LMS Horwich Works, 75.	Vulcan Foundry, Newton le Willows 67.	LNER Darlington Works, 53.
LNER Doncaster Works, 50.	Beyer Peacock & Co, Manchester, 50.	SR Eastleigh Works, 23.

In January 1948 the newly created British Railway BR took into stock 556 engines. With returning ex WD engines that total eventually rose to 666 by 1957.

BR 48774 built North British Locomotive Co, entered traffic August 1940. Works No 24620. Shipped to Persia in September 1941 as WD 41108. Transferred to Egypt/Palestine in 1944 and renumbered 70320. Named LT. W. O. LENNOX whilst with the Middle East Forces on the Egyptian State Railway. Locomotive only without tender returned to UK Derby Works for overhaul after which it was sent to the Longmoor Military Railway (LMR) with a new tender as WD No 501. Sold to BR in July 1957 and numbered 48774. Withdrawn by BR in December 1962 and reinstated in February 1963, again withdrawn by BR in June 1963 and again reinstated in November 1963. Finally withdrawn in July 1965 and scrapped in April 1966.

Ex-WD Stanier 8F 2-8-0 No 501 LT. W. O. LENNOX is seen at the former Longmoor Military Railway site during an open event held on 3 September 1955. The Longmoor Military Railway (LMR) was a British military railway in Hampshire, built by the Royal Engineers from 1903 in order to train soldiers on railway construction and operations, the facility ceased to exist as an operational railway on 31 October 1969. The 8F locomotive is coupled with WD 2-10-0 No 600 GORDON, which is preserved at the Severn Valley Railway (SVR). *Mike Morant Collection*

Sir Wilbraham Oates Lennox VC, KCB

Lennox was born 4 August 1830 at Molecombe House, Goodwood, Sussex. He joined the Royal Military Academy in 1846 at Woolwich. In 1848 he joined the Royal Engineers. Moving through the ranks he served throughout the Crimea Campaign and together with two colleagues he was awarded the Victoria Cross (VC) on 24 February 1857. The award

followed their actions during an attack on the Russia rifle pits during the Battle of Inkerman. After a very distinguished military career he retired in 1888. He was knighted in 1891 and died at his London home on 7 February 1897, and was interred at Woodvale Cemetery Brighton.

Stanier 8F BR No 48774, formerly WD No 501 is seen in a typically work stained condition of the era at Glasgow Polmadie depot in 1960. *Rail Photoprints Collection*

Preserved Stanier 8F BR No 48773 is based at the Severn Valley Railway (SVR) and was built by the North British Locomotive Co, Works No 24607, in 1940. The locomotive was part of a War Department order for use in France, as WD 307. France fell to Germany before the locomotive could be exported, so it was loaned back to the LMS and numbered 8233. The locomotive was later requisitioned and sent to the Iranian State Railways as No 41.109. There it worked on the Trans-Iranian Railway, hauling trains of supplies intended for the Soviet Union, over extremely difficult routes. On 19 August 1942, the locomotive was famously derailed after colliding with a camel, and later in 1944 was converted to oil-burning. In 1946 the locomotive was sent to the British Army's Middle East Forces (MEF) in Egypt where, numbered WD 70307, it worked in the Suez Canal Zone. For a while the locomotive was loaned to Egyptian State Railways but by 1948, in need of a new firebox it was scheduled to be scrapped, but survived. It was shipped back to the UK and overhauled at Derby Works (1952/54) after which going to the LMR as WD No 500. In 1957 it was bought back by BR and numbered 48773. The locomotive then worked right to the end of the steam era in 1968.

Preserved Stanier 8F BR No 48773 is seen at Horse Cove with 'THE STANIER HIND' railtour on 15 May 1998. *John Chalcraft/Rail Photoprints*

For archive rail tour information visit www.sixbellsjunction.co.uk/

'*Rail Photoprints*' have been involved in Railway Photography and Publishing for more than 50 years. For the best in photo files and images of steam and modern traction at work in the UK and further afield contact: https://railphotoprints.uk/

ACKNOWLEDGEMENTS

This is a Perceptive Images 2019 © publication exclusively for Pen & Sword Books Ltd.

Additional editorial material, special images and archive documents were supplied by David Anderson, John Magnall, Mike Morant, Norman Preedy and Pete Skelton.

Photographic libraries whose images have been used include Author, Crewe Archive, LMS Patriot Project, Mike Morant Collection, Norman Preedy Collection, Rail Photoprints Collection, Railway Correspondence and Travel Society Archive (RCTS).

Also: British Army, National Maritime Museum, Royal Air Force, Royal Navy, US National Archive, US Navy and Wikipedia.

A book of this nature could not have been compiled without the co-operation of numerous railway photographers and archivists some of whom are unfortunately no longer with us but in this publication their unique images live on.

Individual photographers whose railway images have been used include Bernard Brown, Phil Brown, Jim Carter, Dave Hewitt, Mark A. Hoofe, David Jones, Fred Kerr, The Metcalf Collection, Len Mills, David Moyle, Railway Images, Mike Stokes Archive, Edward Talbot.

Keith Langston 2019

Dedication

This book is dedicated to the memory of three stalwart railway preservationists, volunteers, authors, photographers and friends who recently passed away.

Malcolm Whittaker *1st December 1940–25 November 2017* (Severn Valley Railway-Hampton Loade Paddock Railway).

Malcolm Ranieri *15 December 1945–12 October 2018* (Stratford Photo Club and Gloucester & Warwickshire Railway).

Norman Preedy *25 April 1943–19 November 2018* (Author and accomplished railway photographer).